UNSETTLING PARTITION: LITERATURE, GENDER, MEMORY

The Partition of India in 1947 marked the birth of two modern nation-states and the end of British colonialism in South Asia. The move towards the 'two nation solution' was accompanied by an unprecedented mass migration (over twelve million people) to and from areas that would become India and Pakistan.

Diverse representations of the violence that accompanied this migration (including the abduction and sexual assault of over 75,000 women) can be found in fictional, historical, autobiographical, and scholarly works. Unsettling Partition examines short stories, novels, testimonies, and historiography that represent women's experiences of the Partition. Counter to the move for 'recovery' that informs some historical research on testimony and fictional representations of women's Partition experiences, Jill Didur argues for an attentiveness to the literary qualities of women's narratives that interrogate and unsettle monolithic accounts of the period.

Rather than attempt to seek out a 'hidden history' of this time, Didur examines how the literariness of Partition narratives undermines this possibility. *Unsettling Partition* reinterprets the silences found in women's accounts of sectarian violence that accompanied Partition (sexual assault, abduction, displacement from their families) as a sign of their inability to find a language to articulate their experience without invoking metaphors of purity and pollution. Didur argues that these silences and ambiguities in women's stories should not be resolved, accounted for, translated, or recovered but understood as a critique of the project of patriarchal modernity.

JILL DIDUR is an associate professor in the Department of English at Concordia University.

JILL DIDUR

Unsettling Partition

Literature, Gender, Memory

UNIVERSITY OF TORONTO PRESS
Toronto Buffalo London

© University of Toronto Press Incorporated 2006
Toronto Buffalo London
Reprinted in paperback 2015

ISBN 978-0-8020-7997-8 (cloth)
ISBN 978-1-4426-1505-2 (paper)

Printed on acid-free paper

Library and Archives Canada Cataloguing in Publication

Didur, Jill, 1965–

Unsettling partition : literature, gender, memory / Jill Didur.

Includes bibliographical references and index.
ISBN 978-0-8020-7997-8 (bound)
ISBN 978-1-4426-1505-2 (pbk.)

1. Indic fiction (English) – 20th century – History and criticism.
2. India – History – Partition, 1947 – In literature.   3. Partition, Territorial, in literature.   4. Gender identity in literature.   5. Violence in literature.   6. Nationalism in literature.   7. Women in literature.
I. Title.

PK5416.D53 2006   823'.91409954   C2005-904567-1

University of Toronto Press acknowledges the financial assistance to its publishing program of the Canada Council for the Arts and the Ontario Arts Council.

This book has been published with the help of a grant from the Canadian Federation for the Humanities and Social Sciences, through the Aid to Scholarly Publications Programme, using funds provided by the Social Sciences and Humanities Research Council of Canada.

University of Toronto Press acknowledges the financial support for its publishing activities of the Government of Canada through the Book Publishing Industry Development Program (BPIDP).

For my family

Contents

Acknowledgments ix

Introduction: Unsettling Partition 3

1 'Making Men for the India of Tomorrow'? Gender and Nationalist Discourse in South Asia 21

2 Fragments of Imagination: Rethinking the Literary in Historiography through Narratives of India's Partition 42

3 Cracking the Nation: Memory, Minorities, and the Ends of Narrative in Bapsi Sidhwa's *Cracking India* 67

4 A Heart Divided: Education, Romance, and the Domestic Sphere in Attia Hosain's *Sunlight on a Broken Column* 94

5 At a Loss for Words: Reading the Silence in South Asian Women's Partition Narratives 125

Conclusion: Recovering the Nation? 157

Appendix A 163

Notes 165

Bibliography 181

Index 197

Acknowledgments

I owe thanks to many teachers, colleagues, and friends for the encouragement and support they have given me during the course of writing this book. I thank my teachers at York University in Toronto, especially my supervisor Arun Mukherjee, Terry Goldie, and Marie-Christine Leps. I am grateful for the support and encouragement I received from Meenakshi Mukherjee at Jawaharlal Nehru University in Delhi while this research was in its early stages. I am indebted to the faculty at the Centre for the Study of Culture and Society in Bangalore, especially Tejaswini Niranjana and Ashish Rajadhyaksha, as well as Alok Bhalla at Central Institute of English and Foreign Languages in Hyderabad, for the opportunity to develop and present some of the ideas in this book at their institutions while I was a visiting fellow at CSCS.

I thank my colleagues, students, and the staff in the Department of English at Concordia University in Montreal for providing me with a friendly and supportive intellectual environment. I thank friends who have inspired and encouraged me while I completed this project: Peter Babiak, Neil Badmington, Ritu Birla, Stephanie Bolster, Jason Camlot, Patrick Carroll, Bina Friewald, Craig Gordon, Allyson Hadwin, Teresa Heffernan, Stacey Johnson, Anna Kasier, Mwikali Kieti, Rita Kothari, David McGimpsey, Radhika Mongia, Anne-Marie Renzoni, Eve Saunders, Yumna Siddiqi, Kate Sterns, Charis Thompson, and Joost Vandenborre. At the University of Toronto Press, many thanks to my editor Jill McConkey for having faith in the manuscript, Barbara Porter for shepherding it through the publication process, and Jim Leahy for copy-editing. I am especially grateful to the Press's anonymous readers for their detailed and insightful comments on the original manuscript. I thank Juliet Dunphy and my research assistant Heather Jessup for helping me prepare the manuscript for review and typesetting.

I acknowledge that chapters 2, 3, and 5 contain some substantially revised material taken from earlier publications: 'Fragments of Imagination: Rethinking the Literary in Historiography through Narratives of India's Partition' in *Jouvert: A Journal of Postcolonial Studies* 1.2 (1997): 27 par.; 'Cracking the Nation: Gender, Minorities and Agency in Bapsi Sidhwa's *Cracking India*,' in *ARIEL: A Review of International English Literature* 29.3 (1998): 43–64; 'At a Loss for Words: Reading the Silence in South Asian Women's Partition Narratives,' in *Topia: A Journal for Canadian Cultural Studies* 4 (2000): 53–71; 'Lifting the Veil? Reconsidering the Task of Literary Historiography,' in *Interventions: International Journal of Postcolonial Studies* 3.3 (2001): 446–51.

Various stages of the research and writing of this book have been funded by Concordia University, the Shastri Indo-Canadian Institute, and the Social Sciences and Humanities Research Council of Canada.

I am grateful for the encouragement and support of my family while I wrote this book. I thank Judy Chan and all the educators at the Concordia Daycare for caring for my child while I did this work. Thank you to Shayle for being patient while I learn to be a parent and an academic at the same time. Finally, I thank Bart Simon for his love, intellectual engagement, and unfailing support of my work.

UNSETTLING PARTITION: LITERATURE, GENDER, MEMORY

Introduction: Unsettling Partition

We experience the 'fictionalization' of history as an 'explanation' for the same reason that we experience great fiction as an illumination of a world that we inhabit along with the author. In both we recognize the forms by which consciousness both constitutes and colonizes the world it seeks to inhabit comfortably.

(White 99)

'It was only after the riots started that people began to recognize that Independence had come, Partition had occurred, India and Pakistan had been established,' said Rashiduddin Khan, a Muslim whose family had owned a shop in the plush market of Connaught Place in 1947. 'To tell you the truth, it was only in the bloodshed of partition that ordinary people saw the shape of independence.'

(Pandey, 'Partition' 2262)

I have heard that many women did not want to lose their honour and chose to die. Many men killed their own wives. I think that is really great because I know that such things make India brave. After all, life and death is a transitory game. Whoever might have died are dead and gone; but at least they have gone with courage. They have not sold away their honour. Not that their lives were not dear to them, but they felt it was better to die with courage rather than be forcibly converted to Islam by the Muslims and allow them to assault their bodies. And so those women died. They were not just a handful, but quite a few. When I hear all these things, I dance with joy that there are such brave women in India.

(Gandhi, '223 Speech at Prayer Meeting' 202)[1]

The partition of India in 1947 marked the birth of two modern nation-states and the end of British colonialism in South Asia.[2] The move toward the 'two-nation solution' was accompanied by an unprecedented mass migration (between eight to ten million people) to and from areas that would become India and Pakistan. It also coincided with the violent deaths of an estimated 100,000 to 500,000 people (Menon, *Borders* 35) and the sexual assault of over 75,000 women (Butalia, *Silence* 3).[3] In Calcutta, Direct Action Day (16 August 1946) – called by the Muslim League to demonstrate Muslim solidarity – was marked by sectarian violence including arson, looting, and the abduction of women. What came to be known as the great Calcutta killing was followed by similar events in September at Noakhali and later in the Punjab and East Bengal from March 1947 onwards.[4] Diverse representations of partition violence and the local consequences of the migration can be found in historical accounts, testimonies, and autobiographies.

The past twenty years have seen a re-evaluation of communalist explanations for partition and partition violence. In particular there has been a previously unprecedented focus on literary and testimonial accounts representing 'local' experiences at the time. While a number of Indian novels in English focusing on this experience have enjoyed a wide readership from as early as 1956 (with the publication of Khushwant Singh's *Train to Pakistan*), it was only after a marked increase in incidents of sectarian violence during the mid-1980s,[5] and in anticipation of the fiftieth anniversary of Indian independence, that an interest in what has come to be known as 'partition literature' came into focus.[6] As Andrew Whitehead observes, 'Partition has proved a remarkable spur to literary endeavour. How could it be otherwise? Several nations born amid turbulence and turmoil ... If little else of value has come out of those dark and dispiriting days ... the corpus of compelling writing is some slender consolation' ('Cross' 19). Some of the best-known collections of short stories available in English include Alok Bhalla's three-volume *Stories about the Partition of India* (1994),[7] Saros Cowasjee and K.S. Duggal's *Orphans in the Storm: Stories on the Partition of India* (1995),[8] Mushirul Hasan's *India Partitioned: The Other Face of Freedom* (1995), and Muhammad Umar Memon's *An Epic Unwritten: The Penguin Book of Partition Stories* (1998).[9]

Renewed attention to fictional accounts of the partition in literary studies was accompanied by a turn toward this same material in historical studies, where literature has been read as offering an alternative 'record' of the period. Mushirul Hasan's *India's Partition: Process, Strat-*

egy, and Mobilization (1993) was one of the first historical studies to include a translation of Saadat Hasan Manto's short story 'Toba Tek Singh' as part of its collection; Gyanendra Pandey's 'The Prose of Otherness' in *Subaltern Studies* (1994) offers a reading of this same story as a 'fragment' of 'everyday' experience that marks 'contested spaces' in partition history ('Defence' 571); and Ian Talbot's work in *Freedom's Cry* (1996) relies on the 'extended use of fictional "representation"' which he argues 'has largely been neglected by standard historical accounts' (xiii). These and other scholars were some of the first to realize that, as historian Antoinette Burton has recently argued, '[t]he pluralization of partition narratives – however belated – offers a rare and politically important opportunity for scrutinizing the various forms and fictions through which memory has been articulated and can therefore be reimagined as a site, a dwelling pace, of legitimate historical practice' (*Dwelling* 102).

Before the late 1980s, literary criticism in English studies had made only tentative efforts to comment on the significance of these narratives. Until recently, literary criticism of 'partition narratives' in English has been limited to a few scattered essays in journals and anthologies on modern India.[10] Nevertheless, critics' praise or disapproval of literature representing the events of partition has played a key role in how the texts were received in their particular national contexts. As Joe Cleary has argued in his comparative study of Irish, Israeli, and Palestinian literature about partition,

> [i]n the case of partitioned societies, cultural narratives play a number of very important functions. They represent one of the media through which the trauma of partition is subsequently memorialised and understood by peoples involved; they can also help either to ratify the state divisions produced by partition or to contest the partitionist mentalities generated by such divisions. (2)

For the most part, early commentary on partition literature characterized it as 'documenting' rather than re-presenting the violence, and thus the interpretive function of reading and writing about the partition, the discursive construction of subjectivity, agency, nationalism, and history that are involved in its narrativization, is not considered. Similarly, literary criticism reliant on 'universalizing' liberal humanist rhetoric to frame discussions of writers' representations of this period sidelined attention to the elite, racist, and patriarchal interests that are often, even in very early literary responses to partition, challenged. What have been pushed to the margins of these types of readings are representations of 'everyday' and local experience that challenge the totalizing logic of bourgeois nationalism and point to a more contingent and polyphonic reading of national identity.[11] One of the central concerns of this book is to explore how literature and literary criticism play a role in bolstering or questioning the production of hegemonic nationalist imaginaries in India, Pakistan, and Bangladesh today.

The role literary criticism has played in silencing some of the challenges to the official record offered by these texts underscores the importance of developing what Suvir Kaul has identified as more 'vigilant or critical reading[s]' of partition literature (13). In the introduction to *Stories about the Partition of India* Alok Bhalla registers a similar imperative: 'I have put together this anthology of stories about the Partition not in order to exorcise the past, but in the hope of initiating an ethical inquiry into the history of my age and place' (x). Bhalla's and Kaul's challenge to their readers raises the question of how a rigorous and 'ethical' inquiry into these events through literary criticism should proceed. The importance of critical reading in this process is underscored by Bhalla: 'The writers of these stories frame the events in a variety of ways and read them according to their own sense of the multi-religious and multi-cultural past of the Indian subcontinent. How we, in turn, read these stories, based upon our own presuppositions, will determine the kind of politics we choose to practice in the future' (xxxiii). *Unsettling Partition* attempts to carry forward the project set out by scholars like Kaul, Bhalla, and others by focusing on the 'performative power' (Miller 8) of language mobilized in the act of reading with an emphasis on how literature intersects with the spheres of knowledge, politics, and history in its representation of India's partition.

Some of the most important work undertaken in connection with the shift in attention to previously unconsidered perspectives on partition includes the pioneering historical research on the gendered nature of the partition violence by Urvashi Butalia, Ritu Menon, and Kamla Bhasin. Beginning with the publication of early essays on women's testimonies, parliamentary records, and interviews with social workers involved in the recovery operations in *Economic and Political Weekly* in 1993, this research culminated in Butalia's *The Other Side of Silence: Voices from the Partition of India* (1998) and Menon and Bhasin's *Borders and Boundaries: Women in India's Partition* (1998). Suvir Kaul underscores the pivotal role this research has played in establishing how '[s]exuality and gender have a *constitutive* centrality here – as critical axes, they provide an understanding that does not simply supplement more orthodox historiography [of partition] but interrogates and rewrites its narratives' (10). A gendered understanding of the partition necessitates a shift in the scholar's attention from the public to the private, from the high political story to the local, everyday account. To be more specific, reading and writing about literature representing women's lives involves straddling both these spheres, making visible the binary construction of the public and private implicated in nationalist discourse, patriarchal power relations, and the way in which women's bodies were singled out as privileged sites of violence at the time of partition.

With the introduction of the issue of gender into a discussion of the history and politics of the partition, a very different kind of story has emerged – different in terms of the understanding of partition it provides and of what it means to write history and read literature about the period. When the trope of 'the citizen' is tracked through the story of partition it becomes apparent that events have a particularly gendered character; the economy of meaning within elite, patriarchal, and racist national imaginaries circulating at the time conflated the sacredness of the nation with the sacredness of Woman, making women both an object of protection and target of violence – both physical and discursive – in the struggle for independence. As the quote from Mahatma Gandhi's 'Speech at a Prayer Meeting' on 18 September 1947 at the beginning of this introduction suggests, dominant representations of 'everyday' experiences of partition focus on the necessity of preserving what is seen as the sanctity of women's sexuality in the private sphere, emphasizing the connection between the defilement of women through sexual assault or separation from their extended family and the defilement of community honour.

It is a testament to the stakes involved in examining the memory of partition that it has taken over forty years for critics to begin to acknowledge how some partition narratives unsettle gendered, monolithic, and objective accounts of this time. Along with the work by historiographers mentioned above (which I consider in more detail in chapter 2) have been several recent publications by literary scholars working in English whose approach to reading partition literature resonates with my own here; Suvir Kaul's edited collection, *The Partitions of Memory: The Afterlife of the Division of India* (2001), while not focusing solely on literature, highlights work that concentrates on the importance of fiction in shaping perceptions of this period in history. As Kaul explains, '[i]nsofar as Partition functions as a touchstone of our culture and polity, each time its stories are made and remade for us by different forms of documentary, fictional and even analytical representation, we learn about our changing social and political values' (9). S. Settar and Indira Baptista Gupta's *Pangs of Partition* (2002) also brings together individual essays on partition literature which, though decribed by editors as merely 'supplement[ing] our knowledge' (12) of the era, go much further to challenge assumed notions about historical discourse. Ravikant and Tarun K. Saint's *Translating Partition* (2001) includes a number of critical essays on partition literature dealing with issues of translation, interpretation, and the mutually constitutive realms of culture and politics. The introduction to their collection identifies several different trends in how partition literature has been read in recent years; it concentrates on partition as 'a watershed, a defining moment' in creative work by writers concerned with the effects of communal ideology in South Asia. 'There came into being,' the editors of this collection argue, 'a body of literature emphasizing that the lessons of the Partition have not been learnt, and that the nightmare could still be upon us' (xxi). As the editors point out, 'the metaphor of madness' that appears in some partition fiction 'could be used as conventional shorthand to communicate a sense of incomprehension' (xvi). It can also 'denote a refusal to understand' (xvi). When 'madness' is used as an explanation for the events of partition in literary criticism, it becomes 'a comfortable way out, for having consigned the irrational to the domain of madness,' and the critic can 'preserve the domain of the rational for himself/herself' (xvi).

In keeping with the pattern characterizing communalist discourse under colonialism, until recently individuals and groups involved in the sectarian violence surrounding the events of partition have been consistently denied conscious agency both for their instigation of and response to violence. Gyanendra Pandey's well-known study *The Construction of Communalism in Colonial North India* argues that during colonial times communalism was perceived by the British as 'the central problem to be overcome in the development of a self-governing, national and democratic polity in India' (5). He tracks how colonial accounts of sectarian violence consistently figured the problem of communal violence as the result of 'religious bigotry and its fundamentally irrational character' (10). In these accounts, the irrationality of this violence was closely related to its local character, setting up an opposition 'between the history of local society – wild, chaotic, liable to unexpected explosions – and the history of the state' (45). The colonial state, on the other hand, was seen as a 'wise and neutral power, ruling almost without a physical presence, by the sheer force of its moral authority' (49). In this way, when documenting violent confrontations between the community and state, colonial authorities could substitute one local riot for another without considering the context in which it occurred and thus gloss over the specificity of a particular event. Pandey contends that the cultural-historical significance of tensions between the colonial state and the local community were emptied out of the records of sectarian violence and substituted with meanings that suited the power/knowledge of colonial rulers (39).

The tendency to attribute partition violence to communalism is evident in some literary criticism on partition narratives. For example, Tariq Rahman praises Bhisham Sahni's novel *Tamas* (perhaps the best-known novel about partition) for its 'successful' representation of 'how people of all religions were caught up in the religious frenzy that could only be solved by partitioning the continent' (70). Similarly, when Alok Bhalla reflects on his own experiences as a child during partition he comments: 'It taught me that a group of people – any people – in their religious passion or tribal pride can always go mad; and that after a time they can relapse into madness again' (xi). The problem with communalist readings of sectarian violence, explains Gyanendra Pandey, is that 'no attempt is made to study the qualities of a specific historical consciousness in this specific time and place – the units of solidarity, the requirements of status, the understanding of honour and shame, in a word the competing and conflicting meaning of "rationality" in an old, highly developed non-capitalist society colonized by an advanced capitalist power' (*Construction* 20).

Translating Partition places a special emphasis on partition literature that reflects an 'ambivalent response to the question of national allegiance' in the work of writers like Saadat Hasan Manto, in contrast to 'a distinct strain' of nostalgia in 'many of the later writings' about partition that 'veer towards the romanticization of the pre-Partition experience' (xvii–xix). In this light, the editors of *Translating Partition* note that 'counter-narratives which focus on the local situation, rather than the national narrative of recovery of "honour" embodied in the abducted women' can be seen as pivotal in opposing 'conventional ways of narrativizing the Partition experience' (xxvi). *Unsettling Partition* concerns itself with these types of counter-narratives – texts that represent how women's bodies and identities became the focus of nationalist discourse and thus trouble both notions of 'recovery' and silences around women's experiences at the time of partition.

While I am concerned with bringing a plurality of views about partition to light – especially those that have been neglected – I am also wary of seeing this process as a way of completing the historical record. The assumptions driving the readings in this study are that it is not only important *what* types of women's experiences are represented (e.g., women who 'sacrifice' their lives in order to protect their honour versus women who live on at the margins of society) but also *how* these experiences are represented. This double focus is key to interrogating and unsettling monolithic accounts of this time. When these events are represented in literature, it is especially important to be aware of the way language renders their experience visible. As Gayatri Spivak argues,

> If we want to read narrative fiction in a specifically 'literary' way, we have to admit that what happens on its pages is language or prose ... Although we often treat narrative literature as if it is gossip about nonexistent people, or something the author is trying to tell us directly, in doing so we go against the specific nature of literature. ('Cultural' 337)

'What happens in literature *as* literature,' Spivak reminds us, 'is the peculiarity of its language' (337). Partition literature has often been read as a kind of 'record' or, conversely, 'gossip,' rather than a literary representation of the historical period. For example, in Saros Cowasjee's introduction to the collection *Orphans of the Storm: Stories on the Partition of India* he repeatedly refers to the stories as 'descriptions' or 'paintings' of the violence. He refers to the '*realistic* portrayal of communal violence as the most representative aspect of the Partition experience' (my emphasis; xii) without exploring the use of realism as a mode of representation with particular socio-historical implications. In contrast to this type of literary analysis, *Unsettling Partition* seeks to emphasize a more 'rhetorically sensitive' (Spivak, 'Cultural' 335) approach to reading partition literature, examining how 'the literariness of literature makes the language itself part of the content' (338).

Hence, rather than attempt to simply seek out a 'forgotten history' of this time, *Unsettling Partition* examines how the literariness of language mediates our perception of history, memory, and fictional representation of experiences connected to this event. It interprets the silences found in women's accounts of sectarian violence that accompanied partition (their sexual assault, abduction, and displacement from their families) not simply as an attempt to conceal a socially damaging experience but as sign of their inability to find a language to articulate their experience without invoking metaphors of purity and pollution. I argue that these silences and ambiguities in women's stories should not be resolved, accounted for, unveiled, or recovered, but, rather, understood as women's inability to subsume their experiences within the project of patriarchal modernity that has produced them in the first place. In this light, the book examines the status of 'truth' in history, literature, and testimony representing women's stories of the emergence of the postcolonial nation-state and considers their implications for nationalist discourse in South Asia today. *Unsettling Partition* considers how narratives concerned with the gendered aspects of citizenship destabilize truth claims about the past, disrupt totalizing accounts of independence and the division of India, and work toward deterritorializing nationalist discourse. In short, this book examines the role that narratives of women's experience play in constructing the memory of India's partition.

One of the overriding practical goals of this project is to contribute in a modest way to the larger project of bearing witness to the experiences of people who lived through the events of partition and reflect on how that process re-orients our understanding of history, politics, and culture.[12] My attempt to do this is informed by the assumption that the notion of 'voice' is fraught with epistemological, ethical, and literary problems.[13] The silence surrounding the gendered violence experienced by 'abducted women' has forced them to re-narrativize their relationship to the state, community, and their own identities in order to make sense of the inscriptions that the violence has left on their bodies and, through this, negotiate their survival. The collapse of meaning that such violent atrocities produce in women's testimonies about this time forces them, as Veena Das argues,

> into a dumb condition that is not only a *sign* of this period but is also a part of the terror itself. It is this fact – that violence annihilates language, that terror cannot be brought into the realm of the utterable – which invites us to constitute the body as the mediating sign between the individual and society, and between the past and the present. (*Critical* 184)

If, as Das claims, the gendered subject's body is a 'mediating sign' between the past and present, literature that represents the 'everyday' experience of women's lives during the nationalist period and partition is a particularly appropriate place to investigate this phenomenon. Literature, as a form of writing that foregrounds the metaphorical and indirect properties of language, points to how that mediation takes place, the discourses available to the subject at any given time, and the specificity of the limits of what can be known about the subject's experience. With regards to partition, Das points out that

> [n]o public space was created in which society could confront the event, in which it could hear from women the nature of their experiences or from men a defence or acknowledgement of the forces that led them to commit such unspeakable crimes. For example there were no tribunals where the guilty were tried; nor were there any court cases in which a theatrical space could have been created for the acknowledgement of the suffering imposed on women – a suffering in which the whole society was accomplice. Neither was it possible to hear of exemplary instances of altruism that could have offered redemptive possibilities. (192–3)

She calls for the creation of 'therapeutic' spaces where the 'reworking of personal histories' can take place that would 'allow private experiences of pain to move out into the realm of publicly articulated experiences of pain' (193). It is my hope that this study will contribute, in a modest way, to the project of creating those spaces.

Because of the stigma attached to women's experiences outside the protection of the patriarchal extended family during partition, and the overriding influence exercised by patriarchal interests over nationalist discourse in India and Pakistan, those invested in maintaining the status quo have been successful in silencing 'abducted' women who are still alive. On the one hand, the state has appropriated the memory of partition to suit its patriarchal, elite, and Hindu-centric agenda. On the other, it appears to be equally true that the victims' community has performed similar manoeuvres to suit its own agenda. 'The militant discourse of the community,' Das argues, 'when it tries to forge itself as a political actor, mimics the state and ends up by reproducing its categories' (205). Further, she points out, 'Both state and community, in claiming the victim, end up simulating the suffering of the victim and thereby making it the victim of their discourse' (209). While some historiographic and historical research has sought to write their stories, this approach fails to address the problem of how *any* attempt to write a meta-narrative is necessarily homogenizing in its articulation. *Unset-*

tling Partition reads decentred and fragmented representations of the 'everyday' events of partition in order to illustrate how they challenge and disrupt meta-narratives and deterritorialize nationalist discourse. These counter-narratives present a different temporality in which 'everyday' life is interrupted and a new order is in the process of being established. I situate the perception of experience in terms of gender, the literariness of language, placing both community and state narratives under erasure in order to allow other narratives to emerge, interrupt, and question the hegemony of the assumed understandings of this period.

I have endeavoured in what follows to avoid the vexed attempt to 'speak for' the victims of partition. Many of the people who experienced partition perished during the upheaval, died in the subsequent fifty years since independence, or now, fifty years later, do not speak about it. Survivors of sexual assault and other kinds of partition violence are especially reluctant to recount memories of these experiences. Furthermore, caution has been expressed by researchers like Anne Hargrove, who points to the danger of 'abducting' women's identities who lived through partition for 'our own scholarly purposes, even when we are trying to write against the state's coercive projects' (2429).[14] She argues, 'we need to reflect upon our efforts to pull women informants back across our own borders and notions of identity' (2429). For these reasons, my project avoids treating any representation of 'experience' as a reflection of 'reality' and insists on the mediating role of language, subjectivity, and materiality in the formation of narratives of identity. Inevitably, the reduction of experience to the personal, private, and subjective property of the individual allows his or her suffering and/or triumphs to be bracketed from the larger historical narrative of the independence. By focusing on the literariness of counter-narratives of partition history, *Unsettling Partition* seeks to redirect the gaze of the reader/researcher away from women's bodies and sexuality (the site surveilled by community and state) and toward the way these narratives intervene in totalizing discourses that have spoken, and continue to speak, for their experiences.

My discussion focuses on several examples of literary representations of the 'everyday' experience of partition, including Rajinder Singh Bedi's 'Lajwanti' (1951), Attia Hosain's *Sunlight on a Broken Column* (1961), Jyotirmoyee Devi's *The River Churning* (1966), and Bapsi Sidhwa's *Cracking India* (1988). It also examines the assumptions that inform scholarly work by bringing together testimonies about the partition by

Gyanendra Pandey, Ritu Menon, Kamla Bhasin, Veena Das, and Urvashi Butalia.[15] All of these texts offer representations of women who negotiate their multiple identities in order to survive the events of partition and point to the differential 'rights' that pertain to the gendered citizen-subject as well as contradictions in state and community nationalist imaginings. By interrupting the 'realist' ideology of these representations of experience, my project rethinks the silence that surrounds the history of the private sphere during partition, its opposition to the public sphere, and discloses the contradictions between women's identities as citizen-subjects and members of their local communities. The so-called secular, democratic, and universal nature of citizenship that the Indian state claimed to establish in 1947 is shown as privileging an elite, masculine, and ethnically homogeneous citizen-subject. To this end, I read competing representations of the violence and displacement that occurred at the time and attempt to disrupt hegemonic accounts that dehistoricize and universalize the conflicts. I argue that the discursive maintenance of a universalizing definition of nationalist identity elides the experience and agency of women in order to contain the threat they pose to a monolithic patriarchal imaginary in the postcolonial modern nation-state. As a counter to this practice, *Unsettling Partition* maps the discursive pressures on the gendered citizen-subject to reconstruct herself as a complement to this normalized subject and examines her strategies of resistance. I consider how literature about the partition poses the question of what is at stake in the universalizing views of citizenship and 'Womanhood' invested in nationalist discourse. In this way, I attempt to highlight how literature prompts us to scrutinize the gendered citizen-subject's compromised position in relation to state and community agendas.

I have chosen to work on this group of texts for a variety of reasons. It is now a well-established view, following Benedict Anderson, that literature serves a major function in the formation as well as contestation of the nation. Each of the texts discussed in this book is engaged, to a certain extent, in this process of rewriting the nation by challenging the construction of Woman as nation. Ania Loomba comments on how 'national fantasies, be they colonial, anti-colonial or postcolonial, also play upon and with the connections between women, land or nations' (215). 'As national emblems,' argues Loomba, 'women are usually cast as mothers or wives, and are called upon to literally and figuratively reproduce the nation' (216). Woman as Mother of the nation is a ubiquitous trope in Indian writing and, as the violence against women at the time of partition and after suggests, the protection, assault, abduction, and recovery of their bodies underscores how their figuration in nationalist discourse is key to understanding this history and its implications for the present.

While many critics have pointed out that women writers and representations of women's experience are just as capable of reinscribing dominant ideologies of the nation as those written by or about men, nevertheless, as Susie Tharu and K. Lalita argue, 'women articulate and respond to ideologies from complexly constituted and decentred positions within them' (*Women* 35). Thus, though these texts representing women's experiences of partition are in different relationships to, and participate in, to different degrees, the reproduction of hegemonic views of the nation, they can also be read 'as *documents* that display what is at stake in the embattled practices of self and agency, and in the making of a habitable world, at the margins of patriarchies reconstituted by the emerging bourgeoisies of empire and nation' (39). Like other work that has been done on women's writing in South Asia, this study attempts to 'dramatiz[e] and clarif[y]' (36) the costs of gendered notions of national belonging which have shown as central to the emergence of nationalist discourse.

'In order to understand the nature of the home that stands under the sign of the mother,' argues Aamir Mufti, 'we must examine closely the inhabitants of that other gendered space, the brothel' ('Greater' 5). Mufti suggests that 'the subaltern figure of the prostitute' serves as a means to 'opening up the familial semiotic of nationalism to interrogation' (4). Following this logic, the women's experiences discussed in *Unsettling Partition* share something of the displaced relationship to 'the sign of the mother' Mufti identifies in the figure of the prostitute; as women whose bodies become sites of sectarian violence but do not die, as abducted and recovered women whose 'pollution' is an accepted fact that they attempt to question, as disobedient daughters who challenge familial expectations about their sexual conduct – these figures 'come to acquire a critical energy that makes visible the representational work of the nation' (6). Like the stories by Saadat Hasan Manto that Mufti discusses in his work, the narratives examined in *Unsettling Partition*, both in their form and content, 'attempt to dislodge, from within, the terms of the attempted nationalist resolution of the question of collective selfhood and belonging' and 'render an account of national modernity that is inscribed not with affirmations of identity and subjectivity, but with displacement and difference' (3–4).

Mufti's essay 'A Greater Story-Writer than God: Genre, Gender and Minority in Late Colonial India' tracks how the 'realist aesthetics' associated with the mid-twentieth-century Indian novel are more accurately understood as a *'national* realism' committed to 'narrating the emergence of this consciousness – the abstract and secular citizen subject – as the highest form of consciousness possible in colonial society' (11). In opposition to this trend, Mufti argues that Manto's choice of the short story form as his primary genre 'puts the terms of this [national] totality in question and holds at bay the resolutions whose "end" is the form of consciousness that is the abstract citizen' (12). While the analyses in *Unsettling Partition* are concerned with a variety of genres that include the novel and represent women's experience of the partition, I argue that each of the texts discussed shares a similar 'ambivalent relationship ... to the forms of national culture that Manto's work exemplifies' (12–13). The link between gender identity and fragmented representations of selfhood, consciousness, experience, memory, understanding, and, consequently, belonging are recurring formal and thematic concerns in each of the texts considered.

The book comprises five chapters. Each one addresses a theoretical issue pertinent to my investigation. Roughly speaking, these sections look at the relevance of theories of gender and nationalism, the linguistic turn in historiography, the discourse of domesticity, and theories of agency and 'voice' to narratives of India's partition. Chapter 1 considers the intersections between gender and the discourse of nationalism in South Asia and suggests how representations of partition might offer a particularly rich expression of this patriarchal community–state alliance. Following Partha Chatterjee and others, I argue that national imaginaries in colonial and postcolonial contexts are posited not in identity with Western models, but in difference. My discussion maps this difference within a critical genealogy of nationalism in South Asia by analysing the effects of the relational, or, in other words, agonistic, production of power/knowledge. I explore how dominant Indian nationalist discourse is organized around the production of two relational and gendered spheres of power/knowledge that Chatterjee terms the material and spiritual domains. This configuration, I argue, is exemplary of the binary construction of nationalist rhetoric that inflects the canonized narrative of partition that my study seeks to problematize. I delineate the need for a more nuanced and contextualized reading of South Asian nationalist discourse, taking into account the way it intersects with the discourses of gender, race, class/caste, and modernity.

This chapter also investigates how theories of nationalism point to the way literature and literary reading strategies can be used to challenge patriarchal and ethnocentric views of the nation.

Chapter 2 explores the power relations expressed in and through figurations of 'everyday' events of partition in recent historiographical scholarship. The main argument that guides this chapter is that historiographers' attempts to problematize a modernist, totalizing perspective of 'H'istory from the state's perspective by including literary representations of the 'everyday' experience in South Asia at the time of partition are insufficiently theorized with respect to their understanding of literary language. In particular, I look at the discursive contradictions and intersections among hegemonic representations of the events of partition and the case of the Indian and Pakistani nation-states' efforts to 'recover' 'abducted' women after independence. Work by feminist historiographers that is conscious of the 'linguistic turn' in historical studies is useful for making visible the assumptions that impinge on representations of women's experience in literary, historical, and oral texts. While I praise historiographers' efforts to articulate a practice of writing history as 'fragmentary' in order to problematize the omniscient, modernist perspective of Historical texts, I am unsatisfied with their deployment of the 'literary' as 'evidence' of the 'everyday.' Finally, I offer a reading of Rajinder Singh Bedi's short story 'Lajwanti' as a model for how the fictional power of texts can be an important resource for understanding the collusion among state and patriarchal and elite interests in the treatment of 'abducted' women. First published in Urdu in 1951 and translated into English by Bedi in 1967, 'Lajwanti' tells the story of the abduction and recovery of Sunder Lal's wife and explores the way her 'pollution' makes visible patriarchal attitudes governing women's identities in postcolonial India.

Chapter 3 picks up on this reading strategy and investigates how partition affected the establishment of a modern nation-state in Pakistan in terms of minoritarian and gendered subject positions. First published in 1988 as *Ice-Candy-Man* and three years later under the title *Cracking India* (1991), Bapsi Sidhwa's novel was one of the first to gain wide attention for its representation of abducted women's experience. I argue that Lenny's narration of her coming of age as a Parsi during the nationalist movement and partition in Sidhwa's novel serves as an analogue for the exercise of agency by groups and individuals whose subject positions are situated outside the dominant order. Sidhwa's text performs a double gesture of highlighting the privileged economic and cultural position of the Parsi community in colonial India despite its minority status, contrasting it with the treatment of the subaltern Sikh, Muslim, and Hindu women, especially Lenny's *ayah*, Shanta, at the time of partition. Despite Lenny's privileged economic position, her 'education of desire' (Stoler 109) under the tutelage of Ayah/Shanta provides insight into the contradictions within her community and society's dominant codes and allows her to subvert the trope of 'the good Parsi' (Luhrmann 1). Finally, I focus on Lenny's figuration of the fluid agency exercised by Ayah with regards to her sexuality and male patronage prior to partition and track the constriction of these same things (as well as the novel's own blindness to the limits of this agency) after the creation of the Pakistani and Indian nation-states. Sidhwa's text, I argue, points to the gendered aspects of modern national imaginaries in which policing women's sexuality is tantamount to policing national borders.

Chapter 4 examines the modernist refashioning of Muslim women's identities in the domestic sphere during the nationalist period leading up to partition, with particular reference to Attia Hosain's *Sunlight on a Broken Column* (1961). I propose that *Sunlight* can be read as a subversion of the popular romance genre that has often been enrolled by nationalist projects. I also investigate the narrative's attention to the reform in Muslim women's identity in relation to female grooming handbooks that were popular in the era in which the novel is set and consider how Hosain's novel satirizes these models for female behaviour. Although Hosain's text produces contradictions of its own around questions of women's sexuality, its focus on the private sphere illuminates links between the recuperation of gender, class, and domesticity and the formation of the modern nation-state.

Chapter 5 responds to recent work on partition narratives concerned with recovering historical evidence about the treatment of 'abducted' women during and after India's partition, and investigates its elliptical quality. I theorize the silence surrounding the details of sectarian violence that recurs in testimonies and literary representations of these events. I argue that the loss of an archive suggested by this silence necessitates that scholars adopt a pedagogy for the study of partition history that moves away from a model that seeks to 'recover' the past and instead focuses on how totalizing representational strategies smooth over ambivalent responses to the birth of the modern nation-state. The desire to 'recover' the experience of 'abducted' women in order to correct the historical 'record' is shown to share the same modernist assumptions that informed the state-sanctioned Recovery Operation. Given that the stated goal of much work on women's experience of partition is to critique the assumptions behind this operation and explore how attention to gender identity can disrupt past and present hegemonic definitions of national identity, a wariness of these kinds of retellings would seem to be in order.

My analysis in chapter 5 meditates on the 'absent-presence' of details concerning sectarian violence at the core of 'abducted' women's narratives and offers a reading strategy that emphasizes the indirect, mediated, and fragmented representational practices that inform all testimony and literature. I offer a reading of Jyotirmoyee Devi's *The River Churning*, first published in Bengali as *Itihashe Stree Parva* in 1966. Set in part in East and West Bengal, this novel tells the story of a young Hindu girl named Sutara who is orphaned by partition violence (which she cannot remember clearly), taken into the care of her Muslim neighbours, and later 'returned' to her extended family in Calcutta only to be rejected by them as 'polluted' when she arrives. I argue that it is an attention to Devi's fragmented figuration of Sutara's traumatic experience of the partition riots – not her realist representational strategies – that makes it possible to render visible the gendered conditions of 'belonging' in the modern nation-state. I conclude that a consideration of the novel's refusal to 'recover' Sutara's experience within the script dictated by patriarchal nationalism suggests a model for challenging the absence of women's and Eastern Indian perspectives from the history of partition without reinscribing the discursive practices that produced this absence originally.

Until recently, a historicist explanation of the events of partition put forward by the Indian and Pakistani states has been allowed to stand as the 'objective' account of what happened and why. Similarly, realist fiction has been interpreted as the unmediated, reflective, and subjective 'T'ruth of partition experience, and the discursive construction of victims and villains, heroes and traitors has gone unremarked upon. Recent attention to women's experiences at the hands of the state and communities in India and Pakistan, however, raises serious doubts about the sufficiency of these narratives. While some historiographic and historical research has sought to write their stories, this approach fails to address the problem of how *any* attempt to write a metanarrative is necessarily homogenizing in its articulation.

In contrast to this approach, *Unsettling Partition* offers readings of decentred, fragmented representations of the 'everyday' events of partition with the hope of both illustrating how they challenge and disrupt meta-narratives and work toward deterritorializing nationalist discourse. These accounts present a different temporality in which 'everyday' life is interrupted and a new order is in the process of being established. I situate the perception of experience in terms of subject positions and the literariness of language, place both community and state narratives under erasure in order to allow other narratives to emerge, and interrupt and question the hegemony of the dominant narrative. The general aims of this investigation are to raise enabling questions about how literary texts and the academic study of literature, culture, and history are enrolled in the production of nationalist imaginaries as well as how they subvert and rewrite them. In what follows, I offer a critical engagement with the politics of gender and nationalism as they are implicated in memories of India's partition.

1 'Making Men for the India of Tomorrow'? Gender and Nationalist Discourse in South Asia

'I want you to understand that you should not be selling foreign stuff. You should not sell English biscuits.'

'All right, sir, hereafter I will be careful, after I dispose of the present stock.'

'If you have any pride as an Indian you will throw the entire stock in the gutter and won't let even a crow peck at it. Do you understand?'

(R.K. Narayan, *Waiting for the Mahatma* 117)

R.K. Narayan's novel *Waiting for the Mahatma* tells the story of an aimless young man, Sriram, who struggles to live up to the teachings of Mahatma Gandhi in order to win the love of his faithful disciple, Bharati. Under Gandhi's orders, Sriram travels around the countryside painting 'Quit India' on the walls of shops and houses in the villages he passes through. A chance encounter with a shopkeeper who boasts of stocking 'Purely English biscuits' (116) draws Sriram into a comical debate over Gandhi's *swadeshi* (self-sufficiency) message that shakes his already fragile commitment to the movement. While Narayan uses what is represented as a trivial issue leading to a ridiculous confrontation to offer a subtle satirization of both the small-minded shopkeeper and the false convictions of Sriram, the incident highlights how the manufacture and marketing of products was inflected with nationalist sentiments during India's struggle for independence.[1]

I was reminded of this fictional incident when I came across an advertisement for Parle's Gluco Biscuits while reading microfiches of English-language newspapers that were published in India as the events of partition and independence unfolded. In the corner of the 3 November 1947 edition of *The Times of India* (see Appendix A), under the slogan

'Making Men for the India of Tomorrow,' is a picture of a group of young boys in an Indian classroom. Three boys are sitting and listening intently as one boy stands facing the class and appears to be giving a speech. The caption below the picture reads, 'The boy who leads on the playground and in the classroom usually grows up to be a leader among men – a statesman. The proud mother sees that Parle's Gluco Biscuits are included in the diet of the young aspirant.' The South Asian boy at the front of the class is dressed in an Indian version of a British prep school uniform. Since its founding in 1929, Parle, an Indian-based biscuit and candy company, has carved a place for itself in the domestic market through a reliance on nationalist rhetoric. As this 1947 ad campaign suggests, the company framed its product as an Indian alternative to British-made biscuits. The 'Parle Story' on the company website describes its inception in similarly nationalistic terms:

> A long time ago, when the British ruled India, a small factory was set up in the suburbs of Mumbai city, to manufacture sweets and toffees. The year was 1929 and the market was dominated by famous international brands that were imported freely. Despite the odds and unequal competition, this company, called Parle Products, survived and succeeded by adhering to high quality and improvising from time to time.
>   A decade later, in 1939, Parle Products began manufacturing biscuits, in addition to sweets and toffees. ('Parle Story')

When this ad appeared in *The Times of India* in 1947, Parle was on the cusp of becoming a nationwide distributor of Indian tea biscuits.

This advertisement epitomizes an aspect of South Asian nationalist discourse (in its revivalist, reformist, and liberal articulations) that appears over and over again in literary and other cultural representations of the events leading up to independence and partition. The gendering of the public and private spheres is quite plain – the schoolroom as the training ground for young boys aspiring to the status of future political leaders and the home as the domain of women, especially mothers, a place for nurturing masculine political power. While the mothers of the boys are not pictured in the staging of their children's entry into the public sphere – the schoolroom imagined as the training ground for future political leaders of the nation – they are hailed on the sidelines as the primary caregivers for these boys at home.[2] Tanika Sarkar, among others,[3] has argued that while this gendering of *ghar* (home) and *bahir* (world) as feminine and masculine respectively has its roots in pre-colonial patriarchal structures governing elite Hindu Bengali (or *bhadralok*) communities, it was first mobilized in nationalist discourse during the nineteenth century in colonial India. As is now well established, in response to colonialism in India, anti-colonial nationalist discourse came to be organized around two relational and gendered domains of knowledge that Partha Chatterjee identifies as 'the material' and 'the spiritual':

> The *material* is the domain of the 'outside,' of the economy and of statecraft, of science and technology, a domain where the West had proved its superiority and the East had succumbed. In this domain, then, Western superiority had to be acknowledged and its accomplishments carefully studied and replicated. The *spiritual*, on the other hand, is an 'inner' domain bearing the 'essential' marks of cultural identity. The greater one's success in imitating Western skills in the material domain, therefore, the greater the need to preserve the distinctness of one's spiritual culture. This formula is, I think, a fundamental feature of anticolonial nationalisms in Asia and Africa. (my emphasis) (*Nation* 6)

This formulation is particularly important for a discussion concerned with how patriarchal nationalist interests situate women as bearers of a reconfigured notion of 'tradition.' The Parle's advertisement encapsulates this discursive manoeuvre; it suggests that the proper nourishment of young Indian boys will give them the constitution to compete physically and intellectually not only with each other, but also with their European counterparts. The masculine subject in the material domain is produced within a Western context (Macaulay's postcolonial schoolrooms) to be schooled in modernist concepts such as civility, rationality, and economics. Though the feminized subject is pushed to the margins of this scene, she is still tethered to its production. Parle interpolates bourgeois women as 'proud mothers' who should ensure that – along with 'traditional' Indian dishes – their family's diet includes modern but locally produced biscuits. Thus, while the 'spiritual' or private domain is constructed as a place free from colonial cultural influence, it is not considered above the need for reform. The mothers addressed by the Parle's Gluco Biscuits advertisement are expected to place their sons' welfares first and build the nation through the dutiful performance of their domestic responsibilities. At the same time they are encouraged to introduce modern food products like Parle's biscuits, legitimated through their indigenous manufacture, into the family diet.

In Chatterjee's words, 'here [in the spiritual domain] nationalism launches its most powerful, creative and historically significant project: to fashion a "modern" national culture that is nevertheless not Western' (6).

Today, Parle boasts that 'Parle-G' – a clever acronym that puns the letter 'G' with '*ji*' (a Hindi suffix denoting respect) – 'are available to consumers [in India], even in the most remote places and in the smallest of villages with a population of just 500' ('Parle Story'). Not just a product consumed by cosmopolitan city dwellers, Parle-G is a biscuit whose homegrown status is certified by distribution to and consumption by villagers. The acronym, suggestive of a blend of tradition and modernity, also continues to inscribe a gendered division between home and the world in ad campaigns where fathers and children are pictured in Western clothes while mothers appear in saris.[4]

Though the gender binary that characterizes nationalist discourse in India has its roots in colonial and pre-colonial patriarchal configurations, here I want to think about it in relation to representations of women's experiences in partition narratives written in the postcolonial era. I argue that these narratives, in their ambivalent relationship to nationalist discourse, highlight the overlap and co-implication of the discourses of gender and nationalism and suggest that the two are inseparable as categories of analysis. My discussion of nationalist discourse in partition narratives follows in the footsteps of feminist researchers like Kumkum Sangari and Sudesh Vaid, whose collection *Recasting Women* is organized around the assumption that 'each aspect of reality is gendered, and is thus involved in questioning all that we think we know, in a sustained examination of analytical and epistemological apparatus, and in dismantling of the ideological presuppositions of so called gender-neutral methodologies' (2–3). In this same vein, in their work on the postcolonial state's treatment of 'abducted' women at the time of partition, Ritu Menon and Kamla Bhasin argue that

> the story of 1947, while being one of the attainment of independence, is also a gendered narrative of displacement and dispossession, of large-scale and widespread communal violence, and of the realignment of family, community and national identities as a people were forced to accommodate the dramatically altered reality that now prevailed. ('Abducted' 3)

The gendered qualities of this 'reality' are inextricably linked to a genealogy of nationalist discourse in which women's 'position[s] as independent, equal citizens in the nation [were] thwarted by the appropriation of "woman" (and its related gendered significations) as a metonymy for "nation"' (Ray, 'Gender' 97).

The discursive understanding of nationalism that underpins Benedict Anderson's analysis in *Imagined Communities: Reflections on the Origin and Spread of Nationalism* makes a particularly useful framework for exploring how literary texts and the academic study of literature and history are enrolled in the production of nationalist imaginaries and gender identity. It is now broadly accepted, following Anderson's research, that the nation may be understood as 'an imagined political community' in the sense that 'the members of even the smallest nation will never know most of their fellow-members, meet them, or even hear of them, yet in the minds of each lives the image of their communion' (6). An imagined community, according to Anderson, is both 'inherently limited and sovereign' (6) as a consequence of the 'finite, if elastic, boundaries, beyond which lie other nations' (7). The birth of national imaginaries in the era of the Enlightenment coincided, Anderson argues, with the decline of 'the legitimacy of the divinely-ordained, hierarchical dynastic realm' (7) and the rise of colonialism. The national imaginary is normalized as a community because, as Anderson points out, 'regardless of the actual inequality and exploitation that may prevail in each, the nation is always conceived as a deep, horizontal comradeship' (7).

Anderson draws an analogy between the concept of 'homogeneous, empty time' (24) as it is represented in narrative realism and the subject's perception of belonging to a (national) community that she or he will never entirely meet. 'Homogeneous, empty time' is, of course, Walter Benjamin's concept for a representation of time 'in which simultaneity is, as it were, transverse, cross-time, marked not by prefiguring and fulfillment, but by temporal coincidence, and measured by clock and calendar' (Anderson 24–5). 'Simultaneity,' Anderson argues, has been normalized in representations of experience in realist novels and newspapers since the Enlightenment (24–5). In other words, characters in realist novels (or news items) move through a 'sociological landscape of a fixity that fuses the world inside the novel with the world outside' and rehearses the idea of a shared time and space between the reader and the text (30). Other forms of realist narrative – like the articles in the

Times of India where I found the Parle's Gluco Biscuits advertisement – can be understood as an '"extreme form" of the book, a book sold on a colossal scale, but of ephemeral popularity' (Anderson 34). As a daily realist narrative representing events in the context of 'homogeneous, empty time,' the newspaper was an ideal place for companies like Parle to have their corporate identities woven into the fabric of the national imaginary. The newspaper – as a product whose value is infused with its time of production (that is, no one wants to read an 'old' newspaper) – becomes part of the national ritual of imaging an anonymous connection with others in the community on a daily basis. The narration of daily life in these terms allows nations (as both 'new' and 'historical') to 'loom out of an immemorial past, and still more important, glide into a limitless future,' thus giving them a sense of destiny foreshadowed by ancient origins (Anderson 11–12).

While Anderson's conception of the nation as a 'cultural artifact' (4) is now well established, many have taken issue with the gendered and universalizing quality of his discussion. The gendered and bifurcated quality of Indian nationalist discourse represents a challenge to Anderson's view that nationalisms around the world borrowed their structures from certain 'modular' forms already established in Europe and the Americas (135). Anderson's universalist stance does not fully engage with the history of colonialism and its relation to the history of modernity and, instead, implies that nationalist imaginaries in nation-states like India and Pakistan are merely derivative of national imaginaries in Europe and the Americas. The irony of this assumption is, as Chatterjee explains, that

> [h]istory, it would seem, has decreed that we in the postcolonial world shall only be perpetual consumers of modernity. Europe and the Americas, the only true subjects of history, have thought out on our behalf not only the script of colonial enlightenment and exploitation, but also that of our anticolonial resistance and postcolonial misery. Even our imaginations must remain forever colonized. (*Nation* 5)

In colonial India, Chatterjee asserts that the national imaginary was 'posited not on an identity but rather a *difference* with the "modular" forms of the national society propagated by the modern West' (5) and that this accounts for its 'success' in India in 1947. Joe Cleary goes one step further to suggest that this may in fact be a common feature of all nationalist discourse. Building on Tom Nairn's widely held view that 'while the nationalist elites in the peripheries construed themselves as the emissaries of Enlightenment and modernization, they simultaneously represented themselves as the heirs and guardians to an ancient and distinctive national traditions,' Cleary contends that 'this ambivalent dialect between "tradition" and "the modern" neither begins with nor is peculiar to nationalism in the peripheries' (54). '[T]he concept of modernity,' Cleary claims, 'can never exist in pure form since it is always constitutively dependent on some concept of the anti-modern' (55). Thus, as Cleary argues, 'the lived experience of modernity – whether in the metropolis or the peripheries – has from the very outset always operated as a dialectical relationship between "modernity" and "tradition," conceived as a relation between two distinct conditions, two regions, two temporalities, two temperaments' (55).

Although this duality within nationalist discourse was highly effective in contesting colonial power, it also, as many feminist readings of the Indian nationalist movement have established, preserved and redeployed elite, patriarchal power.[5] As Parama Roy has pointed out, 'the nation's simultaneous and paradoxical adherence to a primeval past and its turn to the future ... brings together in a mutually uncomfortable but necessary alliance the elements of nostalgia and social and cultural atavism with the notions of modernity and "progress"' (137). Redeploying Anne McClintock's argument that 'the incommensurability of these two sets of terms is resolved "by figuring the contradiction [in nationalist discourse] as a 'natural' division of *gender*"' (McClintock 66; 137) in relation to the history of Indian nationalism, Roy argues that women's identities and bodies come to 'signify nationalism's link to a deep past, its conservative principle' (137). 'Men, on the other hand,' Roy explains, 'stand in for the modernity of nationalism, which is dynamic, aggressive, and revolutionary' (137).[6] Partha Chatterjee observes a similar dynamic in Indian nationalist discourse: 'it was undoubtedly a new patriarch that was brought into existence, different from the "traditional" order but also explicitly claiming to be different from the "Western" family' (9). 'The "new woman,"' according to Chatterjee, 'was to be modern, but she would also have to display the signs of national tradition and therefore would be essentially different from the "Western" woman' (*Nation* 9). Hence, as Chatterjee observes, nationalist discourse in India was not grounded in a 'total rejection of the West' or modernity but rather 'an ideological principle of *selection*' and adaptation ('Nationalist Resolution' 240). In an ironic rehearsal of the colonial construction of the Indian Woman as an object in need of colonial protection against the 'inhuman' and 'primitive' tendencies of Indian men,[7] anti-colonial nationalist discourse positions her as in need of protection from the corruption of Western culture. Sangeeta Ray makes a similar point in *En-Gendering India*, where she argues that

> [t]he Indian woman became a further contested site of appropriation when Indian nationalists sought to advance their agenda by fusing their desire for an independent nation with the independence of the Indian woman, who, they argued, could never achieve her 'pure' status as an equal participant in the domestic or public spheres within the boundaries of a spurious imagined community. (8–9)

In this sense, imperialist and nationalist discourse in India 'became increasingly intertwined as each sought to gain control over the representations of the Indian woman' (9). Susie Tharu's and K. Lalita's work on Indian women's writing reminds us of the differences that class considerations introduce into this problematic. For example, when they reflect on how class distinctions impinge on women's identities they conclude, 'It is difficult to imagine the restrictions on diet and the practices of self-abnegation that haunted the life of the brahmin widow finding place among the lower-caste women, who worked in the fields or at a trade for a living' (151). Similarly, Partha Chatterjee points out that the identity of the 'new' woman was constantly pitted against the '"common" woman who was coarse, vulgar, loud, quarrelsome, devoid of superior moral sense, sexually promiscuous, subjected to brutal physical oppression by males' ('Nationalist' 244). Thus, although women's experiences were informed by this construction, they also stood in contradiction or as a supplement to it.[8]

With the expression of cultural difference relegated to the (feminine) domestic sphere, 'Woman/Mother' and India became synonymous terms, leaving minorities, actual women, and lower castes/classes in a disjunctive relation with the nation. As Tanika Sarkar explains, in response to the 'gradual dissolution of faith in the progressive potential of colonialism' (196) in the mid-nineteenth-century, Hindu revivalists came to see the household as 'doubly precious and important as the only zone where autonomy and self-rule could be preserved' (197). 'Unlike Victorian middle-class situations,' Sarkar explains, 'the family was not a refuge after work for the man. It was their real place of work' (197). In liberal nationalist versions of this gendered division, the metonymic relationship this created between middle-class women and *ghar* (home) placed expectations on them to aspire to an image of femininity that ensured the preservation of patriarchal power and facilitated the adaptation of principles of modernity to dominant Hindu culture. In this sense, Indian nationalists set out to fashion 'new norms ... which would be more appropriate to the external conditions of the modern world and yet not a mere imitation of the West' (Chatterjee, *Nation* 125). The result was a 'marked *difference* in the degree and manner of Westernization of women, as distinct from men, in the modern world of the nation' (126). Changes in the role of women during the nationalist period were carried out under the guise of creating the opportunity for women to realize their essential feminine qualities while recognizing the necessity of adapting what were classified as more superficial cultural practices to the dictates of the modern world. Significantly, as Chatterjee comments, this 'selective appropriation of Western modernity ... continues to hold sway [in India] to this day' (120).

Reconstructions of the 'ancient origins' of Hindu cultural nationalism went hand in hand with an intensification of patriarchal surveillance of elite and middle-class women's sexuality and conduct as wives and mothers. In 'Whatever Happened to the Vedic *Dasi?* Orientalism, Nationalism and a Script for the Past,' Uma Chakravarti traces how the evocation by nationalist discourse of a mythic Hindu-Aryan identity during the nineteenth century produced 'different elements within a complex structure of ideas wherein knowledge about the past ultimately ended in the creation of a persuasive rhetoric, shared by Hindu liberals and conservatives alike, especially in relation to the myth of the golden age of Indian womanhood as located in the Vedic period' (28). The emergence of an archaic and ideal Hindu-Aryan notion of womanhood can be attributed to several interrelated historical narratives that circulated at this time. The first comprised Orientalist texts by European scholars such as H.T. Colebrooke, William Jones, and later Max Muller. These scholars 'saw themselves as engaged in reintroducing the Hindu elite to the "impenetrable mystery" of its ancient lore' (31). The characteristic features of these scholars' work included 'reference to a variety of ancient texts, the special authority given to texts over custom, the search for the "authentic" position as contained in the older and more authoritative texts, and the confusion in reconciling contradictory evidence' (30–1). Though initially the Orientalists did not impose a hierarchy of importance among the texts they studied, there quickly emerged a modernist, homogenizing historical classification of authenticity that privileged particular readings (often with the advice of the indigenous literati) of the Vedas and Upanishads (32). 'The reconstructed past,' Chakravarti comments, 'was increasingly appearing in pamphlets and vernacular journals, made possible with the introduction of printing, and the participants in this were the newly emerging intelligentsia composed of both traditional and modern elements who perceived themselves as interpreters of tradition in a changing situation' (32).

Missionaries, colonial administrators, and European travellers were generally less influenced by this view than by that put forth by Utilitarians like James Mill, whose *The History of British India* sought to investigate the 'peculiarities of Hindu civilization' (synonymous with 'Indian' at the time) and its 'barbaric practices pertaining to women' (Chakravarti 34). Unlike the narrative of ancient glory and present-day degradation that characterized Orientalist scholarship, Mill's book 'deemed Hindu civilization as crude from its very beginnings, and plunged in the lowest depths of immorality and crime' (35). Mill's views lent authority to British legal intervention in Indian society around issues such as *sati*[9] and resulted in his book's strong institutional support. Anxious to counter the negative perception of India's contemporary culture that was being emphasized in accounts like Mill's, Indians like Rammohun Roy and Mritunjay Vidyalankar embraced the double-edged sword offered by the Orientalists and advocated reform. The Hindu reformists took bittersweet comfort in this scholarship because, while it praised the 'ancient past' of their culture as a 'golden age,' it contrasted it with the current 'degenerate' treatment of Indian women and the general effeminacy of Indian men as a result of their submission to colonial rule.

The demonization of Muslims became an increasingly common theme in nationalist texts that emerged in the 1860s, when the Hindu elite in Indian society began to refer to the work of Max Muller in an attempt to naturalize their 'right' to nationhood over all other groups in Indian society. Although already in wide usage, the term Aryan was deployed by Muller to express what he saw as the particular racial qualities of Hindu culture. In these widely read accounts, Aryans are represented as 'the prominent actors in the great drama of history' for having 'carried to their fullest growth all the elements of active life with which [their] nature is endowed' (Muller *Chips* 4; Chakravarti 40). Muller argued that Aryans and Europeans share a common racial heritage, conflating the disciplines of philology and physiology. He writes, 'Though the historian may shake his head, *though the physiologist may doubt*, all must yield before the facts furnished by language' (Muller

History 24; Chakravarti 40).[10] Other Orientalist scholars elaborated on this racial discourse, arguing that 'with the Aryan conquest of India there was a rigid division between the conquering Aryans and the aboriginal people which later resulted in the emergence of mixed castes' (Chakravarti 42).[11] This historical narrative suggests that only those with the 'purest' Aryan blood would demonstrate the superior morality, intellect, and physical vigour of their ancestors.

In this sense the racist recoding of the Orientalist Hindu 'golden age' was informed by a discourse of degeneracy that saw the Aryan race as contaminated by inferior races through miscegenation especially since the Mogul times and in later periods leading up to Independence. One such account referred to by Chakravarti is that of Christian convert M.C. Deb, who attributed the 'sad and deplorable' condition of women in India to 'the ravages of Muslim rule' (38). Chakravarti argues that a language of difference came to dominate Hindu nationalist discourse 'which excluded all "foreigners"' (50). 'Foreigners' in this case meant not only the British 'but also Muslims and lower castes as they were non-Aryan and considered to be of "impure" extraction.' (50).[12] At this time, conservative literary and historical texts began to express a 'new identity of aggressive cultural nationalism' that left behind the universalism of earlier texts and instead reified *select* features of a Hindu past (49).

The dual process of inclusion and exclusion that came to exemplify cultural nationalism throughout much of the nineteenth century and after had specific consequences for perceptions of women's sexuality. Racialized Aryan and Muslim identities that dominated Hindu and Muslim cultural nationalisms were protected from degeneracy through the strict regulation and disciplining of women's sexuality. Totalizing readings of the Vedas by Hindu reformers like Dayananda paid particularly close attention to the issue of female sexuality; Dayananda proposed a regenerated Hinduism, coining the term Arya in place of Hindu to signify the restoration of racial purity to the community (55). The racialized and patriarchal epistemology that underpins Dayananda's reading of the *Rig Veda* is evident in his call for greater scrutiny of women's roles as mothers. As Chakravarti points out,

> Motherhood for Dayananda was the sole rationale of a woman's existence but what was crucial in his concept of motherhood was its specific role in the procreation and rearing of a special breed of men. For example, the *Satyarth Prakash* [Dayananda's overall theory of the state, society, history

and religion published in 1875] lays down a variety of rules and regulations for ideal conception. The birth of the child is also followed by a series of regulations on food, cleanliness, clothing etc. for both mother and child. (56)

There is a resonance here between the evocation of 'motherhood' and the task of 'rearing a special breed of men' and the Parle's Gluco Biscuits advertisement cited at the beginning of this chapter: the mothers referred to in Dayananda's rhetoric were also seen as 'Making Men for the India of Tomorrow.' In addition, Chakravarti notes that, despite Dayananda's belief in the generally destructive nature of women's sexuality, he argues that it is necessary to transform it 'into a force which could be constructively channelized to serve in the regeneration of Aryas' (57). As a consequence, he proposes regulations for everything from the distance between schools segregated by gender, to the best age for marriage with the ideal conditions for reproduction in mind and the management of widows' sexuality through the practice of *niyoga* or levirate (60). The central goal of rules of conduct like Dayananda's was to encourage reproduction among individuals who he thought would produce the 'healthiest' and 'strongest' children, paralleling the emerging bourgeois, patriarchal Hindu hegemonic order.

The intertwining of patriarchal and nationalist interests led to a categorization of women as good or bad according to their ability to live up to notions of idealized womanhood. Gandhi's views on women's 'natural' predisposition for *satyagraha* (nonviolence, or, literally, 'to persist in the truth') are a case in point here; as Kumari Jayawardena argues, in both domestic and civil spheres, 'Gandhi's ideal woman was the mythical Sita, the self-sacrificing monogamous wife of the Ramayana, who guarded her chastity and remained loyal to Rama in spite of many provocations. Sita was "promoted" as the model for Indian women' (96). The universalizing and totalizing view of women that informed Gandhism placed them in the state of 'two-ness' with both Indian and British national agendas. As Ketu Katrak comments,

> The ironic ramification of women's participation in *satyagraha* is that this nonviolent action strategy quite subtly, and insidiously, reinforced the most regressive aspect of women's subordination: their ability to suffer and to persuade through suffering their supposedly higher stature than men. ('Decolonizing' 167)

Katrak argues that Gandhi simultaneously mobilized and then subordinated women by placing strict control over the modality women's participation took in the nonviolent movement ('Indian' 395). Gandhi celebrated the image of the sexually dangerous female contained by strict domestic roles as evidence of the power of discipline to produce change though patience and suffering. The control of women's bodies by restricting their sexuality to a procreative function within marriage was promoted as the ideal for the future of the nation. Given the all-consuming power attributed to women's sexual appetite, Gandhi advocated that married couples take a vow of *brahmacharya*, a pledge to practise sexual abstinence as a 'national service' (397). Not based on an assumption concerning the *mutually* distracting effects of sex on a married couple, this practice was founded on Gandhi's belief in the insatiable sexual desire of women and their destructive effects on men's otherwise rational demeanours.[13]

Although Gandhi invited women to enter the public realm during the nationalist struggle by picketing shops selling British goods and promoting their husbands' participation in nonviolent movement, their identities and actions were governed by expectations that protected patriarchal power relations. As Radha Kumar points out, 'Gandhi was almost hysterical with rage' when a group of sex trade workers organized under the Congress banner

> had been asked to do such Gandhian 'humanitarian' work as helping the poor, nursing, promoting khadi spinning and weaving, etc.; all this was, however, dust and ashes to Gandhi, for the women had not given up their wage-earning work of prostitution itself. The idea of their engaging in 'humanitarian work' before they reformed themselves and 'lived like Sanyasins' was described as 'obscene' by Gandhi, who said these women were worse than an 'association of known thieves,' for they stole 'the virtue of society.' Only through reforming themselves, taking to the charkha and khadi, and welcoming suffering and self-denial, could they be accepted. (83–4)

In essence, Gandhi's conditions for allowing the women to organize as part of his nonviolent movement (which he held up as the only moral way to fight the colonists) required them to adhere to the attitude of a feminized, financially dependent, and sexually 'pure' way of living. Throughout the nationalist struggle women were praised when they adhered to these stereotypes and censured when they deviated from them. Gandhi's use of women's identities is but one example of the many ways they were mobilized at different times and by different groups during the revivalist, reform, and liberal nationalist periods. As Radha Kumar comments, 'The revivalists and extremists had used the images of the mother as victim (mother India, ravaged and depleted by rampaging foreign hordes), and the mother as warrior-protector (mother Kali); reformists and nationalist feminists had used the image of the mother as nurturer, socializer and supporter of men; Gandhi created the image of the mother as repository of spiritual and moral values as a preceptor for men' (82).

It is in this sense that many feminist scholars have argued that the nationalist movement did not really address the conditions of women living under patriarchy in the nineteenth and twentieth centuries in India. As Debali Mookerjea-Leonard explains, 'the pro-women rhetoric of reformist-nationalists did not challenge the patriarchal underpinnings of the prevailing gender regime but reworked it to adapt to the altered social and political circumstances' (15). Joanna Liddle and Rama Joshi's book *Daughters of Independence* provides numerous examples of the gap between the changes in women's legal status as a result of the nationalist movement and their actual effects on women's everyday lives. For instance, they show how the movement to win universal franchise in India was often bolstered by opportunistic and contradictory goals rather than feminist principles. While the Congress Party (dominated by elite men) included universal adult franchise in its platform in 1928, it is apparent that they did so partly with an eye to promoting the idea 'that they were more socially advanced than the British [the suffragette movement in Britain was in full swing at this time] and to counter claims that they were too backward for self-rule' (36).[14] Moreover, giving women the right to vote was not the same as ensuring that they exercised that right, and nationalist leaders knew that many votes would go uncast. Further, in the eyes of patriarchal Indian nationalists, the support for women's franchise in colonial context was seen as the lesser of two evils because 'any increase in Indian political representation was likely to be unfavourable to the British' (36). Thus, while it would be nice to attribute noble motives to Indian nationalists' support for 'women's rights,' it would appear to be somewhat naive.

The limits of nationalist concern with the status of women in Indian society became visible when women tested their 'right' to be treated as 'equal' citizens. When in 1934 the All Indian Women's Conference proposed changes to the Hindu Code that would ban polygamy, legalize inter-caste marriage, loosen restrictions on divorce, and ensure widows an equal share with their sons in their husband's estates (and half the same amount for their daughters), nationalist men retreated into their patriarchal corners. As Liddle and Joshi recount,

> In 1945 the Code divided the Indian political elite, for the Assembly agreed with the principle of sexual equality but found itself in conflict over how to implement it. Agreement was reached on political and economic issues (such as suffrage and employment) but not on domestic issues (such as marriage and inheritance), with the result that the clause forbidding discriminatory marriage and inheritance laws was excluded from the Constitution, and the statement that 'The State shall endeavour to secure that marriage shall be based only on the mutual consent of both sexes and shall be maintained through mutual cooperation, with the equal rights of husband and wife as a basis' was removed from the Code and did not reappear. (37)

As this incident suggests, attempts by women to politicize the domestic sphere represented an attack of male privilege that was otherwise normalized.

The privileging of patriarchal interests can also be seen in the nationalist movement within India's Muslim community during the colonial period with the codification of Muslim civil laws, or *Shariat*. In response to the dangerous malleability of customary law in the patriarchal context of colonial courts, women's organizations advocated legislation governing civil concerns, culminating in the Shariat Application Act of 1937 and the Dissolution of Muslim Marriage Act of 1939. As with the Hindu Code bill, the Shariat Application, which specified women's right to inheritance, was challenged by the landed gentry and was eventually watered down to mollify this group.[15] The Dissolution of Marriage Act (which allowed for divorce in Muslim marriages) – also supported by women's groups – was primarily successful because the *ulemas* (Muslim religious leaders) discovered that women 'were renouncing Islam to seek divorce which was not available under Muslim law' (Chhachhi 160). In the end, the Act limited alimony and restricted rights to *mher* (dower) (thus working against women's material interests) and instituted 'clear sanctions against conversion to another religion, and these functioned to further delineate and consolidate the boundaries of communities' (160). This Act, therefore, 'established a particular family structure – i.e. patriarchal, patrilineal, conjugal as the norm' (160–1) and was readily embraced by conservative authorities because 'it drew the family and crucial areas of gender relations under the jurisdiction of the state' (161). 'It is ironic,' Amrita Chhachhi suggests, 'that these laws have become the battleground for the defence of "authentic" Muslim/Hindu identity [in India today], when historical analysis shows that the process of codification contained a mix of various elements, ranging from interventions by colonial administrators, native interpreters, selected priests and mullahs to pressures from progressive men and women' (161). Far from excluding the private sphere from state control, therefore, there has been a consistent trend in the colonial and postcolonial history of the state to bring it 'under state control and institute a particular family form' (159). Dipesh Chakrabarty has commented on the limits of reform within the domestic sphere, pointing out, 'the line was drawn at the point where modernity and the demand for bourgeois privacy threatened the [elite patriarchal] power and the pleasures of the extended family' ('Postcoloniality' 15).

This overview of the history of mobilizing notions of Indian womanhood in Indian nationalist discourse is intended to help make sense of how women's bodies became sites of violence where different ethnic communities sought to establish their dominance over each other at the time of partition. The suicide, 'martyrdom,' sexual assault, 'abduction,' and social death suffered by women at the time of partition underscore how the metaphorical representation of women's chastity as representative of community honour was read as literal in patriarchal competitions for nationalist power. Furthermore, as researchers like Butalia, Menon, and Das have shown, 'abducted' women, by troubling notions of masculine honour invested in women's chastity, presented a 'new social question' (Canning 383) to patriarchal interests and threatened to destabilize their convergence in the national imaginings of the recently formed postcolonial state. Menon's and Bhasin's research indicates that from the beginning of the partition 'troubles,' representatives of the nation-state were enrolled in the process of 'recovering' 'abducted' women in order to restore masculine honour.

The discursive practices of parliamentarians, families, social workers, and police placed an emphasis on controlling the location and maintaining the sanctity of women's bodies. This practice was central to the production and stabilization of patriarchal nationalist imaginings in postcolonial India. For instance, on 17 November 1947, a resolution was passed by the All India Congress Committee that stated, 'Every effort must be made to restore women to their original homes with the co-operation of the governments concerned' (Menon and Bhasin, 'Recovery' WS4). By the following year, a bilateral agreement was established between India and Pakistan that set out the terms of recovery for abducted persons (read women and children) in both states, and ordinances to proceed with their recovery were issued. Dissatisfaction with the numbers and speed with which women were recovered emerged, and on 19 December 1949, just before the ordinances expired, the Abducted Persons (Recovery and Restoration) Bill was passed in the Indian parliament. As Menon and Bhasin suggest, it is possible to identify the patriarchal, communal, and nationalist discourses that shaped the identity of the gendered Indian citizen in the new nation-state in this bill. An 'abducted person' was defined in the bill as

> a male child under the age of 16 years or a female of *whatever age* who is, or immediately before the 1st day of March 1947, was, a Muslim and who, on or after that day and before the 1st day of January, 1949, [that is, during the time of the migration and violence that accompanied partition] had become separated from his or her family and is found to be living with or under the control of any other individual or family, and in the latter case includes a child born to any such female after the said date. (my emphasis) (Menon and Bhasin, 'Recovery' WS4)

The bill sanctioned the authority of the state to detain 'persons' who were suspected of being abducted, determine their nationality by means of a tribunal established by the Central Government, and use police powers to enforce this decision. As this excerpt from the bill also sets out, adult women were disqualified from designating their national identity themselves, and the state placed a special burden on women who identified themselves as Muslim to legitimate their 'right' to citizenship in India. Adult men, on the other hand, were under no special obligation to do the same because the powers of the tribunal only applied to males under the age of sixteen. Even though some members of parliament objected to these very issues and questioned the bill's legitimacy under the Constitution which would come into effect only one month later (January 1950), it was passed unaltered (WS5).

Contradictions and ambiguities that arose between these state and community investments in the recovery of 'abducted' women appear to have been resolved, at least temporarily, by discounting the agency these women exercised in their 'everyday' experience. However, the material evidence of this agency – in the form of these women's survival in and return from the communities and nation of the Other – became a constant reminder to national patriarchal interests that they had failed to preserve both the women's sexual 'purity' as symbol of community 'honour' and the sanctity of the domestic sphere (an essential component of [male] citizens' identities in postcolonial India). Women's failure to die in the riots resulted in the perception of their tainted chastity (in Jyotirmoyee Devi's *The River Churning* Promode's friend Ajay's frustrated response to the dilemma of 'abducted' women is to 'let them die ... let them be "wiped out"' [118]). 'Abducted' women's survival problematized the dichotomous relation between the civil and domestic spheres at a time when the state was attempting to extend this identity to all castes/classes in Indian society. Urvashi Butalia succinctly articulates this double bind as follows:

> For men, who in more 'normal' times would have seen themselves as protectors of 'their' women, the fact that many of (their) women had been abducted (no matter that some women may have chosen to go, they had to be seen as being forcibly abducted), meant a kind of collapse almost and emasculation of their own agency. Unable to be equal to this task, they now had to hand it over to the state, the new patriarch, the new super, the new national, family. As the central patriarch, the state now provided coercive backing for restoring and reinforcing patriarchy within the family. ('Community' WS19)

As feminist researchers have argued, while the state provided the authority and resources to conduct the Recovery Operation, its 'success' was highly dependent on the attitudes of individual actors at local levels. For instance, Butalia explains that reports of missing relatives (mothers, wives, daughters, and sons) had to be filed by next of kin before the state would intervene on their behalf (WS18). The reintegration of 'abducted' women into their 'original' families and communities also required a complete reconstruction of gendered rituals of purity; women who otherwise would have been shunned by their families as 'polluted' by the possibility or actuality of sexual contact with the Other had their identities reconstructed as 'victims' in exchange for the restoration of their patriarchal patronage. Similarly, the complicity of social workers (the majority of whom were women) was essential to the execution of the Recovery Bill's stipulations. Even though oral testimonies and documents of the social workers' activities suggest a sense of ambivalence about what they were doing, the women themselves seemed to foreclose any consideration of this during the execution of their duties. Instead, they appeared to have compartmentalized their conflicting experiences in much the same way the modern citizen-subject is expected to do with respect to his (and I use the masculine deliberately here) civil and domestic duties. Butalia notes, for example, how Kamalaben Patel, one of three key organizers of the Operation, 'speaks sometimes as an "Indian," other times as a "Hindu," sometimes as a "social worker," as a "nationalist" and sometimes, by her own definition, as a "woman," this last category subsuming, often, all others' (WS20).

Enrolling the coercive arm of the state as its ally provided the patriarchal community with the means of ensuring the triumph of its interests. As Dipesh Chakrabarty argues, 'repression and violence' are as 'instrumental in the victory of the modern as is the persuasive power of its rhetorical strategies' ('Postcoloniality' 21). To this end, ambiguous responses to the recovery of abducted women were often deflected by a rhetoric of idealism allied with the activities of the Recovery Operation.[16] This impulse can be seen in the testimonies of social workers involved in the Recovery Operation. Social worker Damyanti Sahgal, for example, is recorded as saying, 'Of course we felt for the women we were flushing out – sometimes we had to use the police to bring them out. But what we were doing had to be done' (Butalia, 'Community' WS20). The idealism she associates with the Recovery Operation's supposed humanitarian goals is used to justify its violent tactics and elide women's resistance to being 'recovered.'

The practice of 'forgetting to remember' (Bhabha 311) that characterizes popular perceptions of Indian identity underscores the 'split nature' of nationalist discourse. Its contradictory quality is apparent in that the homogeneity of 'the people' (read Hindus), the 'boundedness' of its territory (read the subcontinent), 'entailed in the representation of modern India as the return of the archaic' (Prakash 540). In other words, it hearkens to an ideal past across a history that undermines a modernist, chronological view of progress. Gyan Prakash flags the 'fabulous retroactivity' (555) of this discourse when he asks, 'how can the modern nation emerge continuous with the past when it is evoked as a form of return, as a repetition of the past?' (540). In short, at the same time that the Indian subject evoked a golden past, he also invoked a sense of the present as a time of degeneracy and loss. 'Under this strain,' argues

Prakash, 'the national subject revealed a trace of inadequacy as its retroactive authorization deferred its presence, as the present of the nation was relocated in the past' (546–7). The survival of 'abducted' women after the events of partition represents a similar dilemma for the postcolonial nation-state.

Where Benedict Anderson's work establishes connections between the birth of nationalism and the significance of print-capitalism,[17] here I am concerned with how gendered national imaginaries are imbricated within the discursive structure of narrative. Though Anderson indicates how 'a mythic past functions as a claim to [the nation's] homogeneity' (Prakash 539) in imaginary representations of national identity like the nineteenth-century realist novel, he also neglects to account for the textuality and ambivalence of nationalist narratives or what Homi Bhabha has identified as the 'unruly "time" of national culture' (298). In Bhabha's words, 'Anderson fails to locate the alienating time of the arbitrary sign in his naturalized, nationalized space of the imagined community' (311). This 'alienating time' haunts the national imaginaries in the way 'new-emerging nations imagined themselves antique' (Anderson xiv). As Gyan Prakash elaborates, '[t]he representation of the modern nation as the return to the archaic ... constitutes a profoundly disjunctive process – a process that entails the evocation *and* displacement of the mythic past, a linear history, and a homogeneous people' (540–1). The incommensurability of the past and present in the 'narrative movement' (302) of the national imaginary points to an aporia in Anderson's conceptualization of it as a stable or fixed form of 'homogeneous, empty time.' Modern national imaginaries are thus disclosed as terrains of discursive struggle and contention, marked by critical moments in the policing, production, and contestation of community identity.

Although realist narratives of novels and newspapers help to (re)produce an imagined community, they also exhibit contradictions that produce slippages in that same narrative structure. Recognizing this doubleness in nationalist narratives provides the critic with a means to unpack, as Bhabha writes, 'the complex strategies of cultural identification and discursive address that function in the name of "the people" or "the nation" and make them the immanent subjects and objects of a range of social and literary narratives' (292). The emphasis I place on the instability of meaning in the language of narrative in what follows is an attempt to displace historicism (as a claim to the transparency and objectivity of texts) and provide 'a perspective on the disjunctive forms of representation that signify a people, a nation, or a national culture' (Bhabha 292). Each of the texts discussed in the chapters that follow places itself in an ambivalent relationship with the construction of women's identity as representative of community honour.

In *Of Grammatology*, Derrida argues that while writing can be understood as a *substitution* for speech, it also adds something in its exteriority to the referent, which he calls the 'supplement.' 'Unlike the *complement*,' Derrida argues, 'dictionaries tell us, the supplement is an "*exterior* addition"' (145) and thus represents the overabundance of the signifier in relation to the signified. I think it is important to point out that this overabundance is not relative, but always situated in a worldly context that prevents its signifying force from lapsing into unlimited plurality. As a counter-discourse, therefore, accounts of women's experiences of partition foreground this deconstructive narrative force. The equivocal movement of the narratives discussed here is evidenced in their thematic representations of the disruptive power of anti-colonial nationalism at the same time they place it under erasure with a critique of patriarchal interests. As supplements to hegemonic nationalist discourse, they are *both* 'presence and proxy' – in Bhabha's words – a key to understanding the disruptive potential of national narratives 'within a non-pluralistic politics of difference' (305).

Thus, the Parle's Gluco Biscuits advertisement cited at the beginning of this chapter both promotes and unwittingly betrays a particularly influential construction of the gendered power relations within the bourgeois national family and nationalist discourse in South Asia. While the masculine subject is the focal point of nationalist rhetoric, his identity is disclosed as tethered to his mother's performance of a particular gender identity. The ambivalence within this advertisement's deployment of national discourse is the same ambivalence that haunts the partition narratives discussed in the following chapters. They represent the birth of a nation along with the epistemic violence that split communities, histories, and 'everyday' practices of the self. Moreover, partition narratives can be understood as supplements of South Asian national imaginaries that productively question their totalizing tendencies.

2 Fragments of Imagination: Rethinking the Literary in Historiography through Narratives of India's Partition

[W]hat the historians call a 'fragment' – a weaver's diary, a collection of poems by an unknown poet (and to these we might add all those literatures of India that Macaulay condemned, creation myths and women's songs, family genealogies and local traditions of history) – is of central importance in challenging the state's construction of history, in thinking other histories and marking those contested spaces through which particular unities are sought to be constituted and others broken up.

(Pandey, 'Defence' 571)

Even as we are forced to use the antinomies normalized by the state – Hindu and Muslim, majority and minority, Indian and Pakistani, citizen and alien – our task is to make visible the work of this normalization, to reveal its unfinished nature.

(Mufti, 'Auerbach' 250)

The desire to be able to write an omniscient account of historical events is something most contemporary historiographers have openly abandoned. This shift in disciplinary practice is apparent in recent work on India's partition. Here, historiographers have redirected their attention to exploring 'the particular' rather than 'the general' in an effort to disrupt the state's universalizing and hegemonic historical narratives. To this end, historiographers have turned to literary texts and their representations of what has been called 'the everyday' (Pandey, 'Prose' 221) in search of alternative perspectives to that of the state's central archive. The use of representations of 'the everyday' in historical research not only provides an alternative narrative of historical events but

Narratives of India's Partition   43

also simultaneously brings to crisis 'modernist' assumptions within the discipline of History.[1] It is with this in mind, I think, that Gyanendra Pandey argues that 'the historian needs to struggle to recover "marginal" voices and memories, forgotten dreams and signs of resistance, if history is to be anything more than a celebratory account of the march of certain victorious concepts and powers like the nation-state, bureaucratic rationalism, capitalism, science and progress' (214).

Pandey's attempts to write into history the ambivalences that produce a discourse of modernity have often included references to literary and autobiographical texts. It becomes evident, however, that the historiographer cannot merely use alternative sources for historical research if she or he seeks to question the concept of the nation-state and the power relations implicit in the modernist project of writing History. What is also needed is a thoroughly discursively informed reading and writing practice that is attentive to the literariness of narrative or what Spivak refers to as the 'singularity of its language' ('Cultural' 337). 'Literariness' is a term used by Paul de Man to signify the unmotivated relationship between words and things that is paramount in fictional accounts of the world. De Man argues that '[w]henever this autonomous potential of language can be revealed by analysis, we are dealing with literariness and, in fact, with literature as the place where this negative knowledge about the reliability of linguistic utterance is made available' (*Resistance* 10). 'Literature is fiction,' de Man writes,

> not because it somehow refuses to acknowledge 'reality,' but because it is not *a priori* certain that language functions according to principles which are those, or which are *like* those, of the phenomenal world ... This does not mean that fictional narratives are not part of the world and of reality; their impact upon the world may well be all too strong for comfort. What we call ideology is precisely the confusion of linguistic with natural reality, of reference with phenomenalism. (11)

In effect, without considering the relation between the linguistic construction of 'literary' and 'historical' narratives, historiographers' challenge to modernity is undermined by problematic assumptions disclosed in the (re)deployment of representations of the self, experience, and agency as they are received in and through narrative.

This chapter provides a close reading of 'the literary' as a resource for historical research by tracking the epistemological assumptions about representation embedded in recent historiographical work on partition.

I critique both the assumed differences between 'literary' and 'historical' narratives and the assumed 'value' that each type of text comes to represent for the historiographer reconstructing the events of a particular historical moment. Specifically, I problematize the merely subjective perspective and the transparency of language associated with 'literary' narratives as well as the strictly objective status conferred on 'historical' narratives. Drawing upon the theorization of 'experience' by feminist historiographers Joan W. Scott and Kathleen Canning, I propose a literary approach to reading and writing about India's partition in and through narratives attentive to the dialogic relation between text and context.

To illustrate this approach, I offer a reading of Rajinder Singh Bedi's short story 'Lajwanti,' which depicts the experience of a local community's involvement with the activities of the Central Recovery Operation after partition.[2] As discussed in the previous chapter, this operation was mounted by the Indian government in 1948 to 'recover' women 'abducted' during the migrations that took place and restore them to their 'original' extended families and communities.[3] As Butalia, Menon, Bhasin, and Das have argued, in order to guard the relationship between patriarchal power and pleasure in the domestic sphere and the newly hatched national imaginary in the civil sphere, 'abducted' women had to be returned to the nest of the modern (male) citizen-subject. Bedi's short story is particularly useful for highlighting how the multiple and shifting identities of 'abducted' women were violently (re)constituted as a monolithic site for the containment of contradictions in state and community nationalist imaginings. The goal of this reading, therefore, is to provide an example of how a staged dialogue between literary and historiographical narratives puts pressure on totalizing constructions of the self, experience, and agency and their relation to the notion of citizenship in the modern nation-state. In other words, I am concerned with how '"recovery operations" (of marginalized voices, of memory, of abducted women themselves)' (Wyrick 13) are often embedded in unexamined assumptions about identity, language, and history.

Recently, efforts to 'recover' marginal 'voices' and/or memories of the partition have emphasized the value of including literary sources as 'evidence' in historiographical narratives. More often than not, however, the inclusion of these sources has reinscribed humanist notions of literary production as merely subjective, mimetic, and universal in contrast to the objectivity and specificity associated with historical research. Ian Talbot's work on India's partition exemplifies this practice. In his aptly titled article, 'Literature and the Human Drama of the 1947 Partition,' Talbot deploys literary narratives in his historical analysis with the expressed purpose of complementing his notion of History instead of rethinking it as a whole. The peripheral place Talbot assigns this work is evident in his call for historians to include a discussion of the partition's 'impact' on people's individual lives as something separate from its 'causes' (37). He argues that '[n]ovelists, unlike historians have fully addressed the human agonies which accompanied partition' through their representations of what he terms 'personal experience' (38). To remedy this problem, Talbot recommends that historians study the 'human dimension' of partition by deploying 'a fresh range of source material,' including autobiographical and literary accounts of its events (37–8). 'Personal experience,' in this context, is conceived of as universal, transparent, and outside language, culture, and, ironically, history.

Talbot cautions other historians who might seek to imitate his methodology that

> [t]he novelist's art is subjective by its very nature. All literary sources must therefore be treated circumspectly by historians. It must be remembered that they have been produced by tiny élites in 'traditional' societies. The great writers can of course transcend their own experience and echo the feelings of other classes and communities. But lesser novelists lack this empathy and produce merely stereotypes and stylized emotional responses. (38n11)[4]

In the works he includes in his own discussion, however, he collapses the distinction between the autobiographical and the fictional; presumably, these texts demonstrate the qualities he associates with 'great' literature. It appears that the texts Talbot selects to support his argument are considered more 'reliable' Historical documents (and therefore somehow more objective) based on the empirical verifiability of the writer's 'personal experience.'[5] For example, he prefaces the inclusion of excerpts from Kartar Singh Duggal's novel *Twice Born, Twice Dead* with the information that Duggal came from Rawalpindi, a site of one of the most tragic incidents connected with the partition. Where Duggal's novel includes a representation of a refugee camp, Talbot informs us that Duggal had 'first-hand material to depict the refugees' plight' (48) and that his 'Muslim wife Ayesha worked among the refugees in

Jullundar' (53). Talbot thus reduces the imaginative capacity of the writer to represent the 'everyday' to his or her ability to recycle his or her personal (or spouse's) experiences. The power relations invested in a representation of any experience are negated, and the way language mediates experience remains unexamined. Talbot gives narratives of experience or 'the everyday' the status of a document of 'reality' (albeit, emotional), and a reading practice that situates the perspectives through which texts are written and read is not considered.

Talbot's treatment of literary narratives as a derivative of personal experience is symptomatic of the problems highlighted by Joan W. Scott's critique of historians' use of experience as 'evidence.' Scott points out that '[w]hen it [experience] is defined as internal,' it is understood as 'an expression of an individual's being or consciousness' (782). When consciousness is figured as the origin of experience, Scott argues that historians

> take the existence of individuals [in their narratives] for granted (experience is something people have) rather than to ask how conceptions of selves (of subjects and identities) are produced. It [experience] operates within an ideological construction that not only makes individuals the starting point of knowledge, but that also naturalizes categories such as man, woman, [or Hindu and Muslim] ... by treating them as given characteristics of individuals. (782)

These assumptions are evident in Talbot's conflation of literature with 'personal experience'; the literary texts that he favours in his analysis are the ones he sees as representing their characters' psychological trials. The focus is on the 'Indian subject's consciousness' represented as a natural, homogeneous category that becomes the object of inquiry in an investigation of the internal impact of partition. As Scott elaborates, the subject's knowledge of the events 'reflecting as it does something apart from him, is legitimated and presented as universal, accessible to all. There is no power or politics in these notions of knowledge and experience' (783). Ironically, though Talbot claims that '[t]he authors will be allowed to speak for themselves' (40) in this kind of Historical analysis, 'the authority of the "subject of knowledge" [is measured] by the elimination of everything [particular] concerning the speaker' (de Certeau 218).

Indeed, it becomes apparent that rather than explore the contradictions within and among people's experiences of partition found in literary narratives, Talbot glosses over difference and 'ventriloquizes' or speaks for those people in a monolithic voice. For instance, after citing a loosely contextualized excerpt from Bapsi Sidhwa's novel *Cracking India* (which I return to in some detail in chapter 3) in which Lenny (the narrator) relates how Ranna, a young Muslim boy, escapes death during an attack on his family's village by a group of Sikh men, Talbot comments, 'This account brings out clearly the ferocity and suddenness of the violence in the rural Punjab in August 1947. Standard historical accounts tend to overlook this altogether' ('Literature' 41). A closer reading of Sidhwa's text, however, suggests that there is nothing 'sudden' or entirely unexpected about the attack on the community. On the contrary, each time Lenny visits Ranna's village, her narrative traces a growing tension between Sikhs and Muslims as the partition approaches. While visiting the local fair with Ranna, Lenny notes, 'Other [Sikh] men, who would normally smile at Ranna, slide their eyes past. Little by little, without his being aware of it, his smile becomes strained' (*Cracking* 115). Eventually, relations between the Sikhs and Muslims in the community begin to disintegrate. Lenny's final impression of Ranna's situation before the attack is foreboding: 'The sun has set, but it is still light enough to see. Ranna was leaning against his father when the *granthi* [a local Sikh who is a community leader] spoke. The tone of the *granthi's* voice, the sadness, and the resignation in it, turned the heaviness in Ranna's heart into the first stab of fear' (*Cracking* 116–17).

Though Talbot is interested in what he identifies as the *exceptionality* of Ranna's 'experience' of the attack, his reading elides its specific construction within a larger sociocultural context and the novel's narrative structure. As a result, he ignores the specific discursive construction of Ranna's story from a designated but shifting subject position, generalizes about its details, and suggests that it is universally representative of others' experiences at the time. Thus, Talbot's inclusion of excerpts of literary narratives in his analysis becomes a means of filling gaps or supplementing existing Historical research rather than considering how those excerpts might destabilize the concept of representation in this scholarship as a whole. The concept of Historical research is likened to the process of assembling a jigsaw puzzle composed of pieces marked as 'evidence' that fit together to 'reveal' a larger picture. Historians' neglect of what Talbot terms 'the human dimension of Partition' is cited as the source of 'distortion' (37) or gaps in this picture that would otherwise be completed. In short, Historical representation is characterized as the documentation of a linear and unified account of 'what really happened' as opposed to a practice that recognizes how language and discourse mediate and fragment all experience and textual analysis of the past. In Talbot's view, literary narratives can only be a resource for Historians who want to get the 'human impact' (versus the political or economic impact, for instance) of a particular Historical event, and the History written by scholars like Talbot takes on the semblance of Truth. Instead of examining these literary narratives as interested commentaries on both the causes and effects of historical events, Talbot strips the literary quotations from their textual context and reduces them to confessional chronicles of 'emotional trauma' (49).

Historiographer Gyanendra Pandey's 'fragmentary' approach to writing historical narratives suggests a more promising strategy for integrating a productive critique of the Truth games in modern History. In his essay 'In Defence of the Fragment: Writing about Hindu-Muslim Riots in India Today,' Pandey explains that he came to this approach through his 'experience' of serving as a member of an investigative team for the People's Union for Democratic Rights (PURD) that was sent to investigate the 1989 Bhagalpur 'riots' in India. The difficulties the investigative team encountered while trying to gather 'evidence' about the 'facts' of the occurrences associated with the 'riots' provoked him to rethink the use of narratives of personal experience in historiographical research. Pandey recounts that it was difficult to find people in Bhagalpur who were willing to talk about their experiences – something that victims of sexual assault in particular were reluctant to do. When people were willing to relate their stories, representations of the same incident varied from person to person and different types of questions produced different kinds of answers. The task of re-presenting these silences and conflicting 'evidence' in the team's report drew Pandey's attention to how editorial and interpretive choices shape readers' receptions of what occurred. His decision to self-consciously adopt the 'fragmentary' approach to writing historical narratives, therefore, is an attempt to address these contradictions, gaps, and silences. 'Part of the importance of the "fragmentary" point of view,' Pandey argues, 'lies in this, that it resists the drive for a shallow homogenisation and struggles for other, potentially richer definitions of the "nation" and the future political community' ('Defence' 559). With this, Pandey turns to what he calls fragments of the events in Bhagalpur, including political leaflets, testimonies, newspaper accounts, and, finally, a collection of poetry by Manazir Aashiq Harganvi. He prefaces this last fragment as follows:

Narratives of India's Partition 49

I present this fragment here not as another piece, or even another kind, of 'evidence.' I propose it, instead, as the articulation of another subject position arising from a certain experience (and understanding) of sectarian strife, which may say something about the parameters of our own subject-position and understanding. In addition, this articulation provides a commentary on the limits of the form of the historiographical discourse and its search for omniscience. (569)

In contrast to Talbot's totalizing methodology, therefore, Pandey's fragmentary perspective stresses the 'provisional and changeable character of the objects of our analysis' (560) and attempts to negotiate this provisionality in the way historical narratives are written.

While Pandey's work has been pivotal in bringing more attention to how local accounts of violence problematize the state's narrative,[6] his use of literary sources in his analysis of the Bhagalpur riots and partition violence rely on the same assumptions as Talbot's. These assumptions derail his goal of disrupting historians' 'search for omniscience' in two ways. First, Pandey's narrative contextualizes the poems by Harganvi in a manner that undermines the self-reflexive reading and writing strategies he cites earlier as a necessary component of historiographic interpretation. For instance, the relevance of Harganvi's poetry to Pandey's discussion of the events in Bhagalpur would seem to be derived from the poet's residency in a 'predominantly lower-middle class locality which was not the scene of any of the "great" killings in 1989, but was nevertheless repeatedly attacked, traumatised and scarred forever' (569). In addition, Pandey tells us that Harganvi's poems were 'written for the most part during the first five days of the violence,' and by implication of this immediacy, 'we get some sense of the terror and desolation that so many people in Bhagalpur experienced at this time' (569). Like the rationale Talbot provides for the inclusion of literary selections in his work, the justification Pandey offers for the inclusion of Harganvi's poetry in his historical narrative is based on his perception that the poet had 'first hand experience' of the riots. In other words, Pandey's analysis is concerned more with what he characterizes as the 'authenticity' of Harganvi's representation of the 'riots' than with the critical/imaginative relation this fragment has with the discursive and material conditions that produced the rioting. 'Experience' in this case is 'taken as the origin of knowledge, the vision of the individual subject (the person who had the experience or the historian who recounts it)' and it becomes 'the bedrock of evidence on which explanation is built'

(Scott 777). Moreover, a self-reflexive reading of Harganvi's poetry should not be concerned with authenticating the transparency associated with the narrator's perception of the events in question but, rather, with considering how this transparency is constructed and the power relations that construction makes visible in the sociocultural context.

Second, like Talbot, Pandey does not problematize the mimetic assumptions embedded in his reading of literary representation and representation in general. As de Man argues, however, the literariness of language implies that mimesis is only 'one trope among others, language choosing to imitate a non-verbal entity just as paronomasis "imitates" a sound without any claim to identity (or reflection on difference) between the verbal and non-verbal elements' (*Resistance* 10). Pandey repeatedly deploys Harganvi's poems in his discussion as documentation/information of the events without considering the role language and ideology play in the poems' production of meaning. This reading strategy is most apparent when one of Harganvi's poems is 'described' as providing 'pictures ... of fields of corpses, and the impossibility of counting them' ('Defence' 569). Pandey reads the images in the poem as mere reflections of reality and, as a consequence, elides a discussion of the power relations expressed in and through the figurative language Harganvi uses to re-present his view of the riot's context. Thus, where an excerpt from one of the poems portrays a father's commentary on the sexual assault of his daughter, Pandey challenges his readers to decide if the representation is 'a metaphorical statement of the humiliations suffered by a community, or a literal description of events that occurred' (569). Pandey's question implies that the two interpretations are possible but mutually exclusive. Moreover, the value of this representation of the riots to historians is assumed to be greater if it is read as a 'description.'

On the contrary, I argue that the poems' representation of historical events can be understood as diffracted and metonymical (which recognizes the mutually constitutive relation between the literal and figurative in narrative) rather than as reflective and metaphorical (which understands them as related but independent). Donna Haraway's characterization of the diffracted rather than reflected relation between 'the real' and discourse is particularly appropriate to emphasize the necessarily fragmentary and partial relation between the individual's perception of a historical event and the event itself. 'Diffraction,' Haraway explains, 'does not produce "the same" displaced, as reflection and refraction do. Diffraction is mapping of interference, not of replication, reflection, or reproduction. A diffraction pattern does not map where differences appear, but rather maps where the *effects* of difference appear' (300). Pandey translates Harganvi's poem as follows:

Aur yeh beti jise tum saath
mere kankhiyon se dekhte ho
Beshumar haathon ne loota hai ise.
(And this daughter, whom you observe out of the corner of your eyes, sitting by my side –
How many have looted her.)

('Defence' 569)[7]

The narrator/father of the poem represents the identity of his daughter as a possession to be looted. His rhetorical statement, 'How many have looted her,' is embedded in a patriarchal logic that marks women's identities and bodies as symbols of community honour and 'tradition' and makes them targets for violence during sectarian conflicts. Pandey's analysis, however, is silent about these things. There is no discussion of the narrator's subject position, how he figures his daughter, the power relations this expresses, and/or the way language produces all these effects.

As a critic interested in tracking the intersection of gender and nationalist discourse, I am concerned about the implications that historiography like Pandey's and Talbot's has for reading the agency of women who lived through the events of partition.[8] The enormity of the geographical displacement which Indians experienced during the partition is difficult to comprehend. As mentioned in my Introduction, the migrations and violence related to the possibility of India's partition had been occurring in the Punjab as early as February 1947 and for two years prior in West Bengal. As Ritu Menon and Kamla Bhasin comment, '[b]y the time the migrations were finally over, about eight million people had crossed the newly-created boundaries of Punjab and Bengal, carrying with them memories of a kind of violence that the three communities had visited upon each other that was unmatched in scale, brutality and intensity' ('Recovery' WS3). Murders, looting, 'abductions,' and sexual assault appear to have been frighteningly commonplace occurrences as displaced individuals and communities responded with violence to the threat to their lives, security of their property, and cultural continuity. During this mass migration and violence, thousands of women were separated from their extended families and communities. Some were abducted by those who attacked their families and communities, while others, who were lost or abandoned, simply followed their aggressors, seeing no other alternative in the face of their isolation from community support and protection. From 1948 to 1956, these women became the object of efforts by the Indian Central Recovery Operation, 'which sought to recover those women who had been abducted and forcibly converted during the upheaval, and restore them to their respective families and countries where they "rightfully belonged"' (WS2-3). The quotation marks that Menon and Bhasin place around the phrase 'rightfully belonged' suggest the questionable legitimacy of this judgment. What qualified as the 'rightful' communities, families, and countries for these women appears to have been a particular construction of their identity determined by the state-sanctioned Central Recovery Operation, which Menon and Bhasin argue 'raises serious questions regarding the Indian state's definition of itself as secular and democratic' (WS-3). By focusing on the 'singularity of language' that informs literary and historical representations of 'recovered' women's experiences of the partition, I seek to displace modernist notions of Reason, agency, and identity that represent a limit in Pandey's attempt to disrupt the 'prose of Otherness' he identifies in both colonial and nationalist accounts of India's partition ('Prose' 213). As Ayesha Jalal points out, while Pandey criticizes histories of partition that privilege 'the viewpoint of the state' (214), 'Pandey himself is unsure whether he wishes to undertake a relentless critique of reason as a sign of modernity or make a case for the reason that informs the consciousness of the subaltern agent' ('Secularists' 98).

As in Pandey's discussion of Harganvi's poetry, the limits of his critique of modernity and omniscient history as they relate to partition emerge in his reading of representations of women's experiences. For example, in his essay 'The Prose of Otherness,' Pandey fails to consider how the contradictions that inflect Anees Qidwai's autobiography, *Azadi ki Chhaon Mein* – a text in which she details her involvement with the activities of the Central Recovery Operation – represent a site of resistance to the Operation's patriarchal and nationalist rhetoric and interests.[9] Qidwai worked in the refugee camps and assisted in the 'recovery' of women. The excerpts Pandey provides from Qidwai's autobiography indicate a growing loss of conviction in the 'humanitarian' value of the Recovery Operation. In one excerpt, Qidwai reflects on the predicament of a young girl who had been sexually abused by several men and then 'recovered' to India. She writes:

Today she sits by my side, silent, a question-mark. Her terrified, startled eyes ask me and call out to every human being to tell her who [what] she is? ... She has lost all hope, agility ... youthfulness ... beauty. Will readers be able to tell us whether we acted criminally in bringing them back? Or whether it would have been a [greater] sin not to have brought them?' (Pandey, 'Prose' 217; Qidwai 318).[10]

Qidwai's comments underscore her uncertainty about the stated purpose of the Recovery Operation (i.e., humanitarian). She isolates a serious contradiction in its activities; the Recovery Operation has attempted to write the girl's identity as 'recovered,' and yet she remains as a 'silent' 'question-mark' who continues to 'call out' for answers. Pandey, however, glosses over this ambivalence and characterizes Qidwai's convictions as 'swing[ing] from one position to another,' according to no particular logic ('Prose' 219). I argue that Qidwai's shifting response to the 'reality' of the women's experiences at the hands of the Recovery Operation, the way the seventeen-year-old 'girl' haunts her experience, hints at many contested spaces where Pandey might begin to track resistance to the patriarchal logic of the nation-state. Instead, he forecloses this process, commenting,

> The tragedy of Anees Qidwai's recounting of the pain of Partition, of which the suffering involved in the exchange of abducted women discussed above is but on [sic] example, is that *no resolution at all is possible.* How is one to say, on the question of the 'forcible' recovery and exchange of abducted Hindu, Muslim and Sikh women left on the 'wrong' side of the border, what would be the viewpoint of Reason, what was 'right' and what was 'wrong,' what 'moral' and 'immoral,' what 'sane' and what 'insane'? (my emphasis; 219)

Pandey's conclusion that 'no resolution at all is possible' with regards to the question of whether or not the Indian state was justified in the forcible 'recovery' of women after partition suggests that women can be viewed only as passive victims of History.[11] As Ayesha Jalal comments,

> the most surprising feature of Pandey's essay is its disconcerting implication for understanding the consciousness of women as well as any potential project of feminist history ... It would seem slightly odd to concentrate the new radical historians' fire on the insensitivities, inefficiencies and inactions of the Indian and Pakistani governments in their recovery and

repatriation programmes for abducted women and simply recover the will and reason of the mass actors (still 'protectors and heroes'?!) who had committed the unpardonable crimes of rapes and abductions. ('Secularists' 102–3)

It appears, therefore, that Pandey cites Qidwai's text to confirm his view of the state's actions rather than to problematize the modernist underpinnings of the practice of writing History. This amounts to what Jalal describes as 'uncritically celebrat[ing] the fragment' (101). There is no effort to examine the assumptions shaping the treatment of 'abducted' women before, during, and after their 'recovery' or any attempt to formulate a notion of agency for 'abducted' women outside the liberatory discourse of modernity; hence, Pandey's discussion of the Recovery Operation's representation of these women as passive victims of an apocalyptic event remains unchallenged. He perpetuates the modernist practice of reading the shift in perspective or 'content' of Qidwai's text as the apprehension of the 'prediscursive reality' of partition (i.e., 'abducted' women were *bound* to be the scapegoats of the nation), or, in other words, what Scott has called a 'coming to consciousness' (794). By implication, Pandey chooses to underwrite rather than probe a view of the events that occurred as inevitable and thus reinscribes the conflation of Woman and Nation by indigenous patriarchy. Pandey and his readers are excused from the task of questioning the justice of the treatment of these women by the state and indigenous patriarchy and the implications this has for an understanding of citizenship in India today. Within Pandey's transvaluation of Reason from the state to the (patriarchal) subaltern, 'the constitution of the female subject *in life*' (Spivak, *Critique* 235) is ignored.

The consequences this has in Pandey's reading of partition violence is apparent later in the same essay when he extends his conclusion about Qidwai's narrative to what is arguably the best-known partition narrative, Saadat Hasan Manto's short story, 'Toba Tek Singh.' The *ambiguous* response that Qidwai develops toward the activities of the Central Recovery Operation is interpreted as a *clear* response to its 'insanity.' Pandey juxtaposes this interpretation with what he derives as the 'essential' Meaning in Manto's text (i.e., 'the insane decision to exchange "insane" Indians and Pakistanis') ('Prose' 217). After a lengthy paraphrase of Manto's story concluding with a quote from the final paragraph where Toba Tek Singh is represented as throwing himself on the border between India and Pakistan, Pandey concludes, 'Thus, it seems,

Manto offers a resolution of the paradox that he sets out at the beginning of his story through the suggestion that, in this time of "madness," it was only the "insane" who retained any sanity' (219).¹² Once again, though Pandey sets out to map some of the *ambiguities and contradictions* within the formation of national identities at the time of India's partition, he ends up occluding just those things in his discussion. As Sujala Singh points out,

> even as they [Pandey, Butalia, Bhasin, Menon, Das] critique the closures of the historiographic narratives and recognize the absenses that such accounts enforce, they seem to suggest that literature might be able to breach this repression. In a curious reversal of the traditional binarism which valorizes history as the realm of the real, of facts, removed from the world of fiction, of imaginative fancy, these scholars hail the efforts of writers to document what history has failed to document. (126)

The introduction to Ravikant and Tarun K. Saint's *Translating Partition* offers a more rhetorically sensitive reading of the 'the subversive way in which the motif of madness is deployed' in Manto's story that pushes beyond Pandey's reinscription of sanity or Reason from the state to the subaltern (xvi); 'Toba Tek Singh,' they argue, 'is a triumph of ambivalence and a great story because it proclaims the in-betweenness of its protagonist and his triumph over those who want to fix his identity' (xvi). In effect, 'Manto's searching critique unsettles conventional rationality and its basis for comfort, as well as the consequent and facile exculpation of blame for the Partition' (xvi).

Instead of reading Qidwai's change in perspective concerning the activities of the Recovery Operation as 'the discovery of truth' (i.e., the violence experienced by women at the time of Partition at the hands of the community *and* the state was inevitable), I propose to read it as 'the substitution of one interpretation [of events] for another' (Scott 794). This approach recognizes how Qidwai's reflection on her experiences working for the Recovery Operation provides her with the opportunity to rethink the patriarchal discourse that informs its goals and practices as a whole. Here, it is assumed that 'political consciousness and power [or agency] originate, not in presumedly [sic] unmediated experience of presumedly [sic]' real events but 'out of an apprehension of the moving, differencing properties of the representational medium' – in this case, language (794).¹³ This does not, as Pandey claims, lead to the conclusion that the situation is irresolvable but instead to a more complex (and possibly more just) understanding of the options available to 'abducted' women and how they negotiated their survival. Pandey claims that he will treat these fragments of textual representation 'not as another piece or even kind of "evidence"' ('Defence' 569), but he ends up doing just that; despite his rhetoric of self-reflexivity and his critique of other historiographers who do not integrate this approach into their own work, he fails to theorize the gap between the text and its referent and the way agency comes into play. In Scott's words, '[q]uestions about the constructed nature of experience, about how subjects are constituted as different in the first place, about how one's vision is structured – about language (or discourse) and history – are left aside' (Scott 777). Unwittingly, Pandey's reading of the value of representations of 'the everyday' in literary and autobiographical narratives ensures that women, ineligible for full citizenship in the modern patriarchal nation-state, will continue to be cast as the passive 'victims' of the events of History rather than collective subjects who negotiate their relationship to their context on an ongoing basis and make history.

My reading of the historiographical 'value' of literary narratives also follows from feminist historiographer Kathleen Canning's reading of 'experience' as a re-presentation rather than a record of historical 'reality.' Canning's argument draws on work by labour and feminist historiographers like Alf Lüdtke and Joan W. Scott and defines experience as 'making meanings of events as they happen ... as well as a "self willed distancing" that facilitates a "reframing," "reorganizing," or a "creative reappropriation of the conditions of daily life"' (Lüdtke 304–5; Canning 376–7). The emphasis on 'construing, reframing and reappropriating' in this definition 'implies that subjects do have some kind of agency' (377) in the way they interpret the world from the discourses available to them in their sociohistorical context. I argue that literary texts can also be understood in these terms, and, in fact, their relevance to historical research is enhanced by this critical reading strategy. The tension between text and context that impinges on fictional accounts of partition demands that the reader theorize representations of experience, taking into account the gap between the text and its historical referent. Thus, the inclusion of literary narratives in historiography is not seen as a way of presenting a more 'authentic' or personal view of a particular Historical moment, but, instead, as providing the opportunity to examine 'creative reappropriations of the conditions of daily life' with an explicit attention to the 'double vision of text and context' (Rose 7–8; Canning 380). This 'double vision' creates an awareness of how 'material reality is a force that pressures and destabilizes, the discursive domain requiring representations "to be reworked, shored up, [and] reconstructed"' (Walkowitz et al. 3; Canning 380), and of the role subjects play in that process.

The 'abduction' of women during partition, the geographical displacement, pain, sexual assault, and unplanned pregnancies they suffered, can be understood as examples of material reality putting pressure on the discursive domains of conservative-nationalism, communalism, and patriarchy. As argued in chapter 1, 'abducted' women presented a 'new social question' (Canning 383) to all these domains in the aftermath of independence and destabilized their convergence in the nationalist imaginings of the recently formed postcolonial state. In short, the 'everyday' perspective or experience represented in literary narrativizations of these events should be read as diffractions of historical moments in which nations, communities, families, and individuals engage in a discursive struggle over the interpretation of material reality and the identities of 'abducted' women. The gendered citizen-subject's agency is, therefore, 'a site of mediation between discourses and experiences' (Canning 378) through which she reinterprets the normalized view of 'reality' and transforms the social/political/economic conditions around her. This critical stance puts pressure on representations of 'victims' and 'vanquishers' in partition texts to simultaneously disclose and comment on the discourses of race, class/caste, gender, and nationality that produce these events and designate them as 'inevitabilities.' In a more general sense, the process of 'rewriting, reinscribing and redeploying' History as 'fragmentary' then also becomes the process of rethinking the relationship between historiography and literary criticism.

In the reading of Rajinder Singh Bedi's short story 'Lajwanti' that follows, I suggest that the 'everyday' agency exercised by 'abducted' women falls outside modernist conceptions of 'choice' and can be used to illustrate 'how subjects contest power in its discursive form, and how their desires and discontents transform or explode discursive systems' (Canning 377). I map how the patriarchal modern nation-state contained these rhetorical and material struggles by exploring the contradictions between macro- and micro-physical configurations of power/knowledge and the 'technologies of the self' they produced in the domestic sphere in post-partition India. I argue that it is possible to read Bedi's narrative as a critique of the power relations that inflected the sociopolitical practices surrounding the Recovery Operation.

Born in 1915 in Lahore, India, Rajinder Singh Bedi was 'the son of a

Khatri Sikh father and a Brahmin mother' (Flemming, 'Progressive' 81). Bedi began his career as a writer in English, then Pubjabi, but it was not until he began to write in Urdu that he found his biggest audience (Flemming, 'Interview' 142). He published his first collection of short stories, *Dana-O-Daam* (The Catch), in Urdu in 1936. In a 1972 interview with Leslie Flemming, Bedi comments, 'In order to reach the maximum number of people, I took up Urdu. Besides, Urdu was in vogue; right from my first grades to my later ones, I was taught in Urdu' (142). Bedi spent ten years working as a clerk in a Lahore post office between 1933 and 1943, after which time he briefly took a job with All India Radio (1943–6) (Verma 411). With partition in 1947, Bedi relocated to Delhi and later served for a brief stint as Station Director at Jammu Radio Station in Kashmir in 1949 before settling in Bombay, where he began his film career as a screenwriter for *Badi Bahen* (411). During his career as a scriptwriter, Bedi worked on over forty films while continuing to write fiction, earning him recognition as one of the most important twentieth-century Urdu writers (Verma 411). His short story 'Lajwanti,' published in 1951,[14] and his novella *Ek Chadar Maili Si* (The Soiled Sheet/*I Take This Woman*), published in 1962 (winner of the Sahitya Kala Akademi Award in 1965), are some of his best-known works.[15] Bedi died in 1984.

'Lajwanti' is a particularly interesting partition narrative in that it is one of the earliest literary accounts to focus on the social stigma facing 'abducted' women returned to their families and community through the activities of the Recovery Operation. Bedi's critique of this situation was quite radical for its time and undoubtedly was influenced by his involvement in the Progressive Writers' Association.[16] This group of writers distinguished themselves for, among other things, writing about 'what had been considered unmentionable issues, often involving sex' (J. Feldman 119). In an interview with Flemming, Bedi comments,

> I was very much struck by the earlier phase of the Progressive Movement. The reasons were very simple. First, it had an anti-imperialist slant. We wanted independence at that time, politically speaking. In addition, we wanted this same freedom in our writing. The earlier group called *Angâre* group wrote freely about sex, for instance; whereas we were doing all sorts of prudish things. The Progressive Movement got this liberty for us; we were able then to express ourselves. (147)

The radicalism of 'Lajwanti' with respect to its critique of patriarchal attitudes toward women's chastity might be explained by the way the

Progressives opened up a space for questioning social norms related to sexuality.

Bedi's story is also unique in that 'he uses Hindu imagery and symbolism even though he writes in a language that has increasingly become the province of South Asian Muslims' (J. Feldman 120). In 'Lajwanti' this is evidenced in the references to the story of Sita's rejection by Ram in the *Ramayana* as well as to references to the unhappy lot of the 'widow living in house No. 414,' subject to the strictures of widowhood in an orthodox Hindu community.[17] By addressing a socially taboo subject from a hybrid cultural perspective at a time when identities were being reified along national and communal lines, Bedi's story represents a truly unique reflection of the partition. The anomalous and yet prominent position of Bedi's work in Indian literature adds further weight to Aamir Mufti's view of the Urdu short story as taking 'an exorcising stance with respect to the narrative of Indian selfhood' ('Greater' 12). In his recent essay on Manto, Mufti complicates the link between realism and nationalist literature in late colonial India, arguing it is less about reflecting social reality or mimesis than 'narrating the (national) passage from primitivism to modernity' (12). Urdu literary culture, Mufti argues, has been 'imputed with a minority consciousness and posture in the discourse of the nation' (13) that results in its 'ambivalent' relationship to nationalism in general. As Mufti elaborates,

> [i]ts staging of that selfhood remains ambivalent. Moreover, the fragments it isolates from the stream of life and elevates into form do not merely point towards a totality, however subjective, of which they are part. It puts the terms of this totality in question and holds at bay the resolutions whose 'end' is the form of consciousness that is the abstract citizen subject. (12)

While in Bedi's interview with Leslie Flemming he laments the 'lack of "great novels in Urdu"' (140), 'Lajwanti's' radical critic of social norms concerning women's sexuality seems to lend further support to Mufti's view that '[f]or an enunciation of the "major" claims of nationhood and belonging, Urdu turns to a "minor" epic form, thereby lending those claims an air of contingency' (11).

Set in the Punjab in the town of Ludhiana in the period immediately following partition, 'Lajwanti' tells the story of Sunder Lal's wife of the same name, who is separated from him during the sectarian violence. Lajwanti also refers to the name of a 'touch-me-not' plant that has the unique quality of curling up its leaves when it is touched or brushed.

The plant is popularly named lajwanti because its curling action has been seen as indicative of shyness or shame, hence the root 'laaj,' which refers to shame. The Rehabilitation committee in Sunder Lal's community sings a Punjabi folksong that refers to the lajwanti plant as they march through the area, suggesting an analogy between the plant and 'abducted' women: 'This is the plant of touch-me-not; it shrivels up at a mere touch' (201). The narrator indicates how the song has a special significance for Sunder Lal:

> At early dawn, when Sunder Lal led *prabhat pheris* through the half-awakened streets, and his friends, Rasalu, Neki Ram and others sang in fervid chorus: 'These are the tender leaves of touch-me-not, my friend; they will shrivel and curl up even if you as much as touch them ...,' it was only Sunder Lal whose voice would suddenly choke; and in utter silence, as he mechanically kept pace with his friends and followers, he would think of his Lajwanti whom wanton hands had not only touched but torn away from him – where would she be now? What condition would she be in? What would she be thinking about her people? Would she ever return? ... And as his thoughts wandered in the alleys of a sharp and searing pain, his legs would tremble on the hard, cold flag-stones of the streets. (201–2)

For Sunder Lal, the reference to the lajwanti's curling action has an added connotation; the narrator reports that 'in the past he himself had maltreated *his* Lajwanti often enough and he had not infrequently thrashed her, even without the slightest pretext or provocation' (202) The recoiling action of the lajwanti, therefore, could also be analogous to Lajwanti's response to her treatment by Sunder Lal. Further, it could be argued that Sunder Lal's faltering steps suggest that he has doubts about his own ability to accept Lajwanti back if she is found.

The song would also appear to have an ambivalent connotation for the Rehabilitation committee and the community it is trying to influence; 'abducted' women were seen as polluted, and the ambivalent interpretation of the lajwanti's curling action (from shyness, fear, and/or shame) resonates with the community's ambiguous response to the 'return' of the women. Although the community seemed to respond well to other 'rehabilitation' activities, the narrator comments,

> [b]ut there was one phase of this problem which was yet neglected and the programme that sought to tackle this aspect carried the slogan: 'Reha-

bilitate them in your hearts!' This programme was, however staunchly opposed by the inmates of the temple or Narain Baba and the orthodox, conventional people who lived in that vicinity. (201)

When women like Lajwanti were 'returned' to the domestic sphere of their 'own' communities, they were often seen as 'polluted,' having come in contact with the other community. The folksong, therefore, could also be construed as referring to the consequences of having one's honour defiled: 'This is the plant of touch-me-not; it shrivels up at a mere touch' (201). Indeed the folksong resonates with the response of many people in the community who rejected the women once they returned:

> For a long moment the abducted women and their relatives started at each other like strangers. Then, heads bent low, they walked back together to tackle the task of bringing new life to ruined homes ... But there were some amongst these abducted women whom their husbands, fathers, mothers, brothers and sisters refused to recognize. On the contrary, they would curse them: Why did they not die? Why did they not take poison to save their chastity? Why didn't they jump into the well to save their honour? They were cowards who basely and desperately clung to life. Why, thousands of women had killed themselves before they could be forced to yield their honour and chastity. (204–5)

As this passage suggests, the folksong could be read as suggesting that 'abducted' women *should* 'shrivel up' in the face of their pollution. The survival and return of these women to the community casts aspersions on their virtue and honour (as it is defined by patriarchal codes) and challenges expectations concerning women's sexual passivity outside the domestic sphere of the extended family.

Both the macro- and micro-physical context of post-partition India are well documented in Bedi's narrative. Public exercises of national unity in the civil sphere – a key feature of nationalist thought from its inception in the early nineteenth century (Chakrabarty, 'Difference' 69) – are mimicked by the narrator's journalistic account of how the local 'rehabilitation committee' is established. Ceremoniously, the narrator states how

> [t]o give impetus to this programme, a committee was formed in the *mohalla* of Mulla Shukoor which lay near Narin Baba's temple. Babu

> Sunder Lal was elected secretary of this committee, by a majority of eleven votes. It was the considered opinion of Vakil Saheb, the chairman of the old *moharrir* of Chauki Kalan, and other worthies that there was no one who could perform the duties of secretary with greater zeal and earnestness than Sunder Lal. Their confidence rested perhaps on the fact that Sunder Lal's own wife had been abducted – his wife whose name was Lajo – Lajwanti – the plant of touch-me-not. (201)

The details Bedi's narrative provides about the committee's formation in the context of post-partition India suggest that the 'technologies of the self' that produce the identity of the modern citizen-subject are in full bloom in Sunder Lal's community. Not only is the mutually constitutive relation between the civil and domestic spheres in the life of the individual citizen normalized in this community, it is celebrated; public confidence is expressed in Sunder Lal's dedication to his job as committee secretary *because* of the crisis in his own domestic life.

The disciplinary effect of enrolling Sunder Lal and other community members in the rehabilitation committee is figured in Bedi's text in numerous ways, but I will concentrate on mapping the transformation of Sunder Lal's attitude concerning domestic abuse. Bedi is at pains to make it known that the pre-partition power relation between Sunder Lal and Lajwanti was characterized by a constant reassertion of Sunder Lal's physical and institutional dominance over her as her husband. Bedi's narrative discloses that when Sunder Lal thinks about how he has physically abused Lajwanti in the past, he is ashamed:

> These were the memories that came winging through the years as Sunder Lal went about leading *prabhat pheries* along the streets. And as these pods of nostalgia cracked and opened, Sunder Lal thought: For once, if only for once, I get my Lajo back, I shall enshrine her always in my heart. I shall tell others that these poor women were blameless, that it was no fault of theirs to have been abducted, a prey to the brutal passions of rioters. The society which does not accept these innocent women is rotten and deserves to be destroyed.' (203–4)

Sunder Lal's self-remonstrations disclose a discursive intersection between his sense of emasculation and his view of 'abducted' women as passive victims of the Other. He is figured as afraid that Lajwanti may not want to return to him – even if the Central Recovery Operation is successful in locating her – because of his previous treatment of her. The figuration of this anxiety can be linked to the larger context of the narrative in which male citizens like Sunder Lal are becoming aware of how the modern nation-state both requires and circumscribes their power as 'husband' in the extended family. The enforced separation of civil and domestic concerns in the identity of the (male) citizen-subject relies on women's acceptance of the limited options available to them as subordinates in patriarchal institutions such as the family and the state as well as on the sanction of the community to allow women to return to those positions.[18] When, however, this separation is challenged by the exercise of individual agency by women's survival and/or return (as in 'Lajwanti') at the same time that the title of 'citizen' (in the form of universal franchise) is being extended to all members of Indian society, new 'technologies of the self' must be performed to recoup women's participation. The rehabilitation committee in Bedi's narrative can thus be read as a 'matrix of transformation' where 'techniques of knowledge and procedures of discourse' normalize the 'abducted' female subject as an entirely passive victim who requires the constant protection of the family (Foucault, *History* 98).

This reading highlights the contradictions that arise between micro- and macro-physical interests in the return of 'abducted' women to their 'original' families and nations. After the news of Lajwanti's 'recovery,' Sunder Lal is figured as temporarily overwhelmed by the discursive contradictions involved in (re)constructing his domestic life: 'Sunder Lal shivered with a strange fear and felt warmed by the holy fire of his love' (209). Sunder Lal's contradictory feelings can be interpreted through the incompatible goals that the community and state had set out to achieve through their participation in the Recovery Operation. True, the patriarchal family had invested its agency in the patriarchal nation-state that promised to recover the women whom the (religious) community had failed to protect from 'contamination' from the Other. Nevertheless, in order for this exercise to be read as an act of legitimacy for India's nationalist 'secular' imaginary, the emphasis on women's sexual purity as a symbol of community honour had to be elided (Butalia, 'Community' WS18). Both goals were, ultimately, at cross-purposes with each other. The reconciliation of these conflicting goals could be accomplished only through the denial of 'abducted' women's agency and the (re)inscription of patriarchal power in the domestic sphere.

The precariousness (rather than total success) of the process of recasting women's identities in post-partition India is made visible by the narrative's double focus on the reconfiguration of the power relations between Lajwanti and Sunder Lal when she is returned to him, and on the details of the historical practices of the Recovery Operation. On the one hand, Lajwanti is represented as being aware of her need for patriarchal patronage in order to survive in the community when she expresses her fear about how Sunder Lal will react to her sexual 'contamination.' The narrator comments: 'She and none but she knew Sunder Lal, knew that Sunder Lal had always maltreated her. Now that she was back after having lived with another man, she dared not imagine what he would do to her' (211). On the other hand, Sunder Lal's reception of Lajwanti is torn between his negative reaction to her healthiness and 'well-being' (suggesting that she may not have been as much of a 'victim' of the other man as he would like to think)[19] and the 'new' pressures on his behaviour as a (male) citizen in the modern nation-state to welcome her back as his wife. Though the narrative reports that Sunder Lal is disturbed by Lajwanti's apparent good health and wonders if she truly wishes to return to him, instead his civil responsibilities take precedence over his domestic and the reader is told that '[s]uch were the thoughts that flashed through Sunder Lal's mind as he took the first look at the abducted woman. But he faced these thoughts bravely, sealing them off at their very source' (212). Though Lajwanti is described as 'inebriated with an unknown joy' (213) when she is first returned to her home (after all, Sunder Lal does not beat or reject her), she comes to understand that Sunder Lal's acceptance of her is in exchange for her silence and performance of a new, more disciplined gender identity. Repeatedly, the narrative refers to Lajwanti's desire to talk about her partition experiences with her husband so 'she would let her "sins" be washed away in tears. But Sunder Lal always shrank from hearing her story, so that despite her new freedom Lajo still crouched behind some strange apprehension' (213). Feminist historiographers have noted the stigma attached to recovered women as well as the resulting 'silence' imposed on their experiences by their families and communities. This silence (or conversely, Lajwanti's desire to speak and be absolved of her 'sins') can be read as an analogue for violent foreclosure of narrative ambivalences in the practices of writing History I discussed earlier. Curiously, Aijaz Ahmad reads the silence between Lajwanti and Sunder Lal concerning her experiences as a 'mutual inability to find a language in which the right questions may be asked, the pain expressed and overcome' (*Lineages* 195). It is difficult to accept this reading when the silence encouraged by Lajwanti's husband takes the form of a more sinister (re)constitution of an inequitable power relation that facilitates her patriarchal patronage and the management of his civil and domestic responsibilities.

Thus, even though the ambiguities in the discursive reconstruction of the civil and domestic spheres of the national imaginary are temporarily foreclosed by the violence and idealism of Lajwanti's reconstructed identity, Bedi's text makes the reader aware of this foreclosure. Sunder Lal addresses Lajwanti as *devi* or goddess, placing her identity, agency, and 'everyday' experiences with the other community under erasure. The only information Sunder Lal wants to know about her experiences away from him is, significantly, if the other man had physically abused her; when he learns that he did not, rising to the civil challenge, he claims that he will never beat her again either and declares the subject closed. While Sunder Lal places the 'blame' for the stigma attached to Lajwanti's honour on social conventions, he also invalidates her potential to resist those conventions. According to this reasoning, Lajwanti cannot be held accountable for her experiences because she is constructed as lacking the ability or agency to act in her own self-interest. The narrative suggests, therefore, that the ambivalent terms of Lajwanti's reintegration into the community and nation-state require her to surrender her identity as a woman who can question her husband (albeit, at the risk of a beating) and/or renegotiate the terms of her patriarchal patronage.[20] The narrative states:

> Ultimately, when quite some time had passed, doubt no more remained an intruder but took the place of joy, not because Sunder Lal had again started maltreating her but because he treated her much more kindly than before. It was a kindness that Lajo had not expected from him – she wanted, desperately, to become the same Lajo who would quarrel on a trifle and, all at once, be friends again. Now the question of a quarrel between them did not arise for she was a *devi* and he her worshipper. (214)

Khushwant Singh's, Alok Bhalla's, and Jai Rattan's translations of 'Lajwanti' also note a loss of equity in the couple's relationship. In Bhalla's version the narrator comments, 'She wanted to be Lajo again, the woman who could quarrel with her husband over something trivial and then be caressed' (66). In identical translations of the final section of this same passage Singh and Rattan write: 'She wanted him to be the same old Sunder Lal with whom she quarrelled over a carrot and who appeased her with a radish. Now there was no chance of a quarrel' (Singh 135; Rattan 78). In postcolonial India, where bourgeois conventions produce the domestic sphere as a supplement of the civil sphere, the conditions of possibility no longer exist for the agency Lajwanti exercised prior to the partition. Instead, recalling the folksong, Lajwanti's new identity as a *'devi'* is characterized as a metaphorical assault on her identity: 'So, all that was in Lajwanti's heart remained gagged, stifled. She curled up sobbing in her helplessness and gazing at her body which had become the body of a *'devi'* and not her own – not Lajwanti's' (214). In a review of Bhalla's *Stories about the Partition of India*, Veena Das comments how the 'loss of normality [catalyzed by the events of partition] is rendered with consummate skill as in the figure of Lajwanti whose very elevation as the icon of a near goddess subsequent to her abduction and return, constitutes her sorrow' ('Review' 58). While Das reads Bedi's text in and through the discourse of psychoanalysis, her comment is particularly relevant to my argument in the way it constructs the source of her unhappiness in relation to her experiences *after* her recovery. As the narrator of Bedi's translation states, 'she [Lajwanti] was rehabilitated and she was ruined' (214).

In this chapter I have traced the discursive intersections and disjunctions within and between various historical and literary narratives, in order to foreground a fragmentary, language-centred understanding of the power relations that produced the treatment of 'abducted' women. I have attempted to put pressure on the construction of these women's identities as passive victims of circumstance and to question the universalizing assumptions that inform unified historical accounts about the nationalist struggle. My goal has been to show that the title 'citizen,' despite its universal extension to all members of Indian society, is a contested terrain that has been used to privilege certain actors in relation to the state over others. In my analysis of the formation of a nationalist imaginary at the time of partition, I have argued that the mutually constitutive relation between the civil and domestic spheres in the identity of the citizen-subject is made available to all members of Indian society as a consequence of universal franchise. However, a slippage in this view of the 'citizen' becomes visible with the survival and return of 'abducted' women to their 'original' homes. To contain this threat, the agency of 'abducted' women had to be elided and their identities (re)constituted in the domestic sphere. In this light, the staged confrontation between literary and historical narratives that has propelled this discussion becomes an exercise in 'unraveling the necessary entanglement of history – a disciplined and institutionally regulated form of collective memory – with the grand narratives of "rights," "citizenship," the nation state, [and] "public" and "private" spheres' (Chakrabarty, 'Postcoloniality' 21).

3 Cracking the Nation: Memory, Minorities, and the Ends of Narrative in Bapsi Sidhwa's *Cracking India*

When an end is defined, other ends are rejected, and one might not know what those ends are. So I think what [post-structuralists] are about is asking over and over again, What is it that is left out. Can we know what is left out? We must know the limits of narratives, rather than establish the narratives as solutions for the future, for the arrival of social justice, so that to an extent they're working within an understanding of what they cannot do, rather than declaring war [on the grands récits].

(Spivak, 'Post-modern' 18–19)[1]

In chapter 1, I traced how the trope of 'Woman' became an alibi for colonial *and* nationalist interventions into the everyday lives of South Asians. Feminist critics have demonstrated that concern about women's status in colonial and postcolonial contexts often has less to do with changing the actual material conditions of their lives and more to do with *patriarchal* 'struggles over a community's autonomy and the right to self-determination' (Mani, 'Multiple' 30). For instance, it is now well established that in colonial and postcolonial representations of *sati* (widow immolation) in India, 'women become sites upon which various versions of scripture/tradition/law are elaborated and contested' (Mani, 'Contentious' 115). The women themselves 'are neither subjects nor objects, but rather the ground of the discourse of sati' (117). In chapter 2, I argued that literary reading strategies can help make visible the process through which exclusionary notions of citizenship are normalized and lead to a silencing of ambivalent views of the nation-state. In this chapter I mobilize these two assumptions in a reading of Bapsi Sidhwa's *Cracking India* that focuses on how the narrative's fragmentary and situated relationship to the history of partition offers a critique of nationalist discourse.

My discussion stages a confrontation between the structures of meaning that characterize nationalist discourse and fictional representations of a young Parsi girl, Lenny, and her *ayah* (nanny) Shanta's 'everyday' experience at the time of partition. I argue that the notions of universal citizenship and direct agency are troubled when they are juxtaposed with Lenny's memories of her 'everyday' experiences as a child and adult and the treatment of 'abducted' women. The tension between the historical and fictional events inscribed in Sidhwa's narrative suggest how the discourses of gender, class, and nation overlap and converge to become increasingly restrictive of women's agency as the country faces independence. Whereas before partition, Lenny observes how Ayah/Shanta[2] is able to deflect patriarchal expectations of monogamy and conjugality, after partition, her actions are constrained and her agency and body governed by patriarchal struggles over land and identity. Sidhwa's narrative practice seeks to destabilize patriarchal nationalist discourse and work against the practice of making women the 'ground' in struggles for postcolonial self-determination. At the same time it maps how women's identities, far from being determined by discourse, are 'mediate[d], challenge[d], resist[ed], or transform[ed]' (Canning 377) by their desires and discontents.

As the adult narrator of a fictional autobiography, Lenny is figured as coming to recognize how her memories of the partition and the birth of the Pakistani state are shaped and mediated by her subject position. 'How long does Lahore burn? Weeks? Months?' Lenny wonders (148). Questioning the reliability of her memory, Lenny reflects:

> Despite all the ruptured dreams, broken lives, buried gold, bricked-in rupees, secreted jewelry, lingering hopes ... the fire could not have burned for months and months ...
>
> But in my memory it is branded over an inordinate length of time: memory demands poetic license. (149)

Nandi Bhatia comments on how the trope of memory operates in Sidhwa's novel, arguing that rather than simply 'recovering' an untold story of partition, Lenny's 'questions and queries and her attempt to search for answers constantly interrupt the narrative' (203–4). 'This refusal to impose coherence on the narrative through its fragmentary emplotment,' explains Bhatia, is part of a storytelling technique that can only rely on memories to evoke the past. Memories themselves being fragmentary and changing, the narrative too, as a consequence, veers between bits and pieces of the lives of various characters and presents the past not in fixed or static terms but one that makes itself open to reinterpretation, everytime an untold story is inscribed onto it. (204)

Similarly, Ambreen Hai points out that

in its very form and discursive choices, the text confounds the generic divisions between fiction, history, and autobiography, and between public and private space. Recalling 'real' events experienced by the author herself in a fictive form ... it blurs the distinction between memory and fictive (re)creation, between personal and national experience. (390)

In what follows, I trace how Sidhwa's fictional, partial, and episodic figuration of Lenny's reflection on her childhood experiences represents an effort to make visible the fragmented, nonlinear, and contradictory experience of 'independence' alluded to in the 'cracking' metaphor of her title. While independence brought an official end to colonialism, the premise for the novel – the adult narrator's attempt to make sense of why she is haunted by her memories of this period over forty years later – emphasizes the limited and unequal notion of citizenship that asserted itself in the postcolonial context.

Moreover, while Lenny's narrative undoubtedly focuses attention on an aspect of the partition experience that has been previously ignored by historians, it also resists the idea that literature can become a 'compensatory medium' in attempts to fill the gaps in the historical record (Singh, 'Nationalism's' 127). As Sujala Singh warns, '[a]s questions of narrative are asked of history, but not of fiction, fiction almost becomes the desired "Other" of history' (127). *Cracking India*, I argue, points to the (im)possibility of completing the history of partition with 'firsthand' testimonial or fictional accounts by underscoring the 'unnarratable' (Ray 136) quality of 'abducted' women's experience even while the novel signals the importance of understanding the causes and consequences of their predicament.

First published in 1988 under the title of *Ice-Candy-Man*, Sidhwa's *Cracking India* is one of the most critically examined novels about the partition written in English.[3] Sidhwa's novel was written at a time when interest in the ongoing impact of partition, especially in the lives of women, was just beginning to be explored. In a joint interview with Sidhwa, Urvashi Butalia has explained how '[The anti-Sikh riots which followed Indira Gandhi's assassination in] 1984, for example, acted as a catalyst for many historians to explore histories of violence in India' (Whitehead, 'History' 233). In interviews Sidhwa has stated that her interest in writing about the partition emerged after seeing the film *Gandhi* and feeling the 'Pakistani view' of the partition was misrepresented. In conversation with David Montenegro Sidhwa states, 'I felt, in *Ice-Candy-Man*, I was just redressing in a small way, a very grievous wrong that has been done to Jinah and Pakistanis by many Indian and British writers' (532). It was out of a desire to offer 'the Pakistani perspective,' Sidhwa claims, that she first had the idea of telling the story of partition through the Lenny's eyes, a Parsi girl coming of age during the independence struggle (Whitehead, 'History' 236).

Born in Karachi in 1938, Sidhwa lived in Pakistan until 1985, after which time she moved to the United States and held several teaching positions at American universities (Jussawalla, 'Sidhwa' 261). While continuing to divide her time between Pakistan and the United States, Sidhwa has published four novels, with *Cracking India* garnering the most critical and popular attention. Sidhwa has many biographical qualities in common with the narrator of that novel. Like Lenny she was a young girl at the time of partition. Also like Lenny, Sidhwa is a Parsi woman, and much of her narrative highlights the unique position of the Parsi community in colonial India. Sidhwa, however, is quick to reject autobiographical readings of her novel. While, as children, both she and Lenny suffered from polio, Sidhwa notes, 'the way the book interprets this is quite different from my reaction to it' (Jussawalla, 'Interview' 201). While Sidhwa has stated in interviews that she has used childhood memories of the partition as the basis for some of Lenny's experiences in her novel, she also emphasizes that a simple autobiographical reading of her novel is inaccurate. In an interview with Feroza Jussawalla she states:

> The trouble with the first person child's point of view is that it is very easy to mistake it for autobiography. The child, Lenny, in the book is very distinct from myself. The incidents in her life are often taken from my life, but Lenny is a much more asute child than I was ... So every incident taken from my life, or perhaps from the lives of people I knew intimately, has been embroidered to create the larger reality of fiction. (201)

In her interview with Andrew Whitehead, Sidhwa states, 'I felt it was important that the child be a Parsee child, as I am. Because the Parsees, the Zoroastrian community, which survives in India and Pakistan, is not Hindu, Muslim or Sikh, and that is important' (237). I would argue this view is further decentred by Sidhwa's choice of telling her story from the perspective of an adult narrator reflecting on her community's privileged status in relation to individuals like her *ayah*. As the narrative unfolds, it quickly becomes apparent that the narrator is aware, even as a child, that the Parsi community is undergoing a double-edged identity crisis. The shift in power from a British administration to Hindu- and Muslim-centric states in India and Pakistan respectively, signals the end of the Parsis' privileged relation, despite their minority status, to the ruling class. The novel dramatizes the confusions and contradictions that face a young girl being initiated into the norms of her community and society just as those very norms are being furtively reconstituted to better suit a new set of conditions of power. In this sense Sidhwa's text offers the reader an imaginary peek into the 'location' of the Parsi community as a 'conjunctural sites of underdetermination' (Sangari 872) or, in other words, where the discursive meaning of 'belonging' is under revision. As Ambreen Hai argues, Sidhwa's novel performs a kind of 'border work' (383) in that it 'speaks at once from within and without, producing simultaneously a novel voice addressing Pakistanis from within yet questioning the homogeneity of "within," and a voice addressing Indians from without that overturns the presumption of "without" as Muslim' (389). In addition, Lenny's intimate relationship with her nanny, Ayah, takes her outside the bourgeois circles of the Parsi community and makes her aware of the heterogeneous cultural context of her society at large.[4] Sidhwa's text figures Lenny as questioning the hegemonic structures of meaning that infuse her 'everyday' experiences. Her decentred view of the implications of the end of British rule within her local community helps to defamiliarize the dominant interpretation of history and nationalism at the time of partition and discloses its patriarchal and majoritarian underpinnings.

Lenny's use of narrative as a means for questioning hegemony can be tracked in and through her questioning of the conventional relation between discourse and 'reality.' As partition approaches Lenny recalls how it was difficult for her to comprehend its meaning. As Sangeeta Ray argues, '[t]he term "partition" implies a neat cartographic creation of a new geographic entity that elides the personal and political vicissitudes accompanying such remappings' (*En-Gendering* 131). Repeatedly, Lenny's narrative is represented as troubling the neatness of this process as her statements underscore the magnitude and unacknowledged costs of partition. For instance, when Lenny overhears discussions about partitioning the nation she understands this in physical terms: 'There is much disturbing talk. India is going to be broken. Can one break a country? And what happens if they break it where our house is? Or crack it further up on Warris Road? How will I ever get to Godmother's then?' (101). Later, when Lenny hears her Aunt Mini talk about 'the Mountbatten plan to tear up the Punjab' (121), she comments, 'And the vision of a torn Punjab. Will the earth bleed? And what about the sundered rivers? Won't their water drain into the jagged cracks? Not satisfied by breaking India, they now want to tear the Punjab' (124). Lenny's collapse of the figurative and literal use of the images of cracking, breaking, and tearing draws attention to the way the relation between all words and referents is informed by power relations that express something about the speaker and his or her context. Her confusion highlights the tension between these two aspects of language and, by extension, the thoroughly mediated nature of representation. The creation of two new nation-states may not be accomplished by the material act of 'digging a canal,' as Ayah suggests elsewhere (101); nevertheless, the literalism that informs Lenny's understanding of these metaphorical statements highlights the tension between discourse and materiality. Moreover, as Sangeeta Ray suggests, Lenny's rendering of 'cracking away at the subcontinent makes it clear that such geneses have profound political motives and are inevitably accompanied by ever deepening scars and widening fissures which continue to fracture new nations long after their inception' (132).

Lenny's naive narrative perspective also dramatizes the way the tension between text and context opens up a space for interpretation – rather than the search for Truth – in literary representations of 'everyday' history. The act of narrating her memories gives the adult Lenny the opportunity to reflect on and intervene in the various struggles over the meaning of historical events. For example, as suggested above, it becomes apparent that despite the nation's expression of concern for 'abducted' women's safety and happiness, they were the 'ground' (Mani, 'Contentious' 118) rather than subject or object of nationalist discourse. As discussed in chapter 1, the phrase 'abducted' women refers to women separated from their families and communities during the migrations and sectarian violence that accompanied partition. Public outrage over the presence of 'abducted' women living in the communities of the Other in India and Pakistan after partition placed social pressure on the state to intervene and 'recover' them – regardless of the women's wishes. Some women's resistance to 'recovery' and the problem of what to do with them once they were recovered confronted the national and patriarchal community with one of the first challenges to the seamless presentation of the nation as a universally accessible and equitable expression of the social contract. Ayah eventually becomes one of these 'abducted' women, but Lenny's naive view of her and other women's treatment dislocates the state's and community's attempts to justify their actions and contain the women's ambiguous position.

For example, when the Recovered Women's Camp is first established in Lenny's neighbourhood, she recalls how she assumes 'it's a women's jail, even though they look innocent enough' (201). The manner in which the women are kept under guard, separated from the community ('There is a padlock the size of a grapefruit on the gate, and a large key hangs from the steel bangle around the Sikh's wrist' [201]), initially leads Lenny to believe that the women are guilty of some crime. Indeed, while this may not be the reason for the women's treatment, Lenny's naive observations point to the anxiety surrounding their sexual 'contamination' by the Other community that turns the women into outsiders. Ayah's replacement, Hamida, who has just been released from the camp and sees herself as a 'fallen woman,' tries to explain that the women are 'fate-smitten,' but this does not satisfy Lenny, who recalls, 'I've seen Ayah carried away – and it had less to do with fate than with the will of men' (226). When she asks her Godmother to clarify what Hamida means by calling herself 'a fallen woman,' Godmother explains, 'She was taken away to Amritsar. Once that happens, sometimes, the husband – or his family – won't take her back' (227). Lenny is outraged at the scapegoating of the women; 'It's monstrously unfair,' she thinks, but also notices 'Godmother's tone is accepting' (227). Lenny's interrogation of the normalized assumptions that inform the 'abducted' women's treatment helps to make visible the way patriarchal nationalist interests produce their identities as polluted. Her off-centre view highlights how the women's suffering is both the result of the brutality of their abductors *and* the ostracization they experience when they are 'recovered.'

While Sidhwa has claimed on different occasions in interviews that she sees her membership in the Parsi community as affording her a neutral or objective view of the partition, it is possible to read Lenny's narrative against the grain and track the Parsi community's sympathy with colonial culture.[5] The stories Lenny recounts about the Parsi community's reaction to the possibility and eventuality of the end of colonial rule bring to the fore the history of their opportunistic relationship with the British. The novel's representation of the Parsi community's history in colonial South Asia is shown as fraught with contradictions in that they – like the rest of South Asians in India – are subject to colonial rule but, at the same time, enjoy a privileged relationship with the colonial administration and often express outright admiration for British colonial culture. Questions regarding the privileged identity of the Parsi community at this time and, subsequently, in postcolonial India, have been investigated by Tanya Luhrmann in her book *The Good Parsi*. In this book she tracks the assumptions about the racial and cultural superiority that characterized the Parsi community's identity under colonial rule and its consequences for their postcolonial situation. The 'Good Parsi' in Luhrmann's analysis is a trope for the ideal Parsi colonial subject figured in the political rhetoric directed at the British in order to boost the community's status in relation to other groups in colonial India. This stereotype characterized Parsis as 'charitable, truthful, racially pure, and as like the British as a native community could be' and was invoked to support claims that 'the moral qualities of the Parsis must be classified as more European than Indian, and, like the British, as superior to the moral qualities of the native Indian' (Luhrmann 100).

The original basis for claiming a distinction between the 'native Indian' and the Parsi appears to have been fashioned from a rewriting of the Parsi history and the principles of Zoroastrianism (the religion of the Parsis), to better conform to the values of the colonizer's capitalist Western culture. Support for this reading can be seen in Luhrmann's analysis of the reconfiguration of the attributes most closely associated with the religious texts of Zoroastrianism: truthfulness and purity. During the colonial period, the Zoroastrian concept of *Asha*, a Persian word variously translated as 'Purity,' 'Righteousness,' or 'Truth,' came to be defined in tautological terms with goodness; the commonly invoked aphorism in the Parsi community quoted by Luhrmann is the belief that '[w]hat is good is true, and what is true is good' (100). Luhrmann argues that such a circular definition of 'truth' and 'goodness' allowed the community to substitute the meaning for these words with values that facilitated their assimilation with English culture. This resulted in the Parsi practice of mimicking the colonial culture and placed members of the community in a privileged relation with the colonizer over the rest of South Asians. Furthermore, scholarship on the history of mercantilism in colonial India suggests that '[t]he ability of local [Parsi] merchants to generate reputations as wealthy and trustworthy persons made possible their participation in a vast commercial economy that functioned without legally enforceable contracts or modern financial institutions' (Haynes 342; Luhrmann 101). Luhrmann highlights the significance of this recoded concept of 'Truth' in the context of British rule by pointing out that 'in the rapid economic expansion of colonial west India, in which the Europeans could pick and choose amongst potential partners, Parsi honesty seems to have been entrenched as a status marker to affirm the validity of past profits and to promise them future clients' (101). Commenting on the legacy that the convergence of these redefined codes of conduct have created for Parsis in postcolonial India, Lurhmann observes, 'Parsis pride themselves on their truthfulness and not infrequently contrast their honesty with the dishonesty of non-Parsis' (100).

The concept of 'purity' was also recoded within Zoroastrian/Parsi colonial culture from something that referred to holiness into something more akin to 'racial superiority' (101). During the colonial period, Parsis began to embrace a sense of difference from the indigenous population that hinged on nostalgia for their Iranian ancestry and interpretations of their religion as monotheistic. This origin story includes racist assumptions about the Parsi community's 'white' ancestors, links between Zoroastrianism and Christianity, claims about the Parsis' 'untainted' bloodline, and taboos around intermarriage. Luhrmann argues convincingly that the preoccupation with Iranian heritage at various Parsi community events was born less out of a curiosity about their past and more out of an 'energetic Parsi attempt to detach things Parsi from things Hindu' (102).

The goals of the Iranian Association, founded in India in 1911 by two Parsi religious reformers, are cited by Luhrmann to support this claim. The Association defined its main purpose was to 'maintain the purity of the Zoroastrian religion and remove the excrescences that have gathered around it' (102). The obsessive concern with contamination and degeneration of the community's bloodline stemmed from the precarious position of authority that Parsis occupied in the colonial order of things. The Parsis had a stake in maintaining the appearance of racial distinctions between themselves and the rest of the indigenous population in order to shore up their favour with the British colonizers. Driven by their 'basic uncertainties about who would be granted that privileged status' (Stoler 32) in relation to the colonizer, Parsis could be seen as trying to police the boundaries of the community by identifying those among themselves who transgressed the sexual/cultural/class divide between their community and the rest of the native population. Indeed, Luhrmann points to this 'double' anxiety when she comments that '[t]o call the association the Iranian Association was in fact a polemical claim about who a Parsi "really" was, and a political assertion about the undesirability of anything Hindu' (103).

In this light, Lenny's satirical representation of community culture takes on a much deeper significance than Sidhwa might have imagined. In many ways, Colonel Bharucha, the local Parsi doctor, is the stereotypical 'Good Parsi' that Luhrmann sketches in her book. The dominant community's sense of its racial superiority is first apparent in Lenny's account of Colonel Bharucha's condescending attitude toward the Muslim underclass family that is in his office just before her own doctor's appointment. In this scene, Bharucha asserts a position of cultural, racial, and class superiority when he browbeats the husband whose wife is wearing the veil and at first refuses to speak to the doctor directly. Indignant over the father's ignorance concerning the details of his child's condition, Bharucha scolds him, exclaiming, 'She didn't tell you? Are you a father or a barber? And you all want Pakistan! How will you govern a country when you don't know what goes on in your own house?' (22). Furthermore, he conflates the father's ignorance over the baby's illness with effeminacy and a general lack of authority. In contrast to this effeminacy, Colonel Bharucha exhibits an exaggerated manliness. He 'hollers' patronizingly at Lenny's mother – 'Take her clothes off, woman!' (24) – when she coddles her in the doctor's office, establishing a gruff, abrupt, and impatient manner which characterizes his personality throughout the novel. This 'manliness' is not without its implications for the position of the Parsis under colonial rule. Luhrmann's investigation suggests that 'at the dead centre of the Parsi construction of the self in the economic and cultural arena of the colonial Raj, figured the gentlemanly manliness of the Parsi man, a schema which translated the muscular Christianity, the main argument for British supremacy and their white man's burden, into Parsi terms' (117). The virility and racial superiority of the Parsi community's self-presentation contributed to the British perception of them as a worthy ally in colonial India, and Lenny's representation of Colonel Bharucha's personality epitomizes these traits.[6]

Through Lenny's naive accounts of community meetings she attends with her parents, it becomes clear that the credibility of the superiority (and therefore dominant position) of the Parsi identity is under attack in the nationalist atmosphere of pre-partition Lahore. With the prospect of the British departure on the horizon (the novel opens in 1944 and concludes in 1948) it appears that the privileged position that the community enjoys based on its close cultural, psychological, and economic identification with the colonizer is in jeopardy. Lenny's representations of Bharucha's statements and actions at the meetings suggest this general anxiety. She recounts how

> [a]t the last community dinner, held on the roof of the YMCA building on the Mall, Colonel Bharucha had cautioned (between the blood-chilling whines of the microphone): 'We must tread carefully ... We have served the English faithfully, and earned their trust ... So, we have prospered! But we are the smallest minority in India ... Only one hundred and twenty thousand in the whole world. We have to be extra wary, or we'll be neither here nor there ...' And then, surmounting his uncharacteristic hesitancy, and in thunderous voice, he declaimed: 'We must hunt with the hounds and run with the hare!' (26)

Bharucha's 'uncharacteristic hesitancy' can be interpreted as a symptom of the unstable political and economic situation that the Nationalist Movement has produced in India, but his response that the community 'must hunt with the hounds and run with the hare' suggests that he is not questioning the ethics of its collaboration with the colonizer. Lenny's reference to the crowd's response foregrounds the community's mimicry of the British: 'Everybody clapped and gravely said: "Hear! Hear!" as they always do, reflexively, every time anyone airs a British proverb in suitably ringing tones' (26). The approving exclamations of the crowd, which Lenny indicates are quite common at these meetings, echo British parliamentary rhetoric and illustrate the extent to which the dominant community identity has been assimilated with the cultural values and assumptions of the colonizer. Moreover, this imitation of British cultural practices undercuts Sidhwa's claims about Parsi neutrality. At subsequent meetings the Colonel concludes, 'As long as we do not interfere we have nothing to fear! As long as we respect the customs of our rulers – as we always have – we'll be all right' (48).

A general lack of sympathy for the independence movement is obvious at these meetings, where discussions of Gandhi's Salt March and the appeal to Indians not to buy salt are trivialized by hecklers who ask, 'Who does this Gandhi think he is? ... Is it his grandfather's ocean?' (44).[7] Luhrmann's research confirms this attitude as representative of many members of the community at the time. During her fieldwork she reports how

> [i]n conversation after conversation, Parsis told me that the majority of Parsis had been unhappy with Independence. Old Parsis in particular remembered that the community was uncomfortable with Gandhi and with his insults to the British. The upper class, they said, may have been nationalist, but not the majority, which consisted of deeply committed Anglophiles. (124)

Though Lenny's own parents appear to be somewhat more sympathetic to the independence movement, her naive view of the shifting political terrain around her discloses the opportunism and hypocrisy of the Parsi community's status in the colonial context.

My claim that Sidhwa's narrative maps how women's identities, far from being determined by nationalist discourse, are 'mediate[d], challenge[d], resist[ed], or transform[ed]' (Canning 377) may need some elaboration; the question of what would count as resistance is a difficult one to answer when agency is understood as only direct. Agency continues to be one of the most ill-defined concepts in postcolonial theory and discourse analysis. Because deconstructive practice has been so successful in making visible the 'figurative nature of all ideology' (Poovey 58) – such as the conflation of women's identity with that of the nation – it is easy to forget that these figures are only made visible through the 'interventions of agents who render them contingent and permeable' in the first place (Canning 377). In other words, critics often overlook the fact that the situated action of responding to a text constitutes an intervention into interpretive processes that mediate the experience of reading. Of course, this is a somewhat different notion of agency than the one that has dominated Enlightenment thought, where the individual is supposed to act with full autonomy. Gayatri Spivak has critiqued this kind of agency, most famously, in her essay 'Can the Subaltern Speak?' Spivak argues that the subaltern cannot 'speak,' or in other words, cannot have access to what is understood as direct agency in liberatory discourse, without also reinscribing an Enlightenment notion of subjectivity.

In what is perhaps *the* most controversial contribution to the debate surrounding 'voice' or agency in feminist discourse, Spivak concludes this essay with the statement, 'The subaltern cannot speak. There is no virtue in global laundry lists with "woman" as a pious item. Representation has not withered away' (308). In response to criticism that this argument precludes *any* possibility of agency for the gendered subaltern, Spivak, in a subsequent interview, stresses that her aim was to problematize but not dismiss the concept of agency. She cites her conclusion to this essay as a direct response to Bhuvaneswari Bhadhuri's nieces' representation of her suicide as a case of 'illicit love' despite Bhadhuri's attempts to displace this motive. Spivak reiterates that, even though Bhadhuri committed suicide while she was menstruating (thus, deflecting the interpretation of her death as shame over an unplanned pregnancy) and left a letter explaining her motives, the political 'intent' of taking her own life was overlooked. Spivak states:

> What I'm saying is that even when, whether showing her political impotence or her political power, she tries to speak and make it clear, so that it would be read one way, the women in the family – radical women – decide to forget it. The rhetoric of the ending is a rhetoric of despair. It was at that moment, right after the story, when I said, throwing up my hands, 'The subaltern cannot speak.' (Winant 89)

As I have argued elsewhere with Teresa Heffernan, '[i]t is this unavoidable muting of the subaltern's intent, as a will is constructed for her, that Spivak's work asks us to be attentive to in "our" own work.' (4)

> 'Speaking' for Spivak is a necessarily displaced act. In her recent return to this essay in *A Critique of Postcolonial Reason* Spivak cites Abena Busia's response to 'Can the Subaltern Speak,' which pointed to the fact that in the end, she was able to make the subaltern 'speak.' Spivak explains that Bhadhuri, as a middle-class woman with some access to centres of power, was not a 'true' subaltern, but that, in any case, the goal of her work is not to preclude hopeful investigations of subaltern speech but to foreground how these investigations must acknowledge that '[a]ll speaking, even seemingly the most immediate, entails a distanced decipherment by another, which is, at best, an interception.' (Didur and Heffernan 4; Spivak, *Critique* 309).

Rather than propose that the subaltern is without any kind of agency, Spivak's work suggests that attempts to represent identity or 'voice' ultimately *require* the subordination of the text to the assumptions of the reader. The figurative quality of any 'record' of experience mobilizes multiple and contradictory discourses that must be accounted for if the scholar hopes to avoid unwittingly reproducing 'exploitative and exclusionary' strategies in her own work (Hai 385). Moreover, if the unified rather than split subject remains the focus of the reader's discussion of agency, she or he forecloses recognition of everyday resistance that is neither conscious nor direct. Thus, Spivak's critique and other examples of feminist deconstructions of the unified subject or agent do not negate or dismiss the concept of agency but rather call for its '"critical reinscription and redeployment"' (Canning 373).

The logic of women's actions figured in Sidhwa's novel can be better understood if representations of their experience are reinscribed and redeployed as interpretations rather than mere reflections of 'reality.' As Kathleen Canning points out,

> [t]his emphasis on construing, reframing, and reappropriating [experience] implies that subjects do have some kind of agency, even if the meanings they make 'depend on the ways of interpreting the world, [and] on the discourses available to [them] at any particular moment' ... Indeed, experience, as the rendering of meaning, is inextricably entwined with the notion of agency, with a vision of historical subjects as actors who, in Sewell's terms, 'put into practice their necessarily structured knowledge.' (Weedon 79; Sewell 5; Canning 377)[8]

Canning conceives of agency as 'a site of mediation between discourses and experiences' and 'dispel[s] the notion that discourses are ... shaped by everything but the experiences of "the people the text claims to represent"' (378; Ortner 299).

The concept of direct agency refers to the actions of individuals that are public, self-conscious, and unfettered by social structures – actions taken by an autonomous subject. None of these things can be said to characterize women's agency in *Cracking India*; on the contrary, their actions are generally isolated in the private sphere and mediated by restrictive social discourses that are not necessarily 'self-conscious' in Enlightenment terms. This, in turn, makes it difficult to imagine how women's agency contests the structures and practices of subordination in everyday material and discursive practices. Because examples of direct agency are unlikely in representations of women's everyday experience, there is the danger that their behaviour will be interpreted as passive or dictated by 'ruling ideology.' 'What one needs to keep in mind,' however, as Sumit Sarkar suggests, 'is a vast and complex continuum of intermediate attitudes of which total subordination and open revolt are only the extreme poles' (274). In order to account for 'interventionary possibilities adequate to a thoroughgoing politics of change' (Sangari 867) the critic must question the division between the public and private that characterizes nationalist discourse and recognize their co-implication.

Indirect agency could thus include, as Kumkum Sangari argues, any 'range of actions which take forms that are difficult to fit into commonly understood typologies of organised political activity' (868) but, nonetheless, impact on the flow of power. Douglas Haynes and Gyan Prakash attempt to account for this 'range of actions' in their book *Contesting Power*, where they call for a notion of resistance that 'can be applied to a much wider range of socio-cultural practices and take into account the ways in which the subjectivity of the dominated is constrained, modified and conditioned by power relations' (2). This nuanced understanding of resistance or agency rethinks power as 'constantly being fractured by the struggles of the subordinate' (2). 'Social structure,' Haynes and Prakash argue, 'rather than being a monolithic, autonomous entity, unchallenged except during dramatic instances of revolt, appears more commonly as a constellation of contradictory and contestatory processes' (2–3). In this context, there is no 'pure form' of domination or resistance because 'the two are so entangled that it becomes difficult to analyse one without discussing the other' (3).

The adult narrator's growing awareness of the entanglement of domination and resistance is apparent in her accounts of her experiences at home and in the community. One of Lenny's major preoccupations is her memory of how she came to perceive difference in the way she and her brother were treated by their family and community. From the outset of the novel Lenny is represented as internalizing a sense of inferiority because she is a girl. In physical terms, she remembers how she compared herself unfavourably with her brother: 'I am skinny, wizened, sallow, wiggly-haired, ugly. He is beautiful. He is the most beautiful thing, animal, person, building, river or mountain that I have seen. He is formed of gold mercury' (32). Lenny's apprehension of her brother's favoured status in the family is conveyed in this passage through her choice of comparing him to 'gold mercury' and contrasting him with her own 'ugliness.' The gendered nature of Lenny's perception of herself as ugly as compared with her brother is evident in the derogatory connections she makes between femininity and shame. She explains:

> His name is Adi. I call him Sissy. He is too confused to retaliate the first few times I call him by his new name. At last: 'My name is Adi,' he growls, glowering.
> The next day I persist. He pretends not to notice. In the evening, holding up a sari-clad doll I say, 'Hey Sissy, look! She's just like you!' (32)

Lenny's internalized hatred of her gender identity is exemplified by the taunts she directs at her brother and the hyper-feminine connotation of the doll she goads him with. Her sense of inferiority in relation to her brother is compounded by her skin colour: Lenny's skin colour is noticeably darker than that of her brother, who is able to 'pass' as 'British' in the playgrounds around Lahore. Lenny recalls how Ayah demonstrated pride over this fact, calling Adi her 'little English baba,' and enjoyed the assumptions that strangers made about his White racial heritage. Lenny notes:

> Ayah is so proud of Adi's paucity of pigment. Sometimes she takes us to Lawrence Gardens and encourages him to run across the space separating native babies and English babies. The ayahs of the English babies hug him and fuss over him and permit him to romp with their privileged charges. Adi undoes the bows of little girls with blue eyes in scratchy organdy dresses and wrestles with tallow-haired boys in the grass. Ayah beams. (35)

This quote emphasizes the racial and patriarchal privilege that Adi shares with the White boys when he literally and metaphorically crosses 'the space separating native and English babies.' Trading on assumptions about his racial heritage, he is able to harass the young White girls without reproach and compete as an 'equal' with the 'tallow-haired boys.' Lenny, on the other hand, remembers experiencing anxiety about the consequences of her dark skin. She recounts how

> [e]very now and then Slavesister serves Godmother strong half-cups of steaming tea which Godmother pours into her saucer and slurps. I too take an occasional and guilty sip. Drinking tea, I am told, makes one darker. I'm dark enough. Everyone says, 'It's a pity Adi's fair and Lenny so dark. He's a boy. Anyone will marry him.' (90)

As a girl, Lenny's surplus of pigment is considered a double liability. Her inferior status in a racist and patriarchal society places pressures on her to negotiate patriarchal patronage through marriage and identification with the White colonizer.

Despite this internalized sense of inferiority, Lenny's narrative suggests that she learns how to exercise indirect agency by witnessing and participating in the negotiation of power relations between her parents. Lenny's memories of her parent's interaction with each other figure the dominance of her father in all matters including finances, favour, and family harmony. At the same time, she also remembers the way her mother negotiated her needs with her father, thus exercising some agency – albeit, highly individualized – in how domestic matters will be resolved. In general, it appears that Lenny's mother used her agency in a consensual fashion – in the interest of maintaining her patriarchal patronage – and thus contributed to the perpetuation of elite patriarchal practices. 'Patriarchies,' Kumkum Sangari argues, 'are resilient not only because they are embedded in social stratification, divisions of labour, other political structures, religious/cultural practices, institutions and categories, but also because of the contractual and consensual elements in them' (868). Rather than confront her husband about the various inequities in their relationship, Lenny's mother uses indirect agency to get what she wants without seriously challenging the basis of her subordination. It becomes apparent, however, that even these privileges are not without their costs. The negative effects of this unequal but mutually constitutive relation of subjection are not lost on Lenny, who represents the 'games' her mother and father play over the distribution of the family finances as an amusing, but ultimately degrading, activity. She depicts how her mother chases her father around the bedroom attempting to get money from him for some household expenses, and comments:

> Mother's voice teeters between amusement and a wheedling whine. She is a virtuoso at juggling the range of her voice and achieving the exact balance with which to handle Father. Father has the knack of extracting the most talented performances from us all – and from all those who work for him. (76)

Lenny's attention to the different positions of influence her parents occupy in this negotiation process is evident in the analogy she draws between this 'performance' and the theatre – as well as the employer/

employee relation this relationship mimics (something she consistently forgets in her memory of her relationship to Ayah). While her mother is the performer, 'juggling the range of her voice,' her father is the director, 'extracting the most talented performances from us all.' Though there is an underlying fluidity to the circulation of power in this 'game,' ultimately, her father is in the dominant position. Although a playful mood pervades the scene, Lenny's understanding of the way this process demeans her mother is conveyed through her description of the events; like an animal her mother 'scrambles across the mattress on all fours' as she tries to catch her husband. When she 'warns' him of her determination, Lenny describes her voice as 'tearfully childish' (76). In this scene, Lenny's mother is figured as exercising consensual agency to shore up her access to middle-class domestic security rather than challenge the patriarchal and class conventions that govern her marital relation.

The gendered, unequal, and agonistic qualities of this power struggle take on a darker significance for the adult Lenny, who recalls how she became increasingly complicit in her mother's struggle for favour with her father. Lenny alludes to the fact that her father may have been involved with another woman and indirectly suggests that he beats her mother; Lenny comments, 'But there are other things they fight about that are not clear to me. Sometimes I hear Mother say "No, Jana; I won't let you go! I won't let you go to her!"' (224). One day, Lenny reports, 'I surprise Mother at her bath and see the bruises on her body' (224). When she reflects on their daily ritual of greeting her father as he returns home from work, she is acutely aware of how her mother monitors her father's reaction to her stories, redirecting the conversation to maintain a positive response. When her father expresses annoyance over a story about her brother's behaviour, Lenny recalls how '[s]witching the bulletin immediately, Mother recounts some observations of mine as if I've spent the entire morning mouthing extraordinarily brilliant, saccharinely sweet and fetchingly naive remarks' (88). After reflecting on how her mother called upon her regularly to repeat or invent these kinds of remarks, the adult Lenny figures herself as internalizing her simpering performances: 'And as the years advance, my sense of inadequacy and unworth advances. I have to think faster – on my toes as it were ... offering lengthier and lengthier chatter to fill up the infernal time of Father's mute meals' (88). The 'hellishness' Lenny associates with these interactions between her parents is a far cry from the playfulness connected with the scene discussed earlier. '[In] a narrative,' Spivak comments, 'as you proceed along the narrative, the narrative takes on its own impetus as it were, so that one begins to see reality as non-narrated' ('Post-modern' 19). In her recounting of the details of these lunch-time performances, the adult Lenny's awareness of her inferior status as a woman in a patriarchal society, the different and unequal expectations her parents had for her and her brother, and her mother's subordinate position in the marriage and her own complicity, emerge. The adult Lenny pulls her reader back to the frame of the narrative with a doubly self-reflexive question: 'Is that when I learn to tell tales?' (88). With this move, the narrative self-consciously reminds us of its own limits and sets that stage for examining how Lenny, as a privileged minority in postcolonial Pakistan, may share some responsibility for the failure of the state and community to protect and accommodate the interests of individuals like Ayah.

Another way in which Lenny's narrative comes to question received notions of 'reality' is through her relationship with Ayah. Where Lenny's mother's actions often result in 'overly individualized "private" resolutions' (Sangari, 'Consent' 868) to her subordination, Ayah's initial ability to subvert the codes of chastity and conjugality becomes a radical source of inspiration for Lenny. The subversive potential of Lenny and Ayah's relationship stems from its socially 'unregulated' history. Ayah and Lenny's relatively unsupervised time together allows them to build a bond of unmanaged intimacy that challenges patriarchal, racial, and class conventions. Lenny and Ayah's relationship can be read as an example of an undisciplined, affectionate relationship between a servant and child that Ann Stoler terms an 'education of desire' (109). An 'education of desire' is Foucault's phrase for the process through which the subject learns about the 'correct' expression of his or her sexuality; correct, in this sense, refers to the epistemological assumptions that inform any discourse of sexuality in a given culture. In her book *Race and the Education of Desire*, Ann Stoler takes Foucault's notion of an 'education of desire' and extends its reference to the cultivation of emotional ties between children and their nannies. These ties can be seen as potentially subversive, as in Lenny and Ayah's case, when the 'cultivation of the self' they involve crosses 'carefully marked boundaries of class and race' (Stoler 191). The relatively unsupervised relationship between Ayah and her charge allows Lenny's 'education of desire' to unfold without the usual injunctions against her developing too much familiarity with her nanny. Her narrative figures her growing awareness of the links between the power relations she experiences as a girl growing up in a patriarchal, minority community and the pressures Ayah negotiates as a female Hindu servant living in colonial India and postcolonial Pakistan.

Clearly, part of the fascination that Ayah holds for Lenny is related to her ability to exercise some agency *despite* the subordinate social position she occupies.[9] In the pre-partition world of 1943 Lahore, Lenny perceives Ayah's 'chocolate chemistry' as allowing her to negotiate her desire for sexual intimacy with a variety of men from diverse cultural backgrounds and thereby subvert patriarchal expectations for her behaviour. Lenny notes, for instance, the 'subtle exchange of signals and some of the complex rites by which Ayah's admirers coexist' (29). Once Ayah has made a decision about with whom she will spend her time, Lenny remarks how the other men, '[d]usting the grass from their clothes ... slip away before dark, leaving the one luck, or the lady, favors' (29). Ayah's ability to displace the codes of chastity and monogamy and still maintain the respect of her admirers suggests an alternative to the patriarchal relationships that govern Lenny's mother's life. Lenny likens Ayah's hold over the men in her social circle to 'the tyranny magnets exercise over metals' (29). The type of agonism this metaphor suggests is repeatedly associated with Ayah's influence over the men: 'Ayah's presence galvanizes men to mad sprints in the noon heat' (41). From the naive perspective of a child, Ayah's negotiations with Ice-candy-man and others take on the semblance of a military action in which Lenny learns to participate in order to extract attention, treats, and favours for herself:

> Things love to crawl beneath Ayah's sari. Ladybirds, glow-worms, Ice-candy-man's toes. She dusts them off with impartial nonchalance. I keep an eye on Ice-candy-man's toes. Sometimes, in the course of an engrossing story, they travel so cautiously that both Ayah and I are taken unawares. Ice-candy-man is a raconteur. He is also an absorbing gossip. When the story is extra good, and the tentative toes polite, Ayah tolerates them.
>
> Sometimes a toe snakes out and zeros in on its target with such lightening speed that I hear of the attack only from Ayah's startled 'Oof.' Once in a while I preempt the big toe's romantic impulse and, catching it mid-crawl or mid-strike, twist it. It is a measure to keep the candy bribes coming. (28–9)

This passage depicts Ice-candy-man's seduction of Ayah through storytelling in terms suggestive of a military-like strategy (suggested by the words 'target,' 'attack,' and 'strike') that occasionally leads to the reciprocal expression of desire between them. As Lenny observes, Ayah sets conditions on the manner and circumstances in which she is willing to entertain Ice-candy-man's advances: 'When the story is good, and the tentative toes polite.' In all cases, the emphasis in Lenny's figuration of these encounters is on the unequal but not unmanageable relations of power between Ayah and the men in her social circle.

As argued by Ambreen Hai, Lenny's rendering of Ayah's negotiations with her admirers also unwittingly reveals how

> Ayah is able to consort with her admirers – while taking her young charges to the park – by depending upon Lenny's indulgence and silence bought by 'candy bribes' ... Thus Ayah's servant body and her sexual accessibility make her available not only to surrounding men – over whom she can exert some semblance of power in coquetry and refusal – but also to Lenny's desires (which Ayah cannot withstand). (397)

Significantly, 'the ends' of Sidhwa's narrative, as referred to by the quote from Spivak I began this chapter with, appear to rest with Sidhwa's somewhat romanticized representation of Lenny and Ayah's relationship. Ambreen Hai reads the reception of Sidhwa's novel in light of what she sees as the 'critical climate that sometimes too hastily valorizes' the work of writers who self-consciously position themselves as border crossers and border inhabitants (382–3). Hai questions the novel's status as 'border writing' and suggests that it 'runs aground upon other unforeseen limits that throw that professed border work into disarray' (383). These limits are identified as 'implicit assumptions of gender, class, ethnicity, nationalism, and sexuality' that Lenny's narrative fails to address (383). The common problem, as already suggested in my analysis above, is that 'well-intentioned efforts to represent subalternity' ultimately end up using the subaltern as a site rather than subject of discursive renegotiation (384). While I hope my analysis shows that I share this concern with Hai, I would argue, however, that the adult narrator is represented as in the process of breaching these limits. For example, Lenny's narrative suggests that as an adult she is not unaware of how gendered constructions of ethnic purity cut across class hierarchies; after recalling how, as a child, the mere touch of her and Yousaf's shadows leads a Brahmin Pandit to react with the 'terror, passion and pain expected of a violated virgin,' she comments, 'I experience this feeling of utter degradation, of being an untouchable excrescence, an outcast again, years later when I hold out my hand to a Parsee priest at a wedding and he, thinking I am menstruating beneath my façade of diamonds and sequined sari, cringes' (125). Clearly, rather than isolate the violence of partition as a 'lower-class' experience (Hai 401), as an adult Lenny seems to be in engaged in the process of forging a link between disturbing memories from her childhood and her adult experience of patriarchal and racialized constructions of ethnic identity within her own community in postcolonial Pakistan.

While Ambreen Hai praises Sidhwa's text for undoing some of the binaries I have already discussed above (offering an account from a narrator who is uninitiated in dominant discourses about gender, sexuality, and national identity and whose relationship with her *ayah* allows her to cross, at least temporarily, class and ethnic boundaries), she also registers concerns about what she sees as the text's conceit of performing 'reconstitutive and salutary [work] in revising national history and identity, or in working through collective trauma' (390). 'As the multiply othered victim,' Hai contends, 'Ayah serves finally as a tool to emphasize the goodness of the ethnically neutral and upper-class Parsee (border) women who volunteer to save her and others like her' (391).

While Hai argues this blindness in the novel leads to an uncritical rehearsal of the allegory of Woman as Nation, where 'in replaying the trope it then consolidates – instead of questioning – the gender assumptions of that symbolism' (413), I offer an alternative reading; Hai's reading ignores the novel's consistent refusal to work through or otherwise resolve the traumas connected with the treatment of 'abducted' women.

Lenny's account of Ayah's 'recovery' and the treatment of 'abducted' women in general suggests that the actions of the state and community are governed by the need to recoup the threat 'abducted' women present to patriarchal power relations through their survival.[10] Lenny's memory of the negotiations in her family around what to do about Ayah's situation highlights the competing claims on 'abducted' women's identities that characterized the post-partition context. While Lenny's mother suggests that there is an obvious solution to the fate of 'abducted' women (i.e., 'send kidnapped women, like your ayah, to their families across the border' [254]), it is evident that Ayah's position is not so clear-cut; as 'a wife' (256) to Ice-candy-man she is now inscribed in the patriarchal domestic sphere of Pakistan even while her original religious identity connects her with the patriarchal civil sphere in India. On the one hand, though Ayah's gendered religious identity disqualifies her for citizenship in the Muslim-centric nation of Pakistan, her marriage to Ice-candy-man places her in a contractual relationship in the domestic sphere recognized as protected by the state. On the other hand, her 'abduction' stands as an affront to the (Hindu-centric) patriarchal private sphere in India and counter to the prohibition against conversion and inter-marriage in both communities. When Godmother invites Ice-candy-man to visit her and report on Ayah's well-being, he attempts to gloss over these contradictions by referring to the history of the Hira Mandi district and his legal status as her husband.

Initially, Lenny is impressed by the romantic presentation of Ice-candy-man's identity. Upon his arrival she states: '[B]ehold! The bridegroom comes. Lean, lank and loping, in flowering white muslin, raising dust with his sandled feet, the poet approacheth' (256). While previous events should suggest to Lenny that this new persona is just one more strategic incarnation that Ice-candy-man adopts to suit his purposes, her memory of the meeting indicates that she is still naive and even sympathetic to his desire to dominate Ayah. She writes, 'Astonishingly, we are not amazed at the surge of words pouring from him: so well do they suit the poetic mold of his metamorphosed character' (257). Admitting that some women in the Hira Mandi are exploited because they do not have connections to the 'original' ancestors of the *Kotha* (artists and performers for the royal household), Ice-candy-man assures Godmother, 'we protect our women. We marry our girls ourselves. No one dare lay a finger on them!' (259). Godmother, however, confronts him about his culpability in Ayah's humiliation, dismantling his claim to be her protector. Once again, Lenny's memories of the period reflect an ambivalent view of events rendered in the figurative elements of her statements:

> There is a suffocating explosion within my eyes and head. A blinding blast of pity and disillusion and a savage rage. My sight is disoriented. I see Ice-candy-man float away in a bubble and dwindle to a gray speck in the aftermath of the blast and then come so close that I can see every pore and muddy crease in his skin magnified in dazzling luminosity. The popsicle man, Slavesister and we and our chairs and the table with the fan skid at a tremendous angle to dash against the compound wall and the walls bulge and fly apart. Godmother's house and Mrs. Pen's house sway crazily, the bricks tumbling. (262–3)

Lenny's forced confrontation with the fact of Ice-candy-man's betrayal of Ayah (which is of course, linked to her own) hinges on frequent references to metaphors of vision that are subverted as quickly as they are offered. It is Lenny's admission to Ice-candy-man that Ayah is still living with her family in the house in Lahore that leads to her extrication from her family home. In an interview with Feroza Jussawalla, Sidhwa specifies that 'Lenny's divulgence of her [Ayah's] whereabouts is very crucial in the story, but it is perhaps more crucial in her mind than it needs to be ... the rioters were infallible hunters, and they would have found Ayah' ('Interview' 206). In conversation with David Montenegro, she comments: 'Lenny is growing up – learning, experiencing, and coming to her own conclusions – one of them, that truth, truth, nothing but the truth can lead to a lot of harm, too' (519). While Hai reads the novel as unwittingly aligning the Parsi community with the patriarchal and elite postcolonial nation-state, the narrative's preoccupation with Lenny's exaggerated feeling of responsibility for Ayah's abduction can be read as a symbolic commentary on the failings of the postcolonial state under the rule of solipsistic elite groups. The realization of how she and Ice-candy-man have both coveted and betrayed Ayah in order to satisfy their own desires signals an end to (the adult) Lenny's exculpatory attitude and innocent acceptance of the norms that governed her interpretation of her own motives, the community, and the state. Indeed, Lenny's experience is represented as distorting her vision ('My sight is disoriented'), making 'any claim to [experience's] unmediated transparency impossible' (Scott 794). Although Lenny's narrative represents this moment of substitution as 'a conversion experience, a clarifying moment, after which' she 'sees (that is, understands) differently' as Joan Scott comments, 'there is all the difference between subjective perceptual clarity and transparent vision; one does not necessarily follow from the other even if the subjective state is metaphorically presented as a visual experience' (794). In short, she has what Karen Swann has called 'a vision beyond the visible' (Scott 794). Lenny's use and then subversion of the metaphor of vision in her representation of this experience highlights the new understanding of 'reality' that informs her narrative for the remainder of the book.

In other words, Lenny comes to the realization that the activities of agents like Ice-candy-man *and* the people involved with the Recovery Operation (including the women of her own community) are not self-evident but interested expressions of desire that gain legitimacy through their normalization. In Scott's words, Lenny is figured as coming to recognize 'the complex and changing discursive processes by which identities are ascribed, resisted, or embraced, and which processes themselves are unremarked and indeed achieve their effect because they are not noticed' (792). Lenny no longer takes vision as evidence of an essential meaning or identity that can be apprehended in an unmediated fashion. Instead, the contradictions within Ice-candy-man's self-presentation (a man claiming to worship the woman he subordinates to his desire) are brought out by Lenny's Godmother's critical intervention that 'explodes' or 'cracks' Lenny's naive view of representation, revealing its self-serving, historical, and political implications.

Ambreen Hai takes the position that

[i]n narrating the self-congratulatory, fantasized recovery and restitution of the ravaged Ayah via the intervention of a grandparental matriarch, Sidhwa's belaboured focus on the graphic details of that over-used body deflects attention from and substitutes for what could not be imagined about upper-class female bodies, allowing proximity only by expending its indignation upon the permissible distance of class and ethnic difference. (400)

I would like to suggest, however, that to read the 'recovery' of Ayah in this way requires the elision of the many ways Lenny's account of the treatment of 'abducted' women both refuses to speak for them and attempts to displace the discourse of shame that adheres to their identity. As I have already shown, Lenny comes to be critical of her community's and Godmother's normalized and ingrained attitudes toward these women (attributing their circumstances to 'fate' and euphemizing their condition as 'fallen'). In fact, the outcome of their 'recovery' activities are rendered in an ambivalent light. As Lenny observes the women from the roof of her family home, she describes them as 'moving lethargically between their cots' (202) 'dazed and dull,' and recounts how 'they only look bewildered and rarely smile back' (233). As Sangeeta Ray suggests, '[t]he unnarratable lives of these women undermine the efficacy of the pedagogical narratives of both nations and reveals [sic] the founding ambivalence at the core of every progressive national narrative' (*En-Gendering* 136).

The specific circumstances surrounding Ayah's 'recovery' also render it in a less than celebratory fashion. One could argue that it is only Lenny's refusal to accept the discourse of shame as it is attached to the figure of Ayah that pushes her Godmother to challenge the assumption that Ayah is better off living as Ice-candy-man's wife. When Godmother goes to meet with Ayah, far from forcing her to migrate to India (as the state-run Recovery Operations on both sides of the border did in situations where there was any question about the 'abducted' woman's national identity), Godmother warns her that her family might not take her in (274). Like Colonel Bharucha earlier, Lenny recalls Godmother exhibiting an 'uncharacteristic hesitancy' (273) when she warns Ayah of this possibility. Without prompting, Ayah states: 'I want to go to my family' (273); after further counsel from Godmother, Ayah asserts again, 'Whether they want me or not, I will go' (274) and later 'I have thought it over ... I want to go to my folk' (275). One might be inclined to interpret this moment in the text as the subaltern speaking in some of the troubling ways critiqued in Spivak's 'Can the Subaltern Speak?'; however, this reading of the text is immediately undercut by Lenny's description of Ayah's voice as 'harsh, gruff: as if someone has mutilated her vocal cords' (273). When Ayah arrives at the Recovered Women's Camp she is not described as particularly grateful to Lenny or her family for their intervention; rather, Lenny describes how '[s]he looks up at us out of glazed and unfeeling eyes for a moment, as if we are strangers, and goes in again' (285). Finally, when Lenny recounts how Godmother orchestrated Ayah's 'extradition from the Hira Mandi district,' she describes it in a fashion that belittles rather than celebrates the role of the newly formed Pakistani state; Godmother's effectiveness in removing Ayah from Ice-candy-man's matrimonial home is explicitly attributed to her class position, and not the authority of the state, which is rendered in deflated and ironic terms as 'a toddler nation greenly fluttering its flag – with a white strip to represent its minorities – a crescent and star' (285–6). By this point in the text, the crescent moon on the flag (representing the Muslim majority) has acquired a deeply ambivalent significance; tellingly, Lenny describes the scars of riot victims as resembling 'the shape of a four-day old crescent moon' (206), and the wailing of the women in the camp next to her family home is accompanied by shadows that assume 'the angry shapes of swirling phantom babies, of gaping wounds forming deformed crescents' (224).

Despite the fact that her identity is over-determined by all these discursive structures, Ayah's subject-position is not inscribed in the discourse of salvation or victimization. Lenny's narrative describes how, though her eyes meet Ayah's, she finds them unreadable:

> Where have the radiance and animation gone? Can the soul be extracted from its living body? Her vacant eyes are bigger than ever: wide-opened

with what they've seen and felt: wider even than the frightening saucers and dinner plates that describe the watchful orbs of the three dogs who guard the wicked Tinder Box witches' treasure in underground chambers. Colder than the ice that lurks behind the hazel in Ice-candy-man's beguiling eyes. (272)

Her eyes are both 'vacant' and 'wide-opened,' empty and yet all-seeing. Her new 'watchful' stance is a combination of detachment (suggested by her 'icy' stare) and suspicion produced by the experiences she has had in Pakistan and those she will face in India. Her resolve to leave at the first opportunity, therefore, cannot really be interpreted as an escape from or resolution of these pressures when her behaviour is more guarded than ever.

Lenny's 'education of desire' in her close relationship with Ayah takes her out of the confines of the bourgeois Parsi community and exposes her to the heterogeneity of sociocultural perspectives that lead her to question dominant interpretations of history. Her autobiographical mode of writing indicates that, even as an adult, she continues to question and challenge these things and to consider her own complicity in their transparency. Haunted by the loss of Ayah and the patriarchal and elite dynamic inflecting her abduction, Lenny's story 'takes the form of narrating the independence and birth of nations with all its illegitimate undertones and bourgeois betrayals' (Ray, *En-Gendering* 137). Though partition leaves the nation and community 'broken,' it is clear that Lenny has 'cracked' the patriarchal-nationalist code that (re)asserts itself in the aftermath.

4 A Heart Divided: Education, Romance, and the Domestic Sphere in Attia Hosain's *Sunlight on a Broken Column*

> Home, it has been said, is not necessarily where one *belongs* but the place where one *starts* from.
>
> (Nasta 1)

As I discussed in chapter 1, from the early nineteenth century onwards, middle-class and elite women in India were socialized to assume roles as wives and mothers that were highly implicated in the patriarchal, anti-colonial, and nationalist movement. Nationalist discourse appropriated and further encoded a gendered construction of civil society into (masculine) public and (feminine) private realms, adding new symbolic meaning to gender relationships within the patriarchal family. Feminist critiques of this gendered division of civil society have led to critical investigations into the private sphere and the discourse of domesticity that dominates it.[1] As the work of these scholars has suggested, more attention needs to be paid to texts such as diaries, letters, autobiography, and fiction in order to understand the contours of women's experiences within the public and private realms. While it is undeniable that 'home' in colonial India came to function as a place to offer 'testimony about the ability of the reforming male elite to manage their personal lives' (Burton, 'Girlhood' 8), the women who inhabited this sphere were not simply subordinate to this objective.

In this chapter, I want to demonstrate how elite, patriarchal, and racialized assumptions about citizenship that inform nationalist discourse can be productively critiqued by tracing the contradictions around gender identity in representations of 'everyday' experience in the domestic sphere. In this respect, Attia Hosain's *Sunlight on a Broken Col-*

umn (hereafter *Sunlight*) is an important book for coming to terms with the continuing effects of nationalism and partition in postcolonial India. Set in the northern Punjab between 1932 and 1952, the novel's narrative time frame spans a twenty-year period covering India's transition from a colonial to postcolonial state. It is narrated from the point of view of Laila, a Muslim girl who has been orphaned at a young age and is under the guardianship of her extended family of *taluqdars* (landlords) in Lucknow. The novel portrays Laila's growth from girlhood to womanhood and her experience moving from her grandfather's more 'traditional,' 'orthodox' household to her uncle's more 'modern,' 'reform' household. Although historically, tradition and modernity have been figured as opposites in the dominant discourse of the Muslim community in colonial north India, Hosain's novel, with its attention to the politics of women's education and marriage, suggests this is a false dichotomy used to manage elite, patriarchal, and ethnic interests competing for ascendancy during the nationalist movement and after.

My analysis tracks how Laila's exposure to both so-called traditional and modern contexts alerts her to the contradictions in her community's attitude toward gender issues. Specifically, I will examine how the convergence of both communities' views on women's sexuality makes visible the patriarchal power relations that are normalized within the Muslim community in the pre- and postcolonial context. My discussion sets out to implode the tradition/modernity binary (and its siblings, religious/secular, communal/national, and primitive/rational) by pursuing a reading that concentrates on how women's identities are mobilized in similar fashions in these seemingly discrete discourses. I track how the reform of women's gender identities within the Muslim community in late colonial India was not grounded in an emancipatory politics but, rather, engineered to shore up patriarchal elite interests in the climate of instability that preceded and followed partition and independence. Finally, I argue that the narrative's ambivalent presentation of Laila's attempt to break with her family's expectations for her education and marriage (by pursing a 'love marriage' with Ameer) is analogous with its view of partition and independence. When Laila leaves Ashiana with Asad she not only leaves behind the idealism and modern binaries of her earlier romantic relationship, but also the concept of the nation as a 'bounded unit that inspires passionate attachments' (Skurski 607).

Written from the perspective of an upper-middle-class Muslim woman, Hosain's novel provides a relatively unexamined view of the reconfiguration of Muslim identity in India leading up to independence and partition. Hosain describes the novel as written intermittently over a five-year period from the mid- to late-1950s, and published in 1961 (Khan 17). Hosain migrated to England with her husband and two children in 1947 just prior to the partition and lived and worked there until her death in 1998. The novel has been celebrated as offering a window into the feudal *taluqdari* lifestyle in late colonial India. Anita Desai's introduction to the 1988 Penguin India edition comments extensively on the novel's portrait of 'the feudal society as it existed then, ruled by traditional concepts, sometimes struggling to break or to change them' (xi). Similarly, Mulk Raj Anand's 'Profile of Attia Hosain,' first published independently in 1978 and then as a preface for a 1979 edition of the novel, describes it as the story of 'a society which had become moribund from the effort to preserve the vested interests of the big house' (10). Until recently, apart from these personal and affectionate commentaries (both Desai and Anand were friends of Hosain), *Sunlight*'s unconventional view of events leading up to and following partition has been relatively neglected. However, Antoinette Burton's recently published analysis of the novel's attention to domestic relations and notions of home highlights its significance:

> As an alternative archive of partition, *Sunlight* reshapes the landscape of the historical imagination, offering a modest corrective to local and in turn national history. That it does so by obscuring the actual violence of partition and focusing instead on its architectural ravages speaks so much to the unnarratability of 1947 as it does to Hosain's determination to bring the pressure of family history to bear on the stories the nation tells itself about its origins. (*Dwelling* 134)

Rather than attempt to focus directly on the violence of the era, Burton argues Hosain's novel tracks the consequences of its effects on Laila, her family, and community. When asked in 1991 about what prompted her to write *Sunlight*, Hosain comments 'they [publishers Chatto] kept on at me that you've got to write a novel ... I was also, as I say, by now suffering deeply from this homesickness' (Khan 16). Hosain explains that though her initial impulse was to 'write about that agonizing heart break when we were all split up and a brother could not see a brother and a mother could not be with her dying son and families that had been proud to always collect together when there were weddings or deaths or births or anything, can not be together' (17), she admits, she 'couldn't write it' (17). In the end, she claims to be 'dissatisfied with' the novel she did write but 'handed it in to the agent' anyway (17).[2] In Anita Desai's introductory essay to the 1988 Penguin edition of *Sunlight*, she includes a quote from Hosain emphasizing the centrality of the experience of partition in her life: 'Events during and after Partition are to this day very painful to me' (ix). This may, in part, explain Hosain's decision to remain in England after partition; as she comments in her personal essay 'Deep Roots' (published just after her death in 1998), 'My mind could not accept the division of India, nor could I have belief in the logistics and legalities which subsumed the ideals of freedom and Independence' (22). 'Above all,' Hosain continues, 'Britain was the neutral area where I could still meet those from whom we were now divided by borders of nationality and an artificially nurtured hostility' (23). As Antoinette Burton speculates, *Sunlight* may have been 'borne out of a deeply personal experience of diasporic longing [where] the shadow of history in the form of partition was ever-present in Attia's narratives of alienation and belonging' (*Dwelling* 116). Hosain herself comments, '[p]erhaps, sub-consciously, to console myself for the maiming sense of loss of identity, I began to write. In this at least, I had the best of both my worlds' ('Roots' 23).[3] In short, it is clear that the experience of displacement and liminality has shaped both Hosain's life and her literary vision.

Like Sidhwa, Hosain has much in common with her fictional narrator. The world Laila represents in the novel shares many of the qualities of Hosain's own life. Hosain, like Laila, was born in 1913 in Oudh, part of the United Provinces of British India. Her father Shahid Hosain Kidwai was part of a large extended family of *taluqdars* – orthodox Muslim feudal landowners – and like many of his generation and class, educated in England at Cambridge. Coming from what Hosain herself describes as 'a big house' (Khan 20), she was seen as 'a person of some status' whose family 'enjoyed near princely privileges' (Nabar 124). Her mother Nisar came from an elite Kakori family that Hosain describes as 'intellectual' and 'proud of being people of learning' (Khan 2). Hosain comments:

> My mother grew up with that atmosphere around her, so that I was used to having in our home, as we grew up, people who behaved as if they were in salons where poets could sit – the poets being ones [*sic*] own

relatives because everybody felt that they had to compose poetry or be interested in classical music or anything that had to do with culture. (Khan 2)

Like Hosain, Laila first gains an appreciation for literature and high culture through her parents' social circle while they are alive and later through school and the library of her grandfather. Hosain's parents embraced these high cultural influences in their daily life. Hosain was schooled in English, first at Lucknow's elite La Martiniere School (originally founded for the education of Europeans and Anglo-Indians) and later at Isobella Thoburn College, and was also 'taught Persian, Urdu and Arabic at home' (Nabar 124). Hosain's father died when she was eleven, and she describes her mother as living out the rest of her life in *purdah*, confined to her home. Though as a married adult Hosain abandoned the practice of *purdah*, she comments that it is only because Isobella Thoburn was for girls and women that she was allowed to attend: 'my mother would never have let me go to the university where there were men. We were not in pardha in the sense that we were wearing burqas when we went out but we had a confined kind of life. People who came to visit us in the house were the sons of friends or relations but that was it because my very remarkable mother herself never went anywhere' (Khan 6). In 1933 – the same year Hosain married Ali Habibullah against her mother's wishes (Bondi 8) – she became the first woman from a *taluqdar* family to graduate from college (Burton 'Girlhood' 109). Hosain's marriage, like Laila's, was viewed as controversial because it was a choice made against her mother's wishes. As Laura Bondi reports, 'Attia's mother accused her of having "besmirched the family honour"' and 'never forgave her for what she had done although, as she still insists with a vigour which may sound disproportionate after almost sixty years, she had done "nothing," she was only "fighting for freedom"' (8).[4]

Hosain began writing while in school and was undoubtedly influenced by the climate of social and literary challenge represented by the publication of *Angare* (translated as 'coals' or 'embers') in Lucknow in December 1932 (a collection of short stories written by Sajjad Zahir, Rashid Jahan, Ahmed Ali, and Mahmuduzzafar – individuals who were contemporaries of Hosain and who would go on to be founding members of the Progressive Writers' Association in 1936).[5] Described by Leslie Flemming as expressing 'contempt for contemporary morals' ('Chugtai' 187), the book incited 'outrage' from 'both the religious and civil establishment' (Mahmud 448). As Shabana Mahmud recounts,

> Maulvis issued fatwas (decrees) against the book and the authors. On the floor of the Assembly of the United Provinces questions were asked and demands made for its proscription. Funds were collected for the prosecution of the authors, and the punishments suggested for them included 'stoning to death' and 'hanging by the neck.' (449)

By 13 March 1933 the book was banned under section 295A of the Indian Penal Code for the 'deliberate and malicious intention of outraging the religious feeling' (Mahmud 450), and all but five copies were destroyed. When asked in a 1991 interview with Omar Khan if her work was influenced by 'Sajjad Zaheer [sic] [of the Progressive Writers' Movement] and all of that' (19), Hosain responded, 'No. [I was] totally influenced by the West, I think, in a way but completely about my own cultural backgrounds and patterns of thought' (19). Hosain recalls, 'I did not read much about Urdu literature except what I had to, because it was easier and quicker I mean when from the age of three you were brought up in an English school' (Khan 19–20), but acknowledges that the group did influence her 'thinking politically' (Khan 20). Patrick Colm Hogan argues that this political influence can be seen in Marxist and modernist values in the narrative of *Sunlight* (265).

While these and other details should suggest that Hosain has drawn extensively on her personal experience to write this novel, Hosain herself has been quick to reject a simple autobiographical reading of her novel. When asked in a 1997 interview with Nilufer Bharucha if *Sunlight* was an autobiographical novel, Hosain stated:

> All first novels are autobiographical. But the characters in the book do not have a one-to-one relationship with real-life people. It's the attitudes that are real rather than the people. Its [sic] not purely fictional, it is factional. Laila has something of me in her. (20)

The 'factional' label she gives her work places it in the same category as Bapsi Sidhwa's – straddling multiple genres, times, and locations. In the interview with Khan, Hosain recalls her anger after being told by her agent that Cecil Day Lewis (an editor for the publisher and, later, England's poet laureate) had said 'that it is very autobiographical' (17). Hosain comments, 'I got very angry and I said, what does he mean by autobiographical? Every first novel or any novel will have to be part of oneself and people one knows, but it is not the people and it is not actually the events but it is at the same time yes' (17). Hosain's statements foreground the literary quality of her novel, reminding her readers to be alert to how her first-person narrator shapes the novel's representation of late colonial and early postcolonial Indian society. As Mulk Raj Anand comments, 'Attia had told the story of the big Talukdar household from the intimacy of felt experience and yet from the distant point of recollection, which makes her narrative a work of imagination in the real sense of the word, a novel *qua* novel' (9). More significant, perhaps, is Susheila Nasta's observation that 'Hosain is less concerned with the chronology of either her main protagonist's life – the surface plot – or a linear narration of the fissures of a tortured political history, than with discovering an aesthetic to express the power of memory as a device to both contain and expose the heterogeneity of a broken past' (42). Nasta's comment returns and redirects the reader's attention from the narrator to Hosain's narrative practice, underscoring how it 'open[s] up the unresolved discontinuities of a painful past throught the filters of memory, which can both double and fracture, restrict as well as liberate, perception' (40). More than just an autobiographical account of partition, *Sunlight* investigates the way memory shapes, translates, and unsettles received notions about the past.

Until recently not much critical work has been done on Hosain's forty-three-year-old novel.[6] In an 'early' 1993 essay, 'Multiple Forms of Belonging: Attia Hosain's *Sunlight on a Broken Column*,' Anuradha Dingwaney Needham drew attention to this fact, suggesting that this may have to do with the perception of national identity as seamless and homogeneous and the privileging of narratives of nation/nationalism that are organized around the exclusion of 'certain ideas, certain experiences, certain identities, even certain people' (96). For this reason, Needham calls Hosain's novel 'one instance of (an)other narrative of nation' (95). It could be argued that *Sunlight*'s narrative accomplishes this by representing a Muslim family that is firmly rooted in an Indian context, resistant to seeing itself as alienated from the Indian nationalist movement and, in some respects, challenging ideas of insurmountable differences between Hindus and Muslims that necessitated the founding of the Pakistani nation-state. As Vrinda Nabar suggests,

> Laila, Asad and Kemal [all Muslim characters who remain in India after partition] are important in the context of Independence and the period

following because they debunk fundamentalist distortions about the Hindu-Muslim divide. While it would be simplistic to pretend that irrational suspicion and hatred do not colour attitudes on either side of the border, significantly large numbers of Indian Muslims think of India as 'home,' a choice made without any apparent mental conflict. (133)

As a partition narrative that asserts the belonging of Muslim communities in postcolonial India (albeit with uneasiness), the novel challenges the argument that religious differences were the defining feature of the two nations' identities.

One element of the narrative that has not received much critical attention in the sources already cited is Hosain's treatment of Laila's romantic relationship with Ameer. In fact, much of the novel revolves around Laila's preoccupation with marriage, sexuality, and 'romantic' relationships in their various forms – from Zahra's flirtations with her cousin Asad to her family's servant Saliman's unplanned pregnancy and abandonment by Ghulam Ali, her Uncle Hamid's butler. Indeed, once Laila declares her love for Ameer – a junior lecturer in History at the local university with no significant inheritance – she becomes absorbed with the question of how she will deal with her family's objection to a 'love marriage' below her station. The clichéd sentimentality that characterizes Laila's representation of her interactions with Ameer, whose political convictions seem equally as hazy as Laila's, might lead the reader unfamiliar with this book to assume it is a pulp romance novel. For instance, after recounting how she deceives her guardians about her plans for the evening and then sneaks away for a clandestine meeting with Ameer, Laila writes about their rendezvous with a sentimental flourish worthy of Shoba Dé:[7]

> Ameer held my face between his hands and I blinked back my tears and smiled at him.
> 'I love you very much, Laila.'
> 'I love you too, Ameer.'
> His arms were a circle of safety, and his mouth a seal of tenderness, and in being together there was such purity of completeness that the world dissolved from perception. (240)

The moment of transcendence Laila depicts in this scene is rehearsed each time the lovers overcome adversity in their efforts to be together. This passage is not uncharacteristic of Laila's figuration of her feelings for Ameer throughout the narrative, and the consummation of their romantic relationship is one of the driving forces in the novel's plot.

Of course, it would be misleading to suggest that this kind of sentimentalism is characteristic of Hosain's entire novel. Hosain provides the reader with ample details concerning the sociohistorical context of the time, including the women's lives in the *zenana* (women's quarters), the class and communal issues as they impact on the family, the nationalist movement, her uncle's involvement with the elections for Muslim seats in the Constituent Assembly, and the end of British rule and India's partition. Clearly, Laila's romance with Ameer is embedded in the larger context of the conflicting sociopolitical concerns within her family, community, and emerging nation-state. As a critical account of nationalism, therefore, Hosain's novel tracks the experience of the *ashraf* or rising middle-class Sunni Muslim woman as she moves between the traditional/orthodox and modern/reform communities and experiences the shifting demands placed on her by the patriarchal community. Far from being a peripheral or myopic representation of a particular moment in Indian history, Hosain's novel, therefore, provides the opportunity for feminist scholars to extend their discussions of the co-implication of the public and private and trouble the binary relation between tradition and modernity that informed Muslim nationalism at the time of partition.

A brief critical genealogy of the (re)construction of Muslim identity during the nationalist period helps to place the novel's thematics of marriage and women's education into historical context. There appears to be a consensus among feminist scholars that 'Indian Muslims, prior to the colonial period, were not particularly concerned about defining themselves discursively in religious terms' (Rouse 43). Under colonization, however, Muslim identity underwent a transformation that both narrowed and formalized what were previously customary practices. The debates over social reform in the Hindu community in early and mid-nineteenth-century Bengal (discussed in chapter 1) resonate with events in the Muslim community during the late nineteenth century. As in the Hindu community, Muslim reformist and nationalist ideology was characterized by a 'separation of the domain of culture into two spheres – the material and the spiritual' (Chatterjee, 'Nationalist Resolution' 237). The gendered character of the public and private split in civil society meant that Muslim women were encouraged to make their lives into expressions of what was constructed as 'traditional' and essentially unique to Muslim identity. As Shahnaz Rouse comments:

This set of dichotomies is critical to understanding the nationalist project and its implications for women. For unlike the commonly held separation between 'tradition' and 'modernism,' this suggests the necessary maintenance of a balance – constantly shifting and reformulated – between the two, where 'modernisation' occurs in the material/outer/public world while 'tradition' is maintained in the spiritual/inner/private home. (44)

Rouse's comments make it explicit that nationalist discourse posits a *false* dichotomy between the public and private realms when they are, in fact, relationally constructed. As Barbara Metcalf argues, a close examination of the notion of 'tradition' that informs ideas about Muslim women's education, conduct and domesticity reveals that tradition is 'both variable and recent' ('Reading' 3).

That this binary construct was constantly revised to suit the needs of patriarchal and class interests is evident in debates surrounding the reform of women's education and, later, *Shariat* or Muslim personal law. In the late nineteenth century, for example, social reformers like Sayyid Ahmad Khan encouraged Muslim men to obtain Western education and jobs in the colonial government, but 'remained adamantly opposed to women's education outside the religious mode' (Jalal, 'Convenience' 81). In the 1884 *Education Commission Report* Sayyid Ahmad Khan argues that while 'the general state of female education among Muhammadans ... [was] far from satisfactory,' the government should not adopt 'any practical measure by which ... respectable Muhammadans may be induced to send their daughters to Government schools for education' (81). Ayesha Jalal comments that for Sayyid Ahmad Khan, 'Just as there was no question of allowing the colonial state to tinker with the *Shari'ah*, particularly as it affected the structure of the family, education for women had to begin and end within the secure walls of the domestic arena' (81). However, the revision of this position, while still constructing women as the bearers of cultural authenticity in the private sphere, is evident in the early twentieth century, when elite Muslim men saw the need for more formally educated wives as social companions and political allies. In an effort to meet this need and counter the influence of Christian missionary schools and Hindu revivalists, Muslim women were now encouraged to be educated in institutions (albeit, gender-segregated) outside the home (82). Hence, as this epistemological shift suggests, attitudes to educational reform in the Muslim community were not adopted with an eye to women's emancipation (though, undoubtedly, this move contributed to the advancement of women's interests in South Asia), but to serve the needs of an evolving patriarchal upper middle class. An awareness of this fact seems evident at the level of the narrative in Hosain's novel when Uncle Hamid summons his nieces to advise them about his plans for their immediate futures; when Uncle Hamid declares his support for Laila to continue her education, as if by way of explanation, Aunt Saira comments, 'Young men want their wives to be educated enough to meet their friends and to entertain. Nowadays they lay down all sorts of conditions' (110).

The regulation and revision (rather than the mere 'preservation') of gender roles this education facilitated is evident in guides for domestic behaviour such as Maulana Ashraf Ali Thanawi's *Bihishti Zewar* (variously translated as *Heavenly Ornament* and *Perfecting Women*).[8] Published in the early 1900s, this immensely popular guide for middle-class women outlines in detail how a 'good' Muslim woman should conduct herself with an emphasis on restricting her activities to the 'maintenance' of Muslim identity in the domestic sphere.[9] For this reason, Jalal calls *Perfecting Women* a 'classic example of attempts at controlling and in the process conditioning women's own perceptions of the role ordained for them by Islam':

> Deemed by many to be a mandatory part of the *jehaz* (dowry), it details in meticulous and almost embarrassingly explicit fashion how a good Muslim woman should address and serve her husband, behave towards her in-laws, the mother-in-law in particular, as well as her own kith and kin. Delineating a rigorous set of rules for the most amazingly mundane activities, including how to write letters to the husband, bathe, dress, walk, speak, look, pray, it is a veritable gold-mine for teasing out the inner recesses for the conservative Muslim psyche. ('Convenience' 81)

The emphasis in Jalal's description of Thanawi's book is on how *Perfecting Women* effectively revised the image of the middle-class Muslim woman while still claiming to preserve what was essentially unique about Muslim culture.[10] As Sonia Nishat Amin points out,

> All existing virtues were kept intact; but more practical instruction and advice on cooking, cleaning, child-rearing, home medicine, religious duties, marital duties and rights, travelling, shopping, posting letters, etc. were added. In short, the texts were meant to be the model and guide for the Muslim girl now re-formed, so that she could steer herself and pre-

serve her tradition, religion and purity in changing times, contributing simultaneously to the growth of the Muslim polity by producing ideal citizens. (86)

The unstated goal of these publications was to groom women for service to the *new* patriarchal class while constructing their identities as representative of the 'timeless traditions of Islam' (87).

As my discussion of Hosain's text that follows suggests, these revisions to Muslim women's identities were not adopted uniformly by the Muslim community at any given time. Depending on which set of patriarchal interests are being advanced (traditionalist/orthodox or modernist/reform), these changes in women's conduct were praised or damned as corrupting or preserving the 'essential nature' of Muslim identity. When the figure of 'the middle class woman' is mobilized in the rhetoric of each faction of the community, the binaries of tradition/modernity and anticolonial/assimilationist begin to break down. It becomes evident that in both groups, '[c]ultural and national assertion was to be achieved at the expense of women' (Rouse 50). In all cases, the goal was to 'impress among women of Muslim upper classes their *duty* as Muslims' (51). As Rouse explains,

> Both modernists and religionists focused their activity on the Muslim community, using religious identity as a primary basis for organising resistance-cum-accommodation to colonial rule. Culture – Muslim culture – was the raison d'etre of their efforts. In the public realm, membership in colonial institutions was accepted and even encouraged by both elements. Islamic identity was, however, to be maintained in the private realm, i.e. the family. Both groups favoured education for women but segregated education, emphasizing religious content and domestic training. Muslim identity and respectability were seen to reside in the 'protection' (read segregation and seclusion) of women. (50)

What this convergence suggests is, despite divergent interests, a consensus existed among various patriarchal constituencies that it was necessary to circumscribe women's participation in the public sphere. While the two groups may justify this circumscription in different ways, they share a 'formidable opposition to particular types of learning for women' (Rouse 54). Thus '[t]he difference [between these two groups] does not reside in their respective actions as much as in the rationalisations each group (of men) offered up for them: each is engaged here in a power struggle, vying for consolidation of its own position. Women are treated by each as appendages in this process' (Rouse 53). The struggle between so-called traditional and modern constituencies, therefore, is less about secularity versus religion and more about each group advancing its respective self-interests at women's expense. What both these positions share is a mobilization of elite women's identities as symbolic representations of community identity. Essentially a movement among elites, as Barbara Metcalf has pointed out, the reform movement is 'a story of written texts and of people who read them' ('Reading' 17). In fact, as Metcalf argues, '[w]hile the teachings of the ulema implicitly distinguished Muslim women from non-Muslim women, they explicitly drew the line between the proper, well-brought up Muslim woman and the ignorant one' (6). The main target of their discourse was ' the 'enemy within': the unreformed, uneducated woman who did not know Islamic doctrine, was caught up in expensive and corrupting ceremonial practices, and handled badly the responsibilities of her everyday life' (6).

Hosain's interview with Khan suggests her family was particularly influenced by the ulema's opinions on women's education. When asked about the role religion played in her political life she reveals that her mother 'set up a madrassah [Muslim religious school]. The first of its kind, where my sister went to teach ... she used to go to the school where the girls were taught because my mother said if they were learning the Quran and namaaz [prayer] without understanding, that makes no sense' (7). The divisions between elite and working-class women are further accentuated in *Sunlight*, where 'the servants [like Nandi] who belong to Ashiana make visible the ways in which class and caste constitute respectable girlhood and womanhood in an elite community, offering a contrapuntal note to the counternarratives of gendered colonial modernity that underwrite this bildungsroman *manqué*' (Burton 'Girlhood' 123).

Laila's encounter with the contradictory expectations for women and men in *both* the 'traditional' and 'modern' contexts attests to the 'infinite adaptability of patriarchy' (Rouse 63) within nationalist and culturalist discourse. The thematic figuration of Laila's decentred narrative perspective and the critical distance it gives her from her family and community is established from the outset of Hosain's text. Laila represents herself as a rebellious girl who is remonstrated by her elders for reading too much and for not being more like her cousin Zahra, a 'model' upper-middle-class Muslim girl of marriageable age. Laila notes, on the opening page of the novel: 'Zahra said her prayers five times a day, read the Quran for an hour every morning, sewed and knitted and wrote the accounts' (14). In many ways, Zahra conforms to a model of womanhood promoted by the conduct manuals discussed earlier. Laila, on the other hand, is chastised for reading too much and too widely. She reports how her nanny warns her, 'Your books will eat you. They will dim the light of your lovely eyes, my moon princess, and then who will marry you, owl-eyed peering through glasses?' (14). Laila's insatiable appetite for all varieties of books compared with her cousin Zahra's adherence to the educational goals specified by the Muslim establishment at the time (i.e., she reads only the Quran), forces her to conclude that she and Zahra 'had nothing in common but ... kinship and ... fears' (15). The emphasis the story places on Laila's voracious appetite for unsupervised reading clearly departs from the model of Muslim women's education considered earlier.

The fears Laila refers to here stem from the uncertainty the family experiences while their grandfather, Baba Jan, lies on his death-bed. Until this time, Baba Jan has been the sovereign power in the orthodox/ traditional context of Laila's household. The women in Baba Jan's household practise *purdah* and are subordinate to the men in the family. No one is certain what will happen after Baba Jan's death because his son Hamid, a reform Muslim, has distanced himself from the extended family. The prospect of Baba Jan's loss, therefore, produces fear and anxiety over what mode of power will take effect in his absence. Laila's description of the household conveys the tension that inflects people's behaviour at this time:

> Aunt Abida withdrew into a tight cocoon of anxious silence, while Aunt Majida dissolved into tearful prayers. The quarrels of the maid-servants were desultory and less shrill; the men-servants' voices did not now carry over the high wall; the sweeper, the gardeners and the washerman drank less and sang no more to the rhythm of the drum. Visitors spoke as if someone was asleep next door, and Zahra and I felt our girlhood a heavy burden. Our minds had no defences against anxiety; we were uncertain and afraid. (14)

The uncertainty surrounding the future that is produced by the disintegration of the family and community's sovereign patriarch seems to affect everyone involved. The female members of the family are represented as particularly anxious, recognizing their dependence on patriarchal patronage in order to maintain their class status and material well-being.

The tensions Laila's family experiences as it negotiates a transition from a traditional to reform view of Muslim identity are typical of those experienced by actual *taluqdari* Muslim families at the time. The history of colonialism in the Lucknow region indicates that the privilege of the *taluqdari* community during the period in which this novel is set was under attack. Before the rebellion against the British in 1857, *taluqdars* acted as mediators between small *zamindars* (landowners) and regional rulers (Needham 100). After the rebellion,

> *taluqdars* who survived the events of 1857 without giving unforgivable offence to the British were transformed into urban elites; they were still attached partly to rural bases, functioning as intermediaries between the British colonizers and the peasant and smaller landowners. Whereas many of the 'pre-annexation [pre-1857] *taluqdars* were antagonistic to the British,' the post-annexation, post-1857 *taluqdars* 'bartered away their political rights for secure and enhanced incomes and made possible the century-long *Pax Britannica*' (Needham 100; Oldenburg 218–19).

With the nationalist movement dominated by Hindu concerns, different groups within the Muslim community began to reconstruct their identity in an attempt to maintain their share of power without losing patriarchal control of the domestic sphere. As I argued in chapter 1, though the Indian nationalist movement claimed to be secular in its goals, it relied heavily on the revival of Hinduism. As Amrita Chhachhi and many other scholars have noted, '[m]odern literature in Bengali, Hindi and Urdu was often blatantly communal, depicting Muslims as foreigners and oppressive, lecherous tyrants, while Hindus were portrayed as heroes struggling for positive values' (155). The British exacerbated these communal sentiments by offering official patronage to the Muslim community. These divisions were widened by Gandhi's and the Congress Party's reliance on Hindu symbology in their nationalist platforms. The combined implications of these events meant that the *taluqdari* community's privilege was under attack and the reform of Muslim women's identities became a central strategy for deflecting criticisms of backwardness and primitivism.

Initially, Laila depicts Uncle Hamid's modern/reform lifestyle in sharp contrast to his father's. The interdependent 'traditional' world of the women in the *zenana* – servants, family, and tenants who comprise

Baba Jan's world – is counterposed with Uncle Hamid's modern, individualist, and 'Western' attitudes. Whereas Laila's more traditional Uncle Mohsin taunts her when she cannot remember her 'degree of relationship' (18) to him (as 'the son of my grandfather's father's sister's daughter') (18), he comments that Hamid is 'more a Sahib than the English' (22). Repeatedly, Hamid is represented as a Muslim who has abandoned his community's and family's cultural practices in exchange for British patronage. With Baba Jan's death imminent, Laila reports how 'Aunt Majida moaned perpetually, "When will Hamid Bhai come? At a time like this it is his duty to be with us. Has the government bought him? When will he come?"' (71). The fact that Hamid arrives after his father's death underscores the perception that a break in the family's cultural practices has occurred at this time. Laila's account of how '[h]is presence restrained grief' (86) at Baba Jan's funeral and draws attention to the reformist/modern qualities that Hamid's character epitomizes: 'He was undemonstrative both by nature and because he admired Western forms of behaviour. His relations no longer expected him to conform to traditional patterns; and he was too self-sufficient to care for what they thought' (86). Laila's description of Hamid's 'calculated precision' in manner and appearance, 'his thin grey hair smoothed from the centre parting as if combed a moment before, his thick moustaches neatly clipped,' conveys her perception of his affinity with the mechanistic aspects of modernity (86). Moreover, his Anglicization is suggested by the observation that '[h]e dressed immaculately in Western clothes, and preferred to speak English' (86).

The gendered aspect of this self-presentation becomes apparent when it is contrasted with Laila's description of her Aunt Saira, her uncle Hamid's wife. Although Laila calls Hamid's wife his 'echo,' she also notes that Saira is 'dominated by him' and proceeds to note many points of difference between the two (87). Whereas before Hamid was married he was educated in England, Saira, on the other hand, 'had lived strictly in purdah, in an orthodox, middle-class household' (87). Since Saira's marriage to Hamid, however, '[h]e had her groomed by a succession of English "lady companions"' (87). Here, the 'principle of selection,' which Chatterjee argues is characteristic of the reform movement's construction of women's identities (*Nation* 121), can be seen at work in the figuration of Saira's character. Although Saira dresses in saris, she has also adopted 'discreet make-up, waved hair, cigarette-holder and high-heeled shoes' (87). In fact, Saira is the stereotypical Muslim *mohila* (Amin 71), blending 'Western' and 'Eastern' cultural practices in her appearance, but still equally implicated in patriarchal class-based expectations for her behaviour. 'The "new woman"' of the reform movement, Chatterjee explains, 'was to be modern, but she would also have to display the signs of national tradition and therefore would be essentially different from the "Western" woman' (*Nation* 9). Laila writes, 'Baba Jan had never been able to forgive his son for adopting a Western way of living, bringing his wife out of purdah, neglecting the religious education of his sons and doing all this openly and proudly' (87). As Laila's description of Saira suggests, however, Hamid is closer to Baba Jan in his politics than he realizes; he has merely redeployed Baba Jan's socially conservative views within his own reform views in order to maintain a patriarchal and elite Muslim agenda. Though Saira is depicted as a 'new' woman, she is also subjected to a 'new' patriarchy.

Laila's experience of the expectations placed on her to assume a certain feminine role in the private sphere in both traditional/orthodox *and* modern/reform domestic contexts discloses how patriarchal power relations continue to circulate to equal degrees in both. A prime example of this is the two communities' shared attitudes toward women's sexuality. This is exemplified in the confrontation between Laila and her Aunt Saira and three visitors one afternoon. In this scene, Laila has just returned home from school when her Aunt asks her to meet her three guests. As Laila enters the room, Begum Waheed, a supporter of the Muslim League, Mrs Wadia, an Anglicized Parsi, and her aunt are debating how to organize a reception for the Governor's wife in conjunction with her visit to the local women's park. Laila also notes that there is also a 'hawk-like' woman she has never met before sitting on the sofa, but the woman does not appear to be engaged in the discussion (129). Taking an elite position, Mrs Wadia advocates an admission fee to 'keep out the undesirable elements' from the park during the reception (130). Saira, on the other hand, reminds her '[i]t is a *public* park' established for women in *purdah* (130). Hardly the civic-minded reformer (on numerous occasions Saira distinguishes between herself and others on the basis of 'breeding' [199]), it appears Saira fears the negative impression that limiting admission to the park might have on public perceptions of the Muslim community and her husband's election campaign. Mrs Wadia, on the other hand, uses the discussion to draw attention to the fact that the segregated park is underused by the women; she comments, 'Who comes there unless forced to do so?' (130) and thus attacks what she perceives as the 'backwardness' of the Muslim community as a whole. Begum Waheed, a known reform Muslim, comes to the park's defence by invoking its 'classical' antecedents: 'Purdah women must have a park ... Think of the Mughal Emperors and the gardens they [had]' (131). Saira attempts to placate the two women by changing the subject and offering a conciliatory stance: 'I believe our daughters will find it easier, having the benefit of education. That is why I believe in education for women – to prepare them for service' (131). Mrs Wadia, however, uses this as another opportunity to criticize the Muslim community's 'uncivilized' treatment of women. Laila recounts how Mrs Wadia asks the visiting stranger, '"Begum Sahiba," ... [her] voice was sugar-sweet. "I believe His Highness your brother does not believe in modern education for girls?"' (131). The unfamiliar Begum retorts, 'In Surmai we bring our girls up to be good wives and mothers' (131), further establishing the orthodox attitudes she identifies with.

The verbal irony that characterizes this discussion is cut short when the conversation turns to local gossip concerning an illicit relationship between a Hindu boy and Muslim girl at Laila's school. Significantly, all four women are quick to condemn the Muslim girl for the 'immorality' of her actions, a point that is not lost on Laila. All of the women seem to agree on the unsuitability of a young Muslim girl expressing any agency that might undermine the perception of the Muslim and Hindu communities as culturally exclusive and women as sexually passive. Laila's careful account of the women's conversation and their mutual agreement over the young Muslim girl's immorality – despite their respective traditional, modernist, and reform perspectives – underscores the way patriarchal views are normalized in their assumptions about women's behaviour. In light of this experience, Laila comments how, suddenly, the women 'seemed like paper figures,' to her, 'as hollow as their words, blown up with air. There was nothing in them to frighten me' (133). Laila's comparison between the women and paper dolls and the emptiness she associates with their convictions conveys a lack of respect for their views and their patriarchal construction of women's 'honour.' Outraged at the women's hypocrisy, Laila loses her timidity and defends the girl, comparing her 'love' for the Hindu boy with 'heroines' found in 'novels and plays and poems' (133–4).

While the literature referred to here is left unidentified, there is much in Hosain's own biography that suggests it is primarily English in origin. In interviews and personal essays, Hosain has talked about her own education as being Anglo-centric. In 'Deep Roots' Hosain muses over her decision to write in English over Urdu (which she describes as her 'mother tongue'), signalling the way the English dominated her literary imagination:

> I spoke English from the age of three when I was put in the charge of an English governess, and then, when I was five, went to a school primarily for English and Anglo-Indian girls. At the time in India the best modern education was only possible in such schools. From then on until I graduated fourteen years later, I was taught the same subjects as in any English school. I learnt the beauty, rhythm, flexibility and richness of the English language from reading the Bible, Chaucer, Milton and Shakespeare. (20)

With such a strong emphasis on English literature and culture in her formal education, Hosain laments, 'My vocabulary in my mother tongue was limited – and more so because the pressure of other studies constantly interrupted my studies of our own classics, of Arabic and Persian' (20). When asked by Bondi in a 1991 interview whether *Sunlight*'s preoccupation with the theme of romantic love (something Bondi notes is absent in her earlier collection of short stories, *Phoenix Fled*) was 'imported along with other Western cultural elements' (217), Hosain replies,

> Romantic love? It was not around me, around the traditional people. There was a puritanical way of looking at things. Those people are not the kind of people who ever thought romantically of anything. I used to think – wondering where it was, looking for it – how sad that there is nothing romantic in my civilization! My people are not romantic! It is only those English people who are. (217–18)

Bondi seems to anticipate this response from Hosain, prefacing her statement with the comment 'She [Hosain] stares at me, as if I was stating the obvious' (217). In this respect, perhaps this construction of Hosain could be seen as akin to Mulk Raj Anand's profile of her that Burton describes as the 'modernist fantasy' of 'the emancipated purdha lady who got inside the modernist novel and made it her own' ('Girlhood' 120). In the same way that Burton suggests that it is 'conceivable that Hosain intended to offer a counterimage of purdah that complicated this persistently modernist stereotype' ('Girlhood' 120), I think it is possible to read Hosain's representation of Laila's love relationship as subverting a similar modernist and colonial conceit on this point. As

Patrick Colm Hogan has pointed out, Laila and Ameer's romance is reminiscent of 'the story of Laila and Majnun, the paradigmatic Arabic and Persian story of romantic love frustrated by social denial' (294). Described by Chelkowski as 'perhaps the most popular romance in the Islamic world' (66), it tells the story of Laila and Majnun, two students who fall in love but are prevented from marrying by Laila's father (Hogan 295).[11] Not only do Laila and Ameer's names (Majnun's clan name is Ameer) and the details of their romance tie Hosain's novel directly to this story as an intertext, but as Hogan has noted, 'Hosain alludes to the legend early in the novel, when a vegetable seller refers metaphorically to "the fingers of Laila, the ribs of Majnu"' (Hogan 295; Hosain 58). Such a direct reference to a Persian love story in connection to Laila and Ameer's relationship cannot help but destabilize the accusations that Laila is simply aligning her notion of marriage and sexuality with a colonial culture.[12]

From the outset of *Sunlight*, Laila is figured as torn between two (nationally charged) conceptions of a marriage – arranged and 'love' marriages. Laila's family's discussion of Zahra's impending arranged marriage at the beginning of the novel is followed by Laila's assertion that she 'won't be paired off like an animal' (29) – equating arranged marriage with uncivilized beliefs. In response to this attack, Zahra taunts her: 'I suppose you're going to find a husband for yourself? Maybe you'll marry someone for love like Englishwomen do, who change husbands like their slippers' (30). The potentially random and independent 'choice' associated with 'love' marriage in both the orthodox and reform communities' eyes was seen as threatening the upward mobility of the family as well as attributing women with agency that was incongruent with the nationalist construction of Muslim women as self-sacrificing, religious, and asexual outside the home. The unacceptability of this construction of Muslim women's identities – because of the threat it poses to the extended family and nation – is amply demonstrated by Laila's family's negative reaction to her cousins Zahra's and Asad's flirtations. When, for instance, Asad calls out for Zahra in a fever-induced delirium – 'Zahra, darling, Zahra, don't leave me, don't ever leave me' – Laila is painfully aware of Zahra's mother's disapproval: 'I saw the look of anger in Aunt Majida's eyes, tinged with hatred' (80). Aunt Majida's anger is twofold; one, Asad's precarious class position – as a young orphan with no significant inheritance to hope for – makes him a completely 'unsuitable' choice as a husband for her daughter; two, it could be construed that Zahra has encouraged

Asad's affections (something Laila herself suggests), thus challenging assumptions about Muslim women's sexual passivity and threatening to tarnish Zahra's and, by extension, the family's 'honour.' However, Laila's comment, 'my heart ached for Asad whose love was changed into a sin by conventions,' illustrates her belief that 'love' matches are more 'natural' than arranged marriages (80). While characters like Zahra attribute Laila's resistance to arranged marriage to her Western influence, Laila herself never does this specifically, thus adding to her somewhat displaced relationship to community and nationalist politics. As Burton notes, 'Laila resists the pathways laid out for her by her elders in these terrains, yet she also consistently resists aligning that rebellion with the political unrest that swirls around her' ('Girlhood' 126).

Laila's resistance to the practice of arranged marriage on the basis of its denial of 'human' emotions is developed in part through her response to Zahra's wedding to Naseer, an officer in the Indian Civil Service. For instance, Laila expresses doubts about the contrived rather than passionate foundation of Zahra's arranged marriage. As Zahra prepares for the Islamic ceremony, when she will first see her bridegroom's face in a mirror, Laila comments:

> I felt withdrawn and alien in my thoughts. That moment would have been the same had it been any other reflection Zahra saw. Did no shadow fall across the mirror? No reflection of pained eyes? Was love so pliable? Was it to be recognised only in poems of unrequited suffering? Why question what others accepted? Why was I allowed to become different? (114–15)

Laila's use of the word 'alien' and the series of rhetorical questions that follow suggest that her opposition to Zahra's arranged marriage indicates her growing awareness of how her position sets her apart from the norm in her community. Her use of the shadow image can be read as throwing doubt on the appropriateness of Zahra's marriage and 'traditional' practices in general. Significantly, however, as pointed out by Vrinda Nabar, it is possible to read the narrative's presentation of Zahra's and Laila's actions as 'differently rebellious' and 'allow[ing] the reader at least to think about the idea that liberation might mean a range of things depending on social class and education' (129). For example, Nabar points out that '[o]nce married, Zahra seems to Laila a quite different – and physically assertive – person' (129); indeed, while Laila's characterization of the transformation of Zahra into a 'modern' wife after her marriage expresses cynicism over her new persona, it also registers an awareness of Zahra's newfound freedom. She comments:

> Zahra had changed very much in her appearance, speech and mannerisms ... She was now playing the part of the perfect modern wife as she had once played the part of a dutiful purdah girl. Her present sophistication was as suited to her role as her past modesty had been. Just as she had once said her prayers five times a day, she now attended social functions morning, afternoon and evening. (140)

Laila's description of Zahra's 'transformation' suggests that she has merely exchanged one set of patriarchal expectations for another. At the same time, however, after marrying, Zahra is described by Laila as encouraging her to break away from the 'old-fashioned' rules regarding unmarried women appearing at social functions in public. Laila's comments even suggest a slight envy of Zahra's more relaxed, mildly sexual relationship to her body; as Laila chats with Zahra about joining her at the *taluqdari* reception she observes, 'No more loose, shapeless clothes [for Zahra], no more stooping and hunching of shoulders to conceal and deny one's body' (141).

The false dichotomy between tradition and modernity in the reform community that underpins Zahra's transformation comes to a head for Laila during the *taluqdari*'s reception for the Viceroy. The reception – an expression of the *taluqdari* community's notion of traditional Eastern hospitality – is debunked by Hosain's representation of the opportunism, patronage, and exploitation that inform their relationship to the British and their tenants. For instance, though the President of the Association attempts to represent the relationship between tenants and landlords as one based on reciprocity, he repeatedly confuses the terms 'prosperity' and 'property' in his address to the Viceroy: 'We are aware that the property – er – prosperity of our tenants is our proper – prosperity' (152). The hypocrisy of the pomp and circumstance that surround the *taluqdar*'s celebration of their privileged relationship with the Crown appears to overwhelm Laila. She is figured as dazed by the contradictions in the President's address when she reports how the voice of the speaker

> became a drone. The lights in their brilliance induced patches of blankness in the mind between which were spaced applause, the Viceregal reply,

more applause, more words, the presentation of a gold and silver casket containing the address, more applause, and Zahra saying, 'Laila! Where are you? Asleep with your eyes open?' (152)

In this passage Hosain plays with the images of light and dark, thus undermining Laila's metaphorical association of light with clarity and reason and darkness with irrationality and obscurity.

As the hypocrisy that inflects the speaker's statements begins to erode Laila's faith in the reasonableness of her community, the President's speech becomes like 'blank spaces' punctuated by the occasional round of meaningless applause. After the speech, during the fireworks display, Laila finds herself separated from her family in the now-menacing surroundings of the reception and is seized by a vertiginous state of panic. She recalls:

A rocket flared up and burst in the sky. Another and another ... The man in the black *achkan* was lurching towards me. A scream died in my throat and I ran blindly towards the farthest door crashing into someone coming through it. (153)

She remembers, 'I could see no one I knew. I was so frightened I wanted to cry. I pushed my way back toward the hall. I wanted to get to the Purdah gallery' (153). Left without a sense of belonging in the (modern) bourgeois reform world of the *taluqdari* society, intimidated by the unregulated (masculine) behaviour of the drunkard as he staggers toward her, Laila wishes, not surprisingly, to return to the (traditional and feminine) safety of the Purdah gallery (153).

Just as it appears the catechresis in the tradition/modernity binary that informs Laila's community's identity might be disclosed to her, she retreats into a romantic staging of her meeting with Ameer as 'love at first sight.' When she and Ameer collide, Laila notes that their apologies were in unison. As Ameer walks her through the crowd she comments: 'I felt safe holding his arm ... Staring men no longer mattered' (154). Shortly after, with clichéd sentimentality, she reports how the memory of Ameer's face is superimposed on the fireworks display. Later, when she is introduced to Ameer at her Aunt Saira and Uncle Hamid's tea party, she worries that 'the beating of my heart would be heard' (187). In each of these and all subsequent encounters with Ameer, there is the overwhelming sense that destiny has taken Laila in hand and that their love for each other will provide a complete sense of communion outside the constraints of their community. At this point in the novel, Laila pushes aside the unsatisfactory choice between traditional and reform modes of identity, assuaged by her 'love' relationship with Ameer.

Laila's family's resistance to accepting Ameer as her husband foregrounds the elite and patriarchal assumptions that inform their perspective of marriage. After Aunt Saira realizes that Ameer is Raza Ali's cousin from the 'other branch' of the family with 'no breeding,' Laila becomes acutely aware of how unlikely it is that he will be accepted as a potential suitor (199). When Ameer is invited to dinner after Hamid's success in the elections, Laila notes, 'All through dinner I sensed Aunt Saira's hostility to him' (264). More important, however, Laila suspects that her family will object to the independence she has demonstrated by pursuing the relationship without their consent. She confesses to Ameer:

> I have no courage, Ameer. I have never done anything I really believed in. Perhaps I believed in nothing enough. I have never been allowed to make decisions; they are always made for me. In the end not one's actions but one's mind is crippled. Sometimes I want to cry out, 'You are crushing me, destroying my individuality.' (265)

In this passage and others, it could be argued that the primary issue here is not Laila's expression of love, but sexual agency and self-interest. At this and other moments in the narrative Laila constructs her 'love' relationship with Ameer (and 'love' relationships in general) as an expression of her individuality. Clearly, it is the active and unregulated expression of female sexuality that makes Laila's relationship with Ameer so threatening to the patriarchal community's identity and material security. Thus, it is only when Saira catches Laila and Ameer kissing in the garden of Ashiana (the family home) that the situation reaches a crisis point. Laila comments, 'I saw a naked anger and hatred in her eyes that paralysed me' (266). This same reaction is evident in the orthodox/traditional branch of her family. Laila reports how after her marriage to Ameer, Abida refuses to forgive her for her actions and accuses her of being 'defiant and disobedient,' equating her decision to marry Ameer 'for love' with a loss of the family's honour (312). While her Uncle Hamid claims to object to the match on financial grounds and distances his own objections to her marriage from what he calls her aunts' 'old fashioned' (280) concerns, it results in the same thing: Laila becomes an outcast from the community. Rejected by both reform and orthodox members of the community, Laila concludes:

I had been guilty of admitting I loved, and love between man and woman was associated with sex, and sex was sin ... No one could stop me marrying Ameer if only to prove the purity of love. (312)

Although Laila is able to articulate the way her community's standards conflate love with sex and punish women who appear to exhibit any sexual agency, she (and Hosain) appear to be unable to acknowledge this sexual agency on its own terms. Instead, it is legitimated with reference to another totalizing (and patriarchal) construct – romantic love. While Laila rejects her family's and community's expectations for her sexual purity, she justifies this rejection with reference to another kind of purity – the 'purity of love.' In a 1997 interview with Nilufer Bharucha, Hosain describes herself as a 'Universalist Humanist' (21), and as Patrick Colm Hogan argues about *Sunlight*,

Hosain's implicit advocacy of individual freedom of choice in marriage is not precisely syncretistic. Rather, it is a form of universalism in which societies are seen as different, but human aspirations are the same. For Hosain, love is a human constant. (294)

Thus, while in many ways Laila's desire to be with Ameer gives her the courage to reject her family's bourgeois values and refuse to become 'the repository of her family's masculine honour,'[13] it is not clear that Laila or Hosain sees it in these terms. On the contrary, the novel consistently contrasts the transcendence and equality of 'love' relationships with the patriarchal conditions of arranged marriages, disclosing the rhetoric of 'progress' that underpins Laila's liberal notion of 'change' and the logic of Hosain's narrative.

Hosain rehearses this liberal view of arranged marriages at numerous junctures in the narrative. For example, during a party at Ashiana, Laila's advice to her Hindu friend Sita about 'following her heart' in her feelings for Laila's Muslim cousin Kemal is interrupted by the entrance of Sona Lal, an unhappy socialite who is also in an arranged marriage but competes with Sita for Kemal's attention. As if to foreshadow what the future would offer Sita in an arranged marriage, Laila portrays Sona as bitter and manipulative and describes her reflection in the mirror of the cloakroom where they meet as that of 'a middle-aged woman with slack lines of defeat, the once-inviting eyes dull with despair, the once-passionate mouth dragging with bitterness' (217). She notes how, at the sound of her drunk husband's voice calling her, Sona's face contorts with a 'spasm of hatred' (218). Similarly, Laila's visit to Aunt Abida, who has just had her marriage arranged, is recalled in equally negative terms. For instance, Laila makes a point of mentioning that her aunt's new husband ate with the women only the first day she arrived 'as a concession to me for my first meal in his house' (250). Taking in the scene, she writes, 'As I watched Aunt Abida and her husband, sitting at far ends of the *takht* from each other, silent in the presence of his mother, separate entities whom my imagination could not bring together, I wondered if my aunt had ever dreamed about marriage as I did' (250). Invariably, Laila attributes this to the patriarchal quality she associates exclusively with arranged marriages. Thus, consistently, Laila pits arranged and 'love' marriages against each other as traditional and modern, failed and successful respectively.

This element of the novel and Hosain's comments in interviews on the European origins of romantic love aside, I want to suggest that a more complicated reading of this aspect of the novel is possible with attention to how it is contextualized in the narrative as a whole. Significantly, the idea that 'love conquers all' is not allowed to dominate the remainder of the novel, and in many ways, the collapse of Laila's relationship with Ameer in the final section of the narrative parallels the failure of the nationalist movement to produce a truly inclusive construction of national identity. Commenting on Laila's depiction of 'home' and Ashiana (translated as 'nest') in the novel, Burton argues,

> *Sunlight* is not self-evidently a bildungsroman. It is not teleological, as novels of development invariably are; quite the contrary. Ashiana exhibits degeneration rather than youthful growth: it is disintegrating well before partition – a process Laila is uniquely positioned to appreciate because of her peculiar angle of vision as the orphaned daughter of the house. ('Girlhood' 107–8)

The breakdown of Ameer and Laila's relationship is not unlike the breakdown of the post-independence, post-partition dream of India and Pakistan that Laila is always somewhat distanced from throughout the story. In fact, it could be argued that the totalizing impulse that characterizes Laila's view of her romance is subtly undercut by the narrative's representation of the larger social context throughout. For instance, when Laila goes to meet Ameer for a romantic tryst, she describes how she has to cross 'through the smell, flies, filth, spit, open gutters and ragged crowds in the lanes between the smoke-grimed, rusty-roofed, precarious, pigeon-trap houses of the bazaar and into its wide main street' (220), before she sees him 'standing at the slope where the bazaar ended and opened towards the clean, fashionable world' (220). Unlike the situation at the *taluqdari* reception, here the contrast between the social conditions in the bazaar and the more fashionable marketplace where she meets Ameer is left unresolved. Indeed, there appears to be structural irony built into this scene where, as the couple forms a plan to find a more secluded spot, the coolies seize the opportunity to make some extra money transporting them up the hill. The romantic meeting begins to teeter on the edge of the macabre when Laila reports how 'one of the men moved to the side of the road and leaned against the railings, racked by a fit of coughing, his cadaverous, exhausted face distorted' (220–1). In the face of such poverty and suffering there is something absurd in Ameer's response to Laila's distress when he reassures her, 'There are no simple answers ... But cheer up! You must not look as if you were responsible for his troubles' (221).

The escapist quality of the couple's retreat to the pastoral setting of the hills is reinforced by Laila's observation that 'roads and houses and playgrounds were lost from vision and thought' and 'a sense of peace flowed into the veins of my body' (221). After Laila and Ameer take in the 'visionary summits' of the mountain range before them, they kiss in a moment that Laila considers nothing less than sublime:

> The moment when Ameer kissed me had no beginning; it was as pure and eternal as the snows we had been watching in deep communicative silence. It was part of every moment before it, the moment for which I had been born to become a part of existence before and after it, to know its meaning and fulfill its purpose. I knew a sense of such completeness and harmony that it seemed I was the earth, the sky, the light and the snow. (222)

The timeless, transcendental, unifying, and organic qualities that Laila associates with this moment are plain; the sense of 'completeness and harmony' Laila 'knows' is reinforced by her sense that she has merged with the idealized landscape. Significantly, however, it is the sound of a wood-cutter, a reference to their physical surroundings, that brings them back from the 'great spaceless, timeless distance' (222) to which Laila imagines they have transcended. Put simply, notions of the sublime Laila associates with these moments in her narrative border on the ridiculous when they are contrasted with her view of the events that surround her.

The disclosure of the contradictions underpinning Laila's construction of her relationship with Ameer as 'true love' and their resonance with the contradictions of the nationalist movement are most evident in the final section of *Sunlight*. Here, Laila's narrative is marked by deeper ambivalence toward romance than in any of the other previous sections and, arguably, takes on a self-consciously ironic tone. As Nasta points out, '[a]lthough this last section has most frequently been dismissed by critics as an indulgent "orgy of sentimentality" and an unnecessary adjunct to the novel's already weak chronological structure – it is in fact the coda that explicates Hosain's purpose and provides a 'double screen' for the substance of Laila's earlier recollections' (Nasta 42; Mukherjee, *Twice* 81; Bondi 105). As Burton suggests, 'if we were to understand part 4 simply as the return of the prodigal daughter, we would be in danger of misapprehending both the role of the house and the architecture of the novel itself' ('Girlhood' 132). Not satisfied with Zahra's 'overly individualized "private" resolutions' (Sangari, 'Consent' 868) for maintaining her patriarchal and class privilege, Laila attacks Zahra for characterizing her as naive in her continued commitment to living in India versus Pakistan: 'Where were you, Zahra, when I sat up through the nights, watching village after village set on fire, each day nearer and nearer? Sleeping in a comfortable house, guarded by policemen, and sentries?' (Hosain 304).[14]

Where 'Part Three' ends with Laila poised to leave Ashiana holding Ameer's hand, this fourth and final section opens, fourteen years later, with her returning alone, in the aftermath of the partition, fearing that she might experience an emotional breakdown (272). The 'disintegrating reality' of Ashiana (272) becomes an analogue for Laila's worldview since independence and the partition of India: 'In its decay I saw all the years of our lives as a family; the slow years that had evolved a way of life, the swift short years that had ended it' (273). Laila's sense of dislocation within the family home is intensified by the fact that there were now 'strangers living in the rooms' (272) – refugees from the partition who have been allotted compensation as a result of 'statistical calculation in the bargaining of bureaucrats and politicians, in which millions of uprooted human beings became just numerical figures' (272). With unfamiliar cynicism, Laila brings the reader up-to-date on events that have transpired since the last segment of the novel concluded. It becomes evident that the rejection Laila suffered from her extended family for marrying for 'love' and below her class has not been easy to endure. She recalls how Aunt Abida remained 'cold and unyielding' to her after she married Ameer and notes that 'she had seemed cruel to me beyond reason' (312). When she catches her reflection in a mirror left in her bedroom at Ashiana, she sees her current 'self' as alienated from 'that other when I had last stayed in this room' (313). She recounts how she had begun her married life with Ameer with the sense that nothing in the world mattered except their 'love,' only to discover that 'shadows began to take shape a year after we were married when I told Ameer I was to have a child' (315). There is no small irony in the fact that Laila invokes the image of the shadow and the mirror – the same image she used earlier to cast doubt on the rationale behind Zahra's and Sona Lal's arranged marriages – to express disillusionment with her own marriage. Laila reports how 'We were often short of money, and Ameer was hurt if I suggested I should use mine, or if I did so, trying to hide it from him' (315). The difficulties Ameer experiences living up to the masculine role of 'breadwinner' drive him to join the Public Relations branch in the Army, resulting in his transfer to the Middle East.[15] Laila recalls, 'He was cynical about what he had done, comparing himself to the "rice soldiers" – who had joined the Army without convictions, or even against them, because it was hard to get a good job, or as well paid a one' (316). When Ameer is taken prisoner and later killed trying to escape, Laila becomes completely disillusioned with life; she writes, 'I lived and moved through an endless tunnel with no exit' (317). This image encapsulates Laila's growing sense of alienation from her home and nation as in the post-partition era of the novel. Here, Laila's comments provide much support for Burton's view that '[t]he novel is, in short, a historical argument about the impossibility of dwelling comfortably at home in the wake of the unspeakable violence of the past' ('Girlhood' 106).

While the final section of the novel imposes a kind of closure on Laila's search for domestic happiness and national belonging (she plans to take her young daughter to go to live with Asad, Zahra's previously scorned love interest, who supports Gandhi and the Congress), there is much in the novel that destabilizes this reading.[16] As a reader of an earlier version of this chapter asks, 'what exactly is Asad offering Laila at the end of the novel? How does his sense of an allegiance to another collective (the nationalist one) address the tradition/modernity binary?' In essence, this binary remains intact in Asad's socialist outlook, and it is only the framing of Laila's decision to join him that displaces the possibility of it being (unwittingly) rehearsed in the future. With Ameer's death, Laila decides to act on her desire to be with Asad (someone she has maintained contact with even after he leaves home to pursue his activist and educational goals). Conveniently, in the Persian legend that informs Hosain's novel, Asad is the name for the tribe of 'Laila's kind husband, who accepts that she loves another man and never forces himself on her' (Hogan 296). Here, however, the difference between Hosain's and conventional versions of the Laila and Majnun love story becomes crucial: in Hosain's story, the lovers have acted on their desire to be together, only to be disappointed and disillusioned with the results (Hogan 295–6). Laila in Hosain's novel does not die of the heartbreak of unrequited love but rather survives to pursue another relationship. In the final pages of Hosain's text, as Laila lets go of the idealized construction of her relationship with Ameer, she is better able to confront rather than contain the contradictions and ambiguities of her family's and community's attitudes toward women's sexuality and education. Significantly, Laila and Asad do not name their desire to be together as 'love'; Asad asks her to accept him as a companion with faults and contradictions ('I am no saint, and never have been') (319) as opposed to the idealized lover she saw in Ameer. When Laila leaves Ashiana with Asad she not only leaves behind the idealism and binaries of her relationship with Ameer but also the concept of 'the nation as a bounded unit that inspires passionate attachments' (Skurski 607).

Hence, Hosain's novel draws attention to the interdependent construction of the public and private realms in nationalist discourse by structuring the narrative around what might be considered trivial or peripheral issues in the context of the high political story at the time of independence. Placed in the context of debates within the Muslim community over women's education and 'proper roles' in the civil and domestic realms, I have attempted to illustrate how Laila's narrative perspective implodes the normalized oppositions between tradition and modernity, public and private, Eastern and Western, and community and nation. Hosain represents Laila's growing awareness of the false dichotomy between these terms but also portrays her as overwhelmed by this knowledge and uncertain with regards to how to respond. At numerous points in the narrative, Laila responds to debates about traditional versus modern cultural practices, Islamic versus liberal conceptions of the nation, with the desire to escape. An exception to this sense of uncertainty is her 'love' for Ameer that she represents, at least for a brief time, as the one Truth in her lived experience that she pursues at all other costs. Nevertheless, as the narrative unfolds, even this certainty is short-lived. Eventually, it emerges that the monolithic premises and resulting violent exclusivity that characterize her relationship with Ameer have echoes in the patriarchal nationalist assumptions that have fractured the identity of Laila's, family, community, and nation.

Thus, it is possible to read the organization of Laila's narrative and its thematic concerns of love, education, and domesticity as unsettling the monolithic nationalism that comes to dominate in India and Pakistan at the time of partition. Laila's (failed) attempt to naturalize her choice of husband, form of marriage, and expression of her sexuality dovetails with attempts by nationalists in colonial India, and later Pakistan, to naturalize their exclusionary concepts of the nation. By the end of the novel, Laila sets aside her idealization of 'love' marriages and embarks on a new course in her relationship with Asad. Read on these terms, Hosain's novel can serve as a critique of the discursive links between the discourses of romantic love, patriotism, and national unity in the postcolonial context.

5 At a Loss for Words: Reading the Silence in South Asian Women's Partition Narratives

> I have come to believe that there is no way we can begin to understand what Partition was about, unless we look at how people remember it.
>
> (Butalia, *Other Side* 13)

> The issue is not simply with remembering or forgetting, but rather with *how* the nation remembers to forget, with how, that is, the representations of a remembered past serve an imaginary coherence that remains closed to the other.
>
> (Di Paolantonio 161)

In previous chapters I have attempted to foreground some of the silences and gaps that inhabit literary texts that represent women's experiences of partition. Veena Das's *Critical Events*, Urvashi Butalia's *The Other Side of Silence*, and Ritu Menon's and Kamala Bhasin's *Borders and Boundaries* have all attempted to make sense of the silences that punctuate the testimonies of people who lived through these events. Each of these books has a particular interest in thinking through the implications of silences in testimonies by women who were subject to sectarian violence and experienced social alienation as a result of the discourse of contamination that came to inflect their identities. The exceptionally thought-provoking work by this group of researchers has been instrumental in bringing the treatment of so-called abducted women and the activities of the state-sanctioned Recovery Operation (1947–55) to the attention of scholars and the general public.[1] What these researchers have encountered in their attempts to document and make sense of survivors' memories of this period is a silence about the actual details of the violence. As I have shown in previous chapters, a similar silence is encountered in literature that is purported to represent the events of partition and 'abducted' women's experience. In what follows, I will argue that in both cases this silence serves a pedagogical purpose in reframing our attitude toward partition history.

One such silence can be found in Jyotirmoyee Devi's novel *Epar Ganga Opar Ganga* (*The River Churning*).[2] As Jasodhara Bagchi notes in the introduction to Enakshi Chatterjee's 1995 English translation, the novel was first published in 1967 under the title '*Itihasey Streeparva* (The Woman Chapter in History) in the pages of the Autumn Annual of the reputed Bengali periodical, *Prabasi*' (xxvii).[3] As Jyotirmoyee Devi indicates in the 'Author's Note' to the 1995 English translation, 'Stree Parva' refers to a chapter of the *Mahabharata* and the 'penultimate canto of the epic – the Mushal-Parva' (Mukherjee, 'Pawn' 14) that details Arjun's failure to protect women left alone after the men of the Yadu clan are killed in battle. Jyotirmoyee Devi notes: 'Before his [Arjun's] very eyes, women were insulted and humiliated, some were forced to accompany the bandits out of fear, perhaps some were killed – the chronicler has not been able to give us a complete account' (xxxiv). Obviously, Jyotirmoyee Devi is drawing a parallel between the gaps in the *Mahabharata* regarding this history and the gaps in accounts of women separated from their male relatives during the sectarian violence that accompanied India's partition. Indeed, the final chapter of her novel is titled 'Stree Parva.' While Jyotirmoyee Devi speculates that the silence about these events in the *Mahabharata* may be linked to the masculine gender of the epic's author (she attributes the authorship of the *Mahabharata* exclusively to Vedavyas), she also notes that even if there were women epic poets, 'they could hardly write the stories of their own dishonour and shame. The language for it has yet to be fashioned, so naturally *Stree Parva* does not figure anywhere' (xxxv).[4] As I argue in this chapter, Jyotirmoyee Devi's account of Sutara's experience with her extended family suggests that it is also impossible to write about women's experience of partition violence without lapsing into the vocabulary of dishonour and shame, and thus she refuses to provide a 'conclusive' account of those events. In other words, by leaving the details of Sutara's supposed sexual assault unverifiable to both Sutara and her relatives, *The River Churning* critiques the patriarchal logic of a 'cultural system that dictates that rape signifies a woman's shame and the dishonor of her male protectors' (Hai 401).

Born on 23 January 1894 in the princely state of Jaipur, Jyotirmoyee Devi was the daughter of Abinash Chandra Sen and Sarla Devi (Gupta and Chatterjee v). While her family were elite Rajastanis – her grandfather served as 'the dewan (prime minister) of the maharaja' who '[i]n appreciation of his services ... made him a jagirdar' (a title that was later passed on to her father) – Jyotirmoyee Devi 'never went to school' (v). As her daughters recall, she 'was taught some rudimentary reading and writing and arithmetic. She was taught Bengali and Hindi by tutors at home. She also spent a lot of time in her grandfather's library, which had a large collection of Bengali classics and stocked the important literary periodicals of the time' (v). When she was ten, she was married to a young lawyer, Kiran Chandra, and went to spend thirteen years with his family in West Bengal before he died of influenza when she was twenty-five and he was thirty-seven (v). During this time in Bengal, she became the mother of six children, learned English, wrote her first story (published in 1912), and became part of the 'Bengali community that kept in touch with the literary events' of the region (v). As her daughters bluntly state, '[w]idowhood at the age of twenty-five changed her life forever' (viii). Jyotirmoyee Devi not only lamented the loss of her husband but also commented, 'it seemed as if I'd been reborn in a world of cast-offs or the shudras' (v–vi). While the rest of her life is described as governed by the 'harsh ascetic routine of the upper cast Hindu widow' (vi), she was, however, spared many of the economic difficulties experienced by other women in her circumstances because of her parents' wealth (vi), and it was at this time her work as a writer flourished.[5] As Mahasweta Devi comments, 'she was fully aware of the moral calculus of patriarchy operating behind the petty rules and regulations which circumscribed her, the duties that had been imposed upon her. At first through reading, and later, through writing, she sought liberation for her mind' (x). During her lifetime (she died in 1988) she published over a hundred short stories and seven novels (A. Mukherjee 943), *The River Churning* appearing in print after she was in her early seventies and already well recognized and established as a writer. In some ways, Jyotirmoyee Devi's critique of the treatment of women like Sutara recalls the link Rajinder Singh Bedi makes between Lajwanti and 'the widow living at house No. 414' (208). As argued by Debali Mookerjea-Leonard, '[e]mbedded within this social context, she [Jyotirmoyee Devi] mastered together a keen critique of the constructed nation of gender, and the systemic oppression of women' (3).

The River Churning tells the story of Sutara, a young Hindu girl who is orphaned by partition violence, taken into the care of her Muslim neighbours, and later shunned by her extended family when she is 'returned' to them in Calcutta. As the narrative unfolds, it becomes apparent that while her 'recovery' to India is legitimated by a (nationalist) view of Hindu women as the symbol of community identity and honour, her rejection by her Hindu extended family is also prefigured by this same logic. Unable to verify her chastity after being separated from her family and losing consciousness, Sutara becomes a permanent refugee in her so-called homeland. The novel depicts how Sutara is forced to endure the scorn of her community by becoming a scapegoat whose stigmatization sustains a patriarchal view of Indian nationalism.

While written in Bengali and set in part in West Bengal, it is not clear that Jyotirmoyee Devi's novel can be read as narrative exploring the unique qualities of the Eastern Indian experience of partition.[6] Bagchi and Dasgupta argue that the experience of partition in Bengal is unique in several respects. First, unlike the situation in the Punjab, the migration from East to West 'has turned out to be a continuing process' ('Problem' 12) leading to a more 'porous and flexible' border with people migrating between East and West for various political and social reasons (13). As Bagchi and Dasgupta explain, the 'along-the-border region [has] a composite character of its own which questions the strictly demarcated preconditions of nationalism and the nation state' (13). Second, the intensity and compressed experience of violence in the Punjab 'was not repeated in the East' (12). 'In contrast,' Bagchi and Dasgupta argue, 'the partition of Bengal has produced a process of slow and agonising terror and trauma accelerated by intermittent outbursts of violence on both sides' over the last fifty seven years (12). Finally, 'the two nation theory which proved to be sacrosanct in Punjab,' has been challenged by the language movement in 1952 and the war of independence leading to the establishment of Bangladesh in 1971 (12). The 'one compelling similarity between the experiences in Punjab and Bengal,' argue Bagchi and Dasgupta, is that women 'were targeted as the prime object of persecution' (13).

Jyotirmoyee Devi's novel emphasizes this shared experience by bringing Sutara together with other women from different regions in India who have been rejected by their families for similar reasons. 'Significantly,' as Mookerjea-Leonard points out, 'it is among the women refugees from West Punjab, residing at Delhi, that Sutara, for the first time, feels the bond of community, of being part of a shared history of violence' (37). If the novel does represent a unique perspective on the partition that links it with the East Bengal experience, I would argue it is through the narrative's persistent return to Sutara's incomplete memory of events in Noakhali in 1946. As Shelley Feldman has suggested, the experience of the 1947 partition in 'East Bengal serves as a metaphor for a place that, like women, is constructed as other, invisible, different, and silenced in the real politics of the time' (169). As in the case of women's partition experiences, 'a perspective from East Bengal(is), or one that includes East Bengal as a particular site, adds to Partition analyses an appreciation of the contradictions posed by the events of 1947 and its aftermath' (168). Thus, rather than offering an account of Sutara's experience that subsumes it into the larger history of India's partition and moves on, *The River Churning*'s representation of the absent-presence of events in Noakhali, East Bengal, suggests a pedagogy for thinking about partition history that 'complicate[s] the search for a grand explanation or narrative of the past' (180).

It is the surprising gap in the details of Sutara's experiences during the riots, as in the testimonies of 'abducted' women collected by scholars like Butalia and Das, that preoccupies my reading of *The River Churning*. As noted by Meenakshi Mukherjee, the novel is exceptional for the way it 'conjure[s] up the claustrophobic ethos of stigma without ever mentioning the word "rape" which lay at the core of the plot' ('Pawn' 16). Similarly, Andrew Whitehead comments, 'the novel is deliberately ambiguous about the extent of the assault on Sutara' ('Crosschannel' 19). It is the significance of this silence – the inassimilable gap it represents in Sutara's experience – and what it suggests about literature and literary reading strategies as a practice of historical memory that will be the focus of my discussion here.

Historical memory is a term that Roger Simon defines as a 'public pedagogy of remembrance, [with] a decidedly socially inflected repetition' ('Paradoxical Practice' 9). Central to Simon's definition and my own discussion of historical memory is a notion of remembrance that is not *simply* a retelling or 'a pedagogy of anamnesis, a practice that seeks the recovery of what has been lost, neglected, or misplaced' ('Testimony' 2). While this kind of strategic act of remembrance 'is aligned with the anticipation of a reconciled future in which one hopes that justice and harmonious social relations might be secured' (Simon et al., *Between Hope* 4), it conceals its own will to power and thus ultimately risks encouraging forgetting with regards to the power relations expressed through its own narrative practice. As Simon and colleagues argue, the main educative imperative of strategic remembrance rests on 'a moralizing pedagogy' that can only respond to the failure to remember how the past continues to haunt the present with 'further directives to tell again, and to tell with increased urgency, thereby invoking an absolutist moral demand that one must listen' (4). Given the interested and precarious construction of moralistic views of the past, it would seem that this approach to remembrance raises more epistemological and practical problems about how to address the injustices of the past than it solves.

The kind of pedagogy that historical memory suggests is that of anagnorisis, 'a learning from "the past" that is a critical recognition or discovery that unsettles the very terms on which our understanding of ourselves and our world is based' (Simon, 'Testimony' 4). In the context of literary studies, historical memory as a practice of anagnorisis considers how texts act as a call to witness by disrupting 'our'[7] understanding about 'the past' and its relationship to the present each time the reader engages in the act of reading as remembrance. As Simon and colleagues suggest, '[i]mplicated in this remembrance is a learning to live with loss, a learning to live with a return of a memory that inevitably instantiates loss and thus bears no ultimate consolation, a learning to live with a disquieting remembrance' (*Between Hope* 4). Here, remembrance is no longer a volunteeristic act but 'an *assignment*, not simply a matter of choice' which 'continues to pose questions of what it means to live in the shadows of mass violence' (4).

What the practicalities of this kind of remembrance involve, therefore, is attention not only to *whose* or *what* history is represented, but, indeed, to *how* it is represented and *for what purpose*. These are issues that have preoccupied scholars in postcolonial studies for some time. Subaltern historiographer Dipesh Chakrabarty helps to highlight this particularly modernist and European epistemological problem when he reflects on how the entire practice of writing history is embedded in the colonial project. As Chakrabarty points out, modernist assumptions that inform the academic discourse of history (i.e., modernity as a denial of all other perspectives of time and space) position Europe as the 'sovereign theoretical subject of all histories, including the ones we call "Indian," "Chinese," "Kenyan" and so on' ('Postcoloniality' 1). The things that are written out of this kind of history, Chakrabarty argues, are the 'ambivalences, contradictions, the use of force, and the tragedies and the ironies that attend' the founding of the nation-state (21). As argued in chapter 2, the view that testimony and realist literary accounts can somehow provide a form of 'direct' access to the past that transcends these ambiguities through their reflective and mimetic representational strategies feeds into a modern perception of reality and what Meaghan Morris has described as '[t]he modern ... as a *known history*, something which has *already happened elsewhere*, and which is to be reproduced, mechanically or otherwise, with a local content' (10). In this context, the strategic desire to 'recover' the experience of 'abducted' women in order to enlarge or correct 'our' understanding of history as a descriptive and seamless record of the past risks turning women who testify into informants who allow 'us' to remember the past in comfortable ways and move on. Given that the stated goal of much work on women's experience of partition is to explore how attention to gender identity can disrupt past and present hegemonic definitions of national identity, a wariness of these kinds of retellings would seem to be in order.

While it is only recently that much has been said about the *gendered* nature of partition violence, it has always been widely acknowledged that violence against women took place. Indeed, as feminist researchers such as Das, Butalia, and Menon have shown, debates in the Indian Constituent Assembly, nationalist history, and the media in general have mobilized many gruesome images of women as objects victimized by the other community. The attack on the nation that these images suggest is evident in the importance the Indian state placed on clarifying the status of female refugees as quickly as possible. For example, even before the actual date of independence, in 1946 the Congress Party adopted a resolution that explicitly linked the restoration of civil order to the recovery of women refugees – commonly assumed to be 'abducted.' The resolution read:

> The immediate problem is to produce a sense of security and rehabilitate homes and villages which have been broken up and destroyed. Women who have been abducted and forcibly married must be restored to their homes. Mass conversions which have taken place forcibly have no significance or validity and the people affected by them should be given every opportunity to return to their homes and the life of their choice. (Das, *Critical Events* 60)

The contradiction between the Assembly's resolution that '*people* should be given every opportunity to return to their homes and the life of their choice' but that *women* '*must* be restored to their homes' is symptomatic of the patriarchal norms that privileged the rights of male citizens at the expense of women at the time of partition. As mentioned in chapter 1, this contradiction was underscored a few years later with the definition of an 'abducted person' in The Abducted Persons (Recovery and Restoration) Bill (1949) as 'a male child under the age of sixteen years or a female of *whatever age*' who would then be subject to the will of a tribunal in determining his or her nationality after 'recovery' (my emphasis) (Menon and Bhasin, 'Abducted Women' 8). Though the activities of the Central Recovery Operation were represented as a humanitarian response to the situation women found themselves in as a result of partition violence, these contradictions suggest that they are really better understood as an expression of the kind of 'violence and idealism' which Chakrabarty has argued 'lies at the heart of the process by which the narratives of citizenship and modernity come to find a natural home in "history"' ('Postcoloniality' 22).

Feminist scholarship on 'abducted' women's treatment during and after partition puts pressure on the seemingly benign humanism that underpins the resolution and Bill to disclose it as an alibi for the community and state's manipulation of women's bodies, sexualities, and identities to serve their mutual patriarchal interests. Urvashi Butalia's analysis of the stories published in the *Organizer* (a forum for the views of the Rashtriya Swayamsevak Sangh [RSS] at the time of partition) supports this point.[8] In the 29 December 1949 issue of the *Organizer*, Hindu women are represented as 'spending sorrowful days and unthinkable nights in Pakistan' at the hands of lustful Muslims ('Muslims and Hindus' 67). Similarly, the *Organizer*'s front-page story on 14 August 1947 carried an illustration 'of Mother India, the map of the country, with a woman lying on it, one limb cut off and severed, with Nehru holding the bloody knife responsible for doing the severing' (69). Indeed, there seems to have been no shortage of commentaries on and reports of women's sexual violation at this time. What was absent, however, was any attention to *why* the women were singled out for this treatment on the basis of gender or what implications this might have for the community and state's construction of belonging, citizenship, or national identity in India and Pakistan today.

These are the questions that researchers like Butalia, Menon, Das, and Pandey have attempted to address in their work on testimonies by 'abducted' women, members of their families and community, and social workers involved in the Recovery Operation. In all cases, however, they have come up against a silence concerning the details about women's experiences during the violence itself. What is remarkable about each of the different attempts to break this silence is that continually the silence seems to resist the access of the researcher. For instance,

Urvashi Butalia has documented that '[i]n the remembrance rituals that take place in gurdwaras [Sikh temples] in different parts of the country, the women's 'heroic' steps in offering themselves up for death are valorised, while their abductions [or stories about women who didn't take their own lives] are glossed over' ('Community' WS24). The dichotomous treatment of these women's stories (as either anonymous victims or celebrated martyrs) might suggest that 'abducted' women's stories should be 'recovered' through testimony in order to correct an unbalanced view of history. However, while some survivors' memoirs and testimonies of partition have been collected, they also rehearse the same silence. In *The Other Side of Silence*, Butalia comments that while conducting interviews for her research, frequently there were moments when

> having begun to remember, to excavate memory, words would suddenly fail speech as memory encountered something too painful, often too frightening to allow it to enter speech. 'How can I describe this,' would come the anguished cry, 'there are no words to do so.' At such points, I chose not to push further, not to force the surfacing of memories into speech. Tellings begun thus would be left incomplete. (24)

While Butalia interprets the difficulty the survivors had in recounting their stories as a result of the painful and frightening nature of the memories, other silences seem to be more ambiguous. For example, Gyanendra Pandey recounts that in interviews with survivors of the sectarian violence that accompanied partition, women especially were vague about the details of the events. In an interview with the members of a Sikh family who were present in the villages of Dhamot and Gharoan in East Punjab during the summer of 1947, when attacks and counter-attacks between Sikhs and Muslims took place, Pandey reports how in questions directed at the mother of the family she 'kept turning the questions over to her elder son (the civil servant) and her brother, even though the latter tried to leave the conversation to her and me' ('Community' 2038). While Pandey describes the elder son's statements as a 'sophisticated, rounded account' of the events that summer, by contrast

> [t]he civil servant's mother speaks all too briefly ... She responds repeatedly with the proposition that she has nothing to tell, that she knows nothing about 'politics,' that her son can answer all these questions and if

he has already spoken to me, then surely there is little left to say. She informs me also that 'nothing happened in our village,' that all attacks (against Muslims) occurred 'outside,' that she herself never left her home and therefore knew nothing of what was going on outside, and that there was no discussion of these things amongst the woman inside the homes. (2038)

Pandey claims that the mother's account is typical of many of the women he has interviewed in that it is different from 'the majority of the men's accounts, both in its reticence and repeated avowal of a lack of knowledge and in its sensitivity to the fate of abducted women and children' (2039). While it could be argued that the testimonies given by survivors of partition violence vary depending on the context in which they are interviewed, attempts made to address these kinds of methodological difficulties have failed to produce any definitive version of one individual's experience of sectarian violence.

Most researchers argue that the reason stories about partition violence against women remain incomplete is that the sociopolitical context in India, over fifty-seven years later, continues to make testimony about partition experiences an extremely compromising act for women refugees. However, while there has been much discussion of how the stigma attached to 'abducted' women's stories has created an obstacle for researchers who desire to compile a 'more complete' history of partition, there has been little consideration given to the theoretical problems raised by the fact that many women who experienced sectarian violence died during or since that time without giving testimony. The irrevocable loss or gap in the archive that these women's deaths represent highlights the similarities between the problems of writing a history of partition and other cultural traumas like the Middle Passage or the Holocaust.

The problem of what kind of history can be told in the absence of an archive, progressive notions of time, and mimetic theories of representation is central to Lyotard's discussion of how the practice of writing history has been challenged by the events at Auschwitz. In *The Differend* Lyotard raises the problem of verifying the existence of gas chambers used to kill Jews and other 'undesirable' members of society when to see and 'know' the purpose of the gas chambers would mean to have been a victim of its function. He teases out the problem as follows: Within modernist conceptions of rationality, for the victim '[t]o have "really seen with his own eyes" a gas chamber would be the condition which gives one the authority to say that it exists and to persuade the unbeliever' (3). 'Yet,' Lyotard continues, 'it is still necessary to prove that the gas chamber was used to kill at the time it was seen. The only acceptable proof that it was used to kill is that one died from it. But if one is dead, one cannot testify that it is on account of the gas chamber' (3). '[W]ith Auschwitz,' Lyotard concludes, 'something new has happened in history' where what would be considered conventional historical evidence 'has been destroyed as much as possible' (57). In the face of this loss of an archive and the stakes involved in the practice of remembrance in relation to an event like the Holocaust, Lyotard insists that 'the historian must break with the monopoly over history granted to the cognitive regime of phrases, and he or she must venture forth by lending his or her ear to what is not presentable under the rules of knowledge' (57).[9]

India's partition seems to represent a loss of an archive in these terms: a loss that is permanent, 'always already' incomplete and which requires a new way of listening to the Other if it is not to go unnoticed by the researcher. Learning to hear 'what is not presentable under the rules of knowledge' as it concerns 'the informant in history' is something that Gayatri Spivak characterizes as 'a responsibility toward the trace of the other' that is 'as much a recovery as it is a loss of the wholly other' (*Critique* 198). This is something of the 'double bind' that Spivak argues informs the 'excavation, retrieval and celebration of the historical individual, the effort of bringing her within accessibility' (198). Spivak's deconstructive approach to reading history underscores how the transparency attributed to testimony, historical narrative, and realist fiction produces another act of containment and appropriation. Thus, even when 'abducted' women are interviewed and represented as 'speaking for themselves,' it is impossible to escape the process of exclusion, forgetting, translation, and interpretation that informs their statements.

The way language mediates any attempt to represent experience is often overlooked in discussions of partition narratives that are purported to represent 'abducted' women's experiences. For instance, in 'Telling Tales: Women and the Trauma of Partition in Sidhwa's *Cracking India*,' Deepika Bahri suggests that the gaps in testimonies by 'abducted' women might be filled by literary accounts of their experience. Citing the stigma attached to 'abducted' women's experiences, Bahri raises doubts about the possibility of 'retrieving' this history through testimony when '[b]y all accounts, what remains of women's experiences of personal violation is either a contract of silence or a reference so oblique as to be little more that metaphoric abstraction' (218). Bahri characterizes the metaphoricity or indirectness of these accounts as placing a veil between the 'reality' of these women's experiences and the historian and argues that: 'In the absence of *direct* testimony, fictionalized and second-hand accounts have attempted to capture the elusive experiences of women during this turbulent time' (my emphasis; 218). The perception that there are historical events outside of discourse that, given the right conditions, could be revealed or captured through 'direct' testimony runs throughout Bahri's discussion. In fact, like the final chapter in Bapsi Sidhwa's novel *Cracking India* (1991), her paper is prefaced with a quote from Mohammed Iqbal's poetry, where the speaker calls for 'the (mystic) wine that burns all veils, / the wine by which life's secret is revealed, / the wine whose essence is eternity. / The wine which opens mysteries concealed. / Lift up the curtain, give me power to talk' (217). Bahri concludes: 'It may well be the task of literary historiography to unveil, uncover, liberate from silence and oblivion' these women's stories (228). Similarly, Jashodhara Bagchi reads *The River Churning* as 'intended to lift the veil on a *stree parva* in history – the bloodstained chequered history of "secular" modern India' (xxix). I cannot help but find the call for literary historiographers to 'lift the veil' on this history troubling in light of postcolonial scholarship like Meyda Yegonoglu's that investigates how '[t]he veil is one of those tropes through which Western fantasies of penetration into the mysteries of the Orient and access to the interiority of the other are fantasmatically achieved' (39). If literature representing women's experience of India's partition is read as dispelling the mystery surrounding the details of their personal violation, are literary historiographers not engaging in a similar kind of fantasy?

While some researchers suggest that the gaps in 'abducted' women's testimonies might be filled by imagined accounts of their experience, other work on historical memory provocatively concentrates on its original incompleteness, or what Spivak has called 'loss as loss' in the first instance (*Critique* 217n33). In her return to 'Can the Subaltern Speak?' in *A Critique of Postcolonial Reason*, Spivak argues that chronological and continuous accounts of history need to acknowledge the 'silences between bits of language ... a silence filled with nothing but noise' that disrupts the continuity of historical narratives in any context (239). Rather than papering over the cracks in historical memory – a practice Spivak sees as common in historical writing – the literary historiographer should attend to how literary representations of history emphasize the gaps between and within different perceptions of 'reality' and thus offer a uniquely disruptive view of hegemonic histories. In other words, if the literary historiographer acknowledges that the 'reality' of 'abducted' women's experience is never definitively knowable she must then turn her attention to the gaps in attempts to represent that experience (imaginary or otherwise) in order to understand the power relations that inform its construction.

Initially, Bahri's essay seems to acknowledge this understanding of traumatic experience, citing Cathy Caruth among others to support her argument that literature can serve as a form of testimony about the past. Unlike Caruth and others, however, Bahri's notion of the status of traumatic testimony does not address its fragmented, indirect, and incomplete status. Instead, she argues that Lenny is able to tell a story that transcends the gaps in the historical record and thus Lenny's story allows readers and writers of partition narratives to empathize with the experiences of 'abducted' women like Ayah. Bahri writes,

> Lenny is established by Sidhwa as a sympathetic conduit, giving shape and speech to the suffering that could all too easily lapse into prelinguistic stupor even if it were given permission to express itself. She 'reads' with a concentrated gaze the script in the void where a tangible record of the events and the suffering should have been. Some portion of the horror that Ayah has known passes through Lenny in reaching the reader. (225)

If, as Caruth argues, 'the traumatized person ... carries an impossible history within them, or they become themselves the symptom of a history they cannot entirely possess' (Caruth 'Introduction,' 4), how can the writer, narrator, or reader 'know' the experiences of those who have only a partial knowledge of these experiences in the first place? The assertion that the narrator can somehow 'know' and convey the experiences of those who have been traumatized obscures the partiality of memory and the power exercised by those who claim to represent it without any mediation. In fact, Bahri goes as far as to suggest that Lenny is a mere 'amanuensis,' one who copies or records what is put before her, 'a 'neutral' medium that can carry and convey the suffering that would silence its worst victims' (224). However, the idea that Lenny could occupy a 'neutral' position in the narration of the events of the novel not only serves to reinforce specious claims made by Sidhwa (Kanaganayakam 45) that the Parsi community occupied a neutral position in colonial India (something I argue against in chapter 3), but it also overlooks the novel's own preoccupation with the constructedness of perspective.[10]

This of course raises the following question: Should the goal of the writer, reader, or literary historiographer be to attempt to identify or empathize with (and by implication 'understand') the experience of the Other or, on the contrary, recognize the gap within and between the Other's experience and her own? Simon suggests other ways of approaching the practice of witnessing as a reader of archives, literature, or testimony in ways that account for the unavoidable gaps within and between the Other's experience and one's own and the constructedness of perspective. 'To be present to testimony,' he argues,

> is to be claimed to another in ways that are not reducible to blood ties, geographically local or diasporic identities, or humanistic assertions of empathy. This is because in a witnessing relation, one must always be open to the possibility of unforeseen memory, the possibility of unfamiliar or uncanny connections; connections which disrupt attempts to know what meaning a place or moment may hold. ('Testimony' 4)

For Simon, it is the disruptive, jarring, unfamiliar, and thus unsettling remembrances which reopen 'the certitude of our frames of reference for understanding' the past and its relationship to the present, acting as the 'points of connection' in the witnessing relation (4). While Bahri argues that the narrator of *Cracking India* 'has made us feel Ayah's pain in our bodies, in our veins; she has placed upon the reader the weight of a forbidden story that was never meant to be told' (228), Simon's formulation suggests that the most productive practices of remembrance do not rely on identification with the text but instead emphasize the metaphoricity or indirectness of 'telling' and acknowledge the impossibility of knowing the other's experience. Indeed, while the 'abducted' women have had very little to say about their own experience, there have been no shortage of attempts by the nation-state to write their stories for them.

Cathy Caruth makes a similar point in *Unclaimed Experience*, where she offers a reading of the opening sequence in Alain Resnais's film *Hiroshima Mon Amour*. As she describes, the film opens with a voice-over depicting a conflict between two lovers, a Japanese man and a French woman who has returned from the museum in Hiroshima having seen archival footage of the aftermath of the explosion of the nuclear bomb. After viewing the films, the woman claims to have seen '*everything. Everything*' in Hiroshima (28). This is countered by the man's assertion: 'You saw nothing in Hiroshima. Nothing' (28). Caruth contends, 'the man's denial suggests that the act of seeing, in the very establishing of a bodily referent, erases like an empty grammar, the reality of an event' (28–9). The arrogance (and perhaps obscenity) of the woman's claim to be able to see or understand 'everything' about the nuclear holocaust in Hiroshima by viewing 'direct' archival footage is figured as a betrayal of history in the film. In turn, Caruth suggests, 'it is through the fictional story, not *about* Hiroshima but taking place at its site, that Resnais and Duras [the director and screenwriter] believe such historical specificity is conveyed' (27). It is the 'indirectness of this telling,' Caruth maintains, that creates the possibility of a 'faithful history' (27).

While in the absence of testimony, some scholars see literature as the next best hope for restoring something that has been lost from the historical record, I argue that the silences in 'abducted' women's testimonies are a sign of the original incompleteness of history or an example of 'loss as loss' in the first instance. As Teresa Heffernan has shown with regards to postmodern history, 'it is impossible to translate loss into Symbolic language without acknowledging an even greater loss. In other words, loss is not just an elusive "Thing" but a condition of history, involving an occurrence, which cannot, in any (effective) way be "consciously" named' (2–3). The effort to name or 'recover' the history of 'abducted' women in a definitive way involves a 'suppress[ion] of difference as well as differance' (Spivak, *Critique* 199) and can serve as a permission or freedom to forget. If the role of the (literary) historian after Auschwitz (and perhaps India's partition) is to 'break with the cognitive regime of phrases' and 'venture forth by lending his or her ear to what is not presentable under the rules of knowledge' (Lyotard 57), any attempt to 'capture the elusive experiences of women during this turbulent time' (Bahri 218) in 'neutral' terms would seem to merely reinscribe rather than disrupt present exclusionary conceptions of the nation. 'Within this form of commemoration (the "factual liturgy"),' as Mario Di Paolantonio argues, 'the other has become an object of/for knowledge. This violates the ethical grounds' upon which 'knowledge reveals the desire in the formation of a redeemed national identity: an opportunity for self-confirmation, a history lesson on "who *we* really are"' (164–5). Scholars who claim that it is possible to complete the historical record with literary representations of 'abducted' women's experience risk becoming unwittingly complicit in this kind of exercise of 'self-confirmation.'

The acknowledgment that all 'telling' relies on indirect language and involves gaps and silences as a 'condition of history' points to the importance of literary reading strategies and literary texts as a potential resource for historians and scholars interested in making sense of testimonies by women who lived through the events of partition. Literature, as a form of writing that highlights the figurative and indirect properties of language, is a particularly appropriate place to consider how experience is mediated and the specific limits of what can be known about that experience. Veena Das makes a similar point in her discussion of how 'the language of pain' that informs representations of 'abducted' women's experience of collective violence relies on a particular poetics. This poetics emerges, Das argues, with the inversion of the common relationship between language and mourning as a result of 'the investment of sexuality into the project of nationalism' ('Language' 71) that placed a burden on women to remain silent or speak indirectly about their experiences after they were 'recovered.' 'Rather than bearing witness to the disorder that they had been subjected to,' Das states, 'the metaphor that they [the women] used was a woman drinking the poison and keeping it within her' (85). In the course of Das's interviews, 'a woman would say that she is like a discarded exercise book in which the accounts of past relationships were kept – the body, a parchment of losses. At any rate, none of the metaphors used to describe the self that had become the repository of poisonous knowledge emphasized the need to give expression to this hidden knowledge' (84). Das's discussion emphasizes the metaphoricity of women's statements about the violence they experienced and explains how the patriarchal practice of using their bodies as surfaces for nationalist inscriptions is subverted by this representational strategy: 'The bodies of the women were surfaces on which texts were to be written and read – icons of the new nations. But women converted this passivity into agency by using *metaphors* of pregnancy – hiding pain, giving it a home just as a child is given a home in the woman's body' (my emphasis; 85). Here and elsewhere, Das's discussion of women's testimonies emphasizes how the women are empowered by their use of indirect or figurative language when they speak about their experiences of collective violence. Das reports:

> When asking women to narrate their experiences of the Partition I found a zone of silence around the event. This silence was achieved either by the use of language that was general and metaphoric but that evaded specific description of any events so as to capture the particularity of their experi-

ence, or by describing the surrounding events but leaving the actual experience of abduction and rape unstated. (84)

As I have argued above, the attempt to account for the significance of women's resort to figurative and metaphoric expressions of their experience – or what can also be called indirect telling (89) – is key to disrupting modernist conceptions of this history. Perhaps, as Das suggests, '[s]ome realities need to be fictionalized before they can be apprehended' (69).

Just exactly how this indirect approach to representing women's experience of the sectarian violence can lead to other ways of knowing the history of partition is the focus of my discussion of Jyotirmoyee Devi's *The River Churning*. The gaps or silences in women's testimonies and literary narratives like Jyotirmoyee Devi's resonate with Lyotard's description of 'the differend.' In Lyotard's words,

> The differend is the unstable state and instant of language wherein something which must be able to be put into phrases cannot yet be. This state includes silence, which is a negative phrase, but it also calls upon phrases which are in principle possible. This state is signaled by what one ordinarily calls a feeling: 'One cannot find the words,' etc. A lot of searching must be done to find new rules for forming and linking phrases that are able to express the differend disclosed by the feeling, unless one wants this differend to be smothered right away. (13)

Lyotard's definition of the differend conceptualizes the 'feeling' that 'one cannot find the words' as a condition of the discourse that orders 'reality' and refuses questions or statements that challenge its ontological basis. A recognition of these 'feelings' places an obligation on the role of the reader in the witnessing relation to conceptualize new ways of knowing that avoid splicing the story of the Other and smoothing out the awkward questions it raises about 'reality' within the logic of modernity. My reading of Jyotirmoyee Devi's novel foregrounds these 'feelings' or moments of disruption within its narrative strategies, displaces the urge to recover 'abducted' or 'polluted' women's stories, and allows new forms of knowing to emerge. The novel encourages this reading in that it appears to strive to 'make its inadequacy present' (Simon, 'Testimony' 4). It provides a fragmented view of one 'abducted/polluted' woman's experience after 'recovery' through a realist narrative that is constantly interrupted by the gap in Sutara's experience during the sectarian violence. In Jyotirmoyee Devi's text the details of abducted women's experiences during the partition violence are impressionistic and fragmented, thus undermining the reflective quality of the realist genre she adopts for the rest of her narrative. At the same time, however, the reader comes away with 'an assignment' (in Simon's terms) to pursue a better understanding of the patriarchal, elite, and Hindu-centric interests that have been normalized as secular, universal, and national in India today. In other words, this double movement between the details and the limits of their construction in Jyotirmoyee Devi's narrative permits '*history* to arise where *immediate understanding* may not' (Caruth *Unclaimed*, 11) and thus suggests an ethics for witnessing or reading that focuses on the opacity rather than transparency of language as well as the partiality of all knowledge.

The partiality of 'abducted' women's experience and historical narratives in general is both a performative and thematic concern of Jyotirmoyee Devi's text. The novel opens as Sutara, a college history teacher in Delhi, reflects on the absence of anything like a *Stree Parva* (women's chapter) in history writing and contemplates the implications of an 'official circular that had come to this partly government controlled college giving clear directions regarding the history syllabus, specifying the books and authors to be taught' (1). Later she recalls the questions her students have asked her that day concerning the 'truth and falsehood as presented in history books' (4). As she ponders these questions, her memories of partition violence that occurred in Noakhali, the small village where she grew up, begin to return. Sutara recalls the community's diverse character in which both Hindus and Muslims, rich and poor, lived together in relative peace. With the approach of partition, however, her family learns of riots in Calcutta through a letter from their relatives, and that same evening, violence breaks out in their own community. That night, after Sutara's father returns from investigating a fire at a neighbour's house, he orders her mother to take their daughters into the corner room of the house and bolt the door from the inside. He warns them, 'Don't come out of the house even if someone calls or bangs on the door' (7). Sutara's memories of this incident are characterized by confusion over her parents' fear and why they are asked to barricade themselves in the house.

Eventually, when the fire reaches Sutara's house, the narrative recounts that her mother emerges to set the livestock free but is intercepted by the family's Muslim servants and 'a few other unknown faces' (8). In the confusion of the attack Sutara recalls,

> The cows were mooing desperately, so Mother rushed to the cowshed.
> Sutara started after her when suddenly she heard her sister scream and fall to the ground. From near the shed where Mother was wrenching the flap door open she heard a shrill cry. 'I'm coming,' she called.
> But she could not make it. Dark shadowy figures surrounded her, some tried to grab her by the hand. Breaking free she rushed to the pond at the back and jumped into the water.
> In the light of the spreading fire everything was now visible. One of the ruffians went after Mother ... But Didi [Sutara's sister] did not stir. Was she dead?
> What happened to Didi? Sutara couldn't tell. She wanted to reach mother and began to run, but stumbled and fell. Then everything went blank. (8)

The narrative of the attack breaks off here and is never 'completed' in the course of the novel. The 'blankness' that Sutara associates with these events, along with an anxiety, a loss of a sense of time, and questions about whether her family members are dead or alive, is rehearsed throughout the novel. In addition, though the narrative states, 'in the light of the spreading fire *everything was now visible*' (my emphasis), Sutara is unable to 'know' if her sister is alive or dead, thus displacing the connection between sight and knowledge.

The disjunction between sight and knowledge is reiterated throughout *The River Churning*. After Sutara regains consciousness and is staying in the care of Tamij's family (her Muslim neighbours), the narrator comments, 'Days went by, Sutara lost count' and again, 'Sutara lost count of days and nights' (10–11). Sutara's disorientation is figured as accompanied by anxiety from an indefinable source and a 'loss' of memory that disturbs her:

> She had not recovered from the tremendous shock she had received. It had shaken her to the core. The exact nature of the blow which had stunned her physically and mentally was unknown to her – she was only aware of something terrible having crushed her existence out of shape.
> She could not clearly remember what had happened, but the dreadful memories of that night kept returning like a nightmare. Did she fall to the ground or was she pushed down? What happened after that? Who rescued her and when? For how long had she been running a fever? (16)

When Sutara is first able to walk about, she wanders outside and sees the ruins of her family's property in the distance and is haunted by 'invisible scenes in her mind which she could not get rid of' (19). Jyotirmoyee Devi's paradoxical representation of Sutara's experience – of being haunted by memories that she cannot remember – figures the events of partition in a traumatic, elliptical mode and raises questions about the possibility of 'capturing' her experience in modernist accounts of the birth of the Indian nation-state.

The disruption Sutara's 'return' causes in her family (which comprises the larger part of Jyotirmoyee Devi's narrative) attests to the unsettling effect Sutara's subject position has for patriarchal history in the post-partition sociopolitical context. The patriarchal discourse of contamination that legitimates Sutara's treatment by her extended family is simultaneously displaced and made visible by her refusal to confirm the source of their anxiety regarding her return. From the first letter Sanat (Sutara's brother) sends after learning about his parents' deaths during the sectarian violence, there is a sense that 'something is amiss'; the narrative states: 'Sanat lamented the death of his parents, briefly mentioned his sister. If she wanted to return, they had to think of how to bring her over. But the letter displayed no particular anxiety toward her' (16). Even though the nation-state in Jyotirmoyee Devi's novel has a stake in recovering Sutara, the dominant Hindu community is depicted as plainly at odds with how to (re)integrate her into the domestic sphere. The tensions in this scenario resonate with those generated between the community and state in actual cases of 'recovery.' Urvashi Butalia summarizes the conflict between the two constituencies at the time of partition (and after) as follows:

> For the community it was the woman's sexual purity that became important, as also her community and/or religious identity. For the state, because the women the state was rescuing were already in a state of sexual 'impurity' having often lived with their captors, this problem had to be pushed aside, and their religious identity made paramount. ('Community' WS18)

Measures were put in place to try to facilitate the 'repurification' of these women, such as the separation of women from 'illegitimate children,' the invalidation of any 'forced' intermarriages and conversions, and the provision of abortions (illegal at the time), euphemistically known as 'medical treatments' (WS18–19). Aware of the community's resistance to reintegrating women the government had 'recovered,' 'the ministry of relief and rehabilitation is said to have issued a pamphlet which quoted Manu [the creator of the *Manavadharmasatra*] to establish that a woman who had sexual involvement with someone other than her husband became purified after three menstrual cycles, and hence her family could accept her back' (WS18).[11] Where possible, the idea was to erase any material or discursive evidence that reminded the community of the women's experience with the Other. Failing that, it was essential to portray their involvement with the Other as passive. Each of these measures was designed to facilitate what Das calls a 'social forgetting' of 'abducted' women's experiences ('Composition' 70). In the case of one woman Das interviewed, it became apparent that the entire community avoided discussing her experience with the Other. As Das points out, 'by refusing to elicit speech on her experience in the village where she was ambushed, and allowing her to socially "forget" her experiences, the society allowed her to be treated as a woman whose life could unfold itself in accordance with a traditional telos' (70).[12] While this practice allowed the woman to avoid Sutara's fate, it came at the price of her silence, denial of her experience, and acquiescence to a 'traditional telos' (i.e., patriarchal expectations) for her behaviour.

The importance of (re)constructing an aura of purity around 'recovered' women is exemplified in repeated appeals by Gandhi and Nehru.[13] In these statements, they encouraged extended families to reclaim their 'recovered' female relatives and spoke about 'polluted' and 'abducted' women as their own daughters. 'Repurification,' like 'recovery,' was held up as a national goal which 'abductees' (women) and 'abductors' (men) could achieve by the former submitting to the Recovery Operation's infrastructure and the latter admitting their guilt. In the 8 March 1947 edition of the *Times of India* it is reported that Gandhi made a 'post-prayer speech' that spoke to this issue. The article states:

> It had been conveyed to him, he added, that there were Muslim women even now kept perforce in Hindu homes. If that were true, and if of course such women were still living, he would expect every one of them to be restored to their homes.
>
> [Gandhi stated:] It was not enough that Hindus should express lip repentance or compensate the sufferers by means of money. What was really needed was that their hearts should become pure. ('Leaguers')

The possibility of Muslim women being held 'against their will' in the homes of Hindus threatened to soil the purity of the Indian nation-state by bringing their 'abductor's' honour under scrutiny. Unlike 'abducted' women, however, 'abductors' (men) had access to complete re-purification by releasing their 'captives.' Veena Das argues that 'despite the rhetoric on barbarism of men who abduct women, this "lapse" by men is seen as temporary' and that by returning abducted Muslim women, Hindu and Sikh men could regain their lost purity (*Critical* 70). Despite the government's efforts, many women were permanently stigmatized.

This is certainly the experience of Sutara in *The River Churning*. There are no external signs of Sutara's pollution; nevertheless, the letters from Sutara's extended family indicate that her reception in India will not be pleasant. Eventually, when Tamij and his son Aziz bring her to Calcutta, the extent of her rejection becomes clear. As she greets her brother's mother-in-law, she is warned not to touch her ('No, no, don't touch me now. You have not changed your clothes' [31]). The narrative states:

> She could overhear Boudi's mother's sharp tones, 'Are you out of your mind? Her clothes have been polluted by the touch of a Muslim household. Why did you have to go and take her in your arms?' ...
> 'Don't we have a deity in the house? And Brahmin widows come here also. How can you have her pollute everything?' (31–2)

When Sutara's nieces offer to take her to her room, Boudi's mother intervenes and instructs the servant, 'See that she does not sit on the bed. She must be purified with Ganga water first. God knows what kind of forbidden food she has eaten there' (33). Because Sutara has lived with a Muslim family after the sectarian violence and the loss of her family, her 'pollution' is assumed without discussion. Later in the novel, it emerges that Sutara is also considered sexually contaminated; discussions of marriage are cut short by Subha's mother's euphemistic references to 'other problems' (71) that would diminish her prospects for a good match. Even though there is no conclusive evidence that Sutara was sexually assaulted (she is found unconscious and described as 'feverish' and 'aching all over' in the days following the incident [9–10]), it appears the patriarchal fantasies are powerful enough to assume this is the case unless proven otherwise. Later in the narrative, when Sutara returns to Pakistan to visit Tamij's family, Aziz (Tamij's son) recalls his own memories of the night her family home was attacked. He recounts how he, his father, and brothers arrived *after* the attack when 'there was not a soul in sight ... Baba was looking for Sutara and the rest. Suddenly he saw a bundle of clothes under the porch. He went near and found it was Sutara lying in a pool of blood' (100). While Aziz's mother would like Sutara to come and live with their family in Pakistan and marry one of her sons, Sutara, Aziz, and his brother all reject this idea, citing both the events of that evening and 'Hindu-Muslim antagonisms' (102) as insurmountable barriers between them. Similarly, when Promode informs his mother of his desire to marry Sutara her main objection is, 'Nobody knows what actually went on there' (124). Indeed, Jasodhara Bagchi suggests that Sutara's sexuality 'is the great "unspoken" in the novel, yet it remains the stake in the sinister game in which the community teams up with nationhood, in order to keep alive the caste-class *entente* of the hegemonic group in independent India' ('Introduction' xxvii). 'It is best,' Mookerjea-Leonard argues

> not to read/dismisss Jyotirmoyee Devi's syncopated, circumlocutive writing as reticence or, as residual prudery of a post-Victorian novelist, because the use of the Bengali equivalent for 'rape' is not rare in her writings, especially in her essays. Rather, the veiling of the bodily trauma through language constitutes a counter-discourse to the economy of display of woman (41).[14]

What the narrative does make abundantly clear, however, is how, repeatedly, the gaps in Sutara's story are written for her and at her expense. Community and state conflicts over what to do about/with Sutara are resolved by casting her as a passive victim who was polluted by a lustful Muslim Other, thus sealing her fate as an outcast.[15] Sutara's 'failure' to recall her experience with the Other, her 'recovery' by the state but rejection by the community are represented by Jyotirmoyee Devi's text as a loss that disrupts the perception of the present.

Sutara's experience suggests that enforcing these patriarchal codes was often the role of women in the community who sought to maintain their own patriarchal patronage by distancing their identities from those considered polluted. Jyotirmoyee Devi's narrative singles out the women in Sutara's family – especially the older generation – as the instigators of Sutara's alienation from the family. For instance, it is the 'lady of the house' (35) who constantly reminds everyone of Sutara's pollution and ensures that she is kept away from the food, kitchen, and family gatherings. Similarly, the older women in the family express repeated concern over the consequences that the stigma attached to Sutara's honour will have for the marriage of their daughters. They are the ones who consistently uphold the rituals of purity that marginalize her connection to the family.

These incidents gesture toward the opposition between the treatment of protected and (therefore 'pure') women and 'abducted' (hence 'polluted') women. Often, women who were shielded from the violent events of partition feared being tainted by the stigma attached to 'abducted' women. While the younger women in the family are uncomfortable with Sutara's treatment, they eventually acquiesce to their elders' views. Although Subha invites Sutara to attend her wedding, she and her sister Probha comply with the humiliating treatment she receives from Subha's mother and her peers. For example, when Subha's mother insists that Sutara eat separately and leave the wedding as quickly as possible, the narrative states, 'The two sisters heard the order without comment' (63). Later, when Amulya Babu inquires why Sutara is eating alone, the narrative reports, 'Bibha and Boudi [Sutara's cousins] had no answer but the seniors came to their rescue' (63). The disruption and embarrassment precipitated by Sutara's presence at Subha's wedding is so significant that she never attends another family wedding. Clearly, the women play a significant role in maintaining the rituals of purity that exclude 'abducted/polluted' women like Sutara and help to preserve the moral order that creates their difficulties. 'Thus,' as Butalia concludes in her discussion of women's agency during partition, 'our understanding of agency too needs to take into account notions of the moral order which is sought to be preserved when women act, as well as the mediation of the family, community, class and religion' ('Community' WS24). Though patriarchal structures cast women as the bearers of 'tradition,' 'honour,' and 'purity,' women themselves contributed to the perpetuation of this practice in order to maintain their patriarchal patronage at the expense of the women concerned.

Ironically, the characterization of this internalized disciplinary behaviour as 'common-sense' allows the 'master of the house' (33), Basu, to appear to be a benevolent soul who only reluctantly complies with the women's treatment of Sutara. When his sister explains, 'it would be better if Sutara kept herself at a distance from the kitchen and the store' and reminds him, 'we Hindus have some code of daily rituals. It does not allow such girls to be accepted back' (42), he even attempts to put up some resistance; he cites instances when the family has eaten food at the local Muslim restaurant. His wife, however, maintains:

'Well, men will do such things. You break conventions in the home and also outside' (42). Similarly, at Subha's wedding, the narrative figures Babu as 'irritated and silent' (63) when he sees how Sutara is treated, but adds 'he did not pursue the matter' (64). Buffered by the women's enforcement of the patriarchal codes that underpin Sutara's treatment, Amulya Babu can afford random acts of kindness. Whenever the women's opposition hints at how the maintenance of these codes preserve his own privilege, however, he defers to their judgment and reconciles himself with the thought, 'One could not possibly shoulder everyone's responsibilities' (49).

This treatment makes it clear that Sutara's contact with the Muslim community outside the bounds of her family's domestic sphere threatens the status quo in her community. Her survival in the absence of community protection threatens to make visible the gendered structure of the social contract and thus challenge the legitimacy of the community and state's claims to represent a homogeneous constituency. The temporary solution to coping with this threat in Sutara's extended family is to send her to boarding school:

> Sanat heaved a sigh of relief, though he made no comment. Subodh and Sudhir, too, kept quiet.
>
> 'I think this is the best thing for the time being,' said Bimal at last. 'Let her pass out of school, then we'll see what can be done.'
>
> About what could be done, none of them was quite sure. But the crisis was stalled for the time being. Spend some money. Send her to boarding school. (49)

Clearly, the boarding school is used by Bibha's family as a 'surface of absorption' (Donzelot 25; Das, *Critical* 57) for their unwanted niece. It allows them to conform to the restrictive codes of conduct expected of the citizen-subject in the preservation of the 'spiritual sphere's' purity. This becomes most evident during the holidays, when Sutara and many of the other girls at the school do not return home for a visit: 'The boarding house had to be kept open for some orphaned girls who were exiles, fugitives, with no place to go to' (56). It is not that the girls do not have living relatives or friends, just that they are unwelcome in their homes. Further, the narrative indicates that '[f]rank discussions' among the girls concerning their background 'were forbidden in the school' (57). The school is thus placed in a tactical alliance with the community and state. Because of this taboo, it is only when Sutara works as a teacher at Yajnaseni College (a reference to Draupadi in the *Mahabharata*) (Mookerjea-Leonard 27) that she learns other women share the experience of losing their family and being ostracized. At this point, Sutara begins to identify patterns in and links between her treatment and others and is 'amazed to learn that Muslim women had had to face the same trauma' (86). Here, Jyotirmoyee Devi's focus on the treatment of 'abducted' and 'polluted' women precludes the idealization of any nation and instead shifts the reader's attention to the intersections and contradictions among patriarchal, community, and state concerns.

Sutara's exclusion from the pool of marriageable women in the nation, because of her 'polluted' status, leaves her in a state of alienation from the nation-state and her community. This exclusion is discussed by members of the community as a necessary evil to maintain a homogeneous and stable representation of the nation-state. For instance, during a discussion among Promode and his friends about what do to with the 'problem' of 'abducted' women, his friend, Ajay, comments, 'Will you stop this, please? Let them die first, let them be 'wiped out.' We have got our government, that is the main thing' (118). It could be argued that in the Indian context today, Ajay's desire to wipe out the history of 'abducted' women in order to protect the patriarchal community/state alliance is fulfilled.

Sutara's struggle to be 'independent,' therefore, is in direct conflict with the patriarchal and Hindu-centric codes that have produced her dilemma in the first place. The narrative's account of how she gets a teaching job at the college and settles into new lodgings emphasizes the contradictions she experiences:

> Although Sutara found a place to stay, it was neither a home nor a household and least of all a nest created by a woman's love and care. But it was a room, a room of her own, and hers through her hard-earned money. Did that make it a home? She knew, only too well, the bitter truth that she would never have a home. But at least her brothers would no longer have to finance her. She would be a burden no more. Did that mean she was now independent? Do women ever become independent? Does anyone worry about her?' (69)

The allusion to Virginia Woolf's *A Room of One's Own* highlights the irony of Sutara's newfound 'independence.' Though Sutara accomplishes a level of self-reliance that would make a man in her position highly marriageable, she finds herself increasingly isolated from social events, and marriage is not even considered a possibility. In this context, the liberal notion of 'independence' emerges as inappropriate in relation to the feminine subject.

Despite attempts by the state to promote the reintegration of 'abducted' women back into the gendered space of the domestic sphere, in many instances the community's perceptions of these (Hindu) women's 'contamination' left them ostracized from society as a whole and relegated them to a life of silence as permanent refugees. Sutara's attempt to get her friend Kaushalyavati (another boarder at the school) to empathize with her frustration over her rejection by her extended family also falls flat. Sutara tries to compare her situation as a Hindu in Pakistan after partition to India's foreign diplomats, 'visiting other countries, eating with all sorts of people' (78). Kaushalyavati responds, 'Bibiji, how can you compare such people, ministers and ambassadors, with us! They are rich and powerful' (79). Kaushalyavati's comments underline how class and gender privilege allow some Hindus to transgress cultural norms that are maintained at the expense of those less 'rich and powerful.' The exclusivity of the so-called universal and secular Indian identity is driven home for Sutara when Promode and Sudhir (her brothers-in-law) come to pay her a rare visit at her college. The narrative records how Sutara 'was beside herself with joy. After all, the ties of language, of kinship, of region, are deep and strong. She had tried to disown them thinking they were superfluous, that she was that all encompassing person, an Indian' (79). Far from allowing her to assume the profile of the 'all encompassing person, an Indian,' Sutara's banishment prevents her from identifying with any sense of community or nationality. Indian citizenship has become an empty promise for Sutara; as an outcast, she cannot share the sense of belonging women's citizenship derives from its naturalized referent in the domestic sphere of the Hindu extended family and community. Ultimately, the identity of the 'all encompassing person, an Indian' and the secular, liberal, and pluralist assumptions it implies are exposed as elite patriarchal rhetoric used to prop up the production of Sutara's alienation in the first place.

To a reader familiar with the *Ramayana*, Jyotirmoyee Devi's novel is easily recognizable as a retelling of the story of Rama's doubts concerning Sita's fidelity after her rescue from Ravana.[16] Jyotirmoyee Devi's novel makes a direct allusion to this aspect of the epic when Promode, Sutara's cousin, discusses his frustration over the treatment of women refugees with his friends. The differences between Sutara's situation and Sita's, however, are underscored by Promode and the events of

Jyotirmoyee Devi's narrative. Where in Valmiki's well-known version of the story Sita offers to walk through fire to prove her faithfulness to Rama, in *The River Churning*, Sutara is unable to undergo a similar test of her purity. Her inability to remember the events of the attack on her family and herself absolutely precludes the possibility of deflecting the aspersions concerning her 'honour' in this context.[17] Similarly, as Promode points out, while Sita eventually asks Mother Earth to swallow her up in the ground, thus ending her exile, women like Sutara who survived the partition violence remain in exile until their deaths. Promode emphasizes the never-ending ostracism these women experience when he describes the women refugees as eking out 'a most precarious existence on the margins of society' (118). Thus, while Jyotirmoyee Devi's text resonates with this larger cultural narrative, it also subverts it by refusing to offer any conclusive 'evidence' of Sutara's pollution *or* purity and rejects the idea of death and reincarnation as the ultimate solution to the women's bad experiences in this life. 'Thus,' as Mookerjea-Leonard suggests, 'Jyotirmoyee Devi situates Sutara within the 'woman-as-nation' paradigm, but in her writings the fallen woman is the symbolic representation of the nation' (39).

Though Promode's proposal to marry Sutara (which comes at the end of the novel) seems to bring her back into the domestic sphere of the nation, the narrative resists this sense of closure. Sutara's proposed marriage to Promode comes at a time when he is planning to leave the country. Thus, while Promode's proposal returns Sutara from exile in her own so-called homeland, it is only a partial return. Promode appears to propose the marriage out of a combined sense of affection and guilt for how his family and nation have treated Sutara. His proposal to Sutara exudes a sense of his patriotic and patronizing impulses in its reference to the sympathy he feels for her: 'I hope you won't say no. We talk of you often, Subha and myself. We like you so much. I don't know about love, but we felt so sorry for you. Can you try to like us?' (129). Promode's plans to live as an expatriate allow him to make the ultimate patriotic sacrifice; as a son of the nation planning to live in exile he marries Sutara and removes her from the nation rather than directly challenge her treatment by the state and community. In this light, the novel's multiple references to a composite Hindu-Muslim culture in India, such as the location of Sutara's college in Old Delhi near the Red Fort and the scene of Promode's proposal to Sutara in Qudsia Bagh – a garden named after Emperor Muhammed Shah's wife – serve only to underscore the irony of Sutara's treatment by her extended family.[18]

As they leave the park where he has proposed to her, the narrative records:

> He was filled with sympathy. What he did not know was that Aziz [Tamij's son and now a Pakistani citizen] had had identical feelings for her. They got into a taxi. Promode wished he could make her his very own that minute. He wanted to draw her close and whisper, 'I am taking charge. I'll look after you.' (132)

The narrator's reference to Aziz deflates the sense of patriotic righteousness (not to mention paternalism) Promode expresses through his gesture to Sutara. On the contrary, the narrative suggests that Hindu and Muslim, Indian and Pakistani are equally haunted by the implications of Sutara's treatment despite the liberal ideals their nations espouse. Sutara wonders at Promode's motives: 'What she wanted to ask was, are you doing this out of pity? Charity? Was this love? Was this kindness? But she could not bring herself to utter these thoughts' (130). Jyotirmoyee Devi's narrative leaves these questions unanswered, ending the novel as Promode leaves Sutara in the boarding house where she has been living. Though the narrative concludes, 'Today, suddenly, she realised that she was at the end of a long nightmare even though she had not really been aware of living ... For the first time she felt she was not a respected college professor, but a young, dreamy girl' (133), all is not resolved. As Sutara gazes out across the college courtyard, the 'solitary and indifferent' eucalyptus trees remind her of the presence of the other 'inmates' (i.e., 'polluted' women) who will remain at the hostel after she leaves (133). The narrative reads: 'No branches or flowers to redeem them. Storms could not bend them' (133).[19] Thus, this somewhat 'fairy-tale' ending for Sutara (premised on the acceptance her marriage will provide for her in wider society) is undercut by the information that she will leave the other women behind. Moreover, these women are not portrayed as victims without agency but, rather, as strong and resilient women – 'Storms could not bend them.' Menon and Bhasin report that many women who were 'recovered' can still be found in 'rehabilitation centres and shelters even today, in Punjab and Haryana' ('Abducted' 4). Those who managed to elude the recovery process were often able to rebuild their lives and integrate into the communities and families they found themselves in after the violence and migration. [20]

What I want to stress as I conclude this reading of *The River Churning* is that the absence of details regarding the violence Sutara experienced returns throughout the narrative as flashbacks disrupting Sutara's perception of time and sense of belonging. It also underscores her inability to remember what happened that night. For example, when Sutara finally discusses with her friend Kaushalyavati the sectarian violence that took place at the time of partition, she realizes for the first time that she, her mother, and her sister may also have been the target of sexual assault. The narrative states, '"What did they do with the women? Did your milkman tell you?" Scenes from that terrible night floated before her – the screams of Ma and Didi, Didi's terror-stricken face. Now she understood the full import of it' (86). Even after comparing her experience with others, Sutara's flashbacks to the events leading up to her blackout become increasingly impressionistic and fragmented as she becomes preoccupied with whether or not her family members are dead. For instance, the narrative figures Sutara as panicked when she accompanies a group from the college on a pilgrimage and is asked to participate in a Hindu ceremony where rice and water are made as offerings to relatives. When she is asked if her parents and siblings are alive, the narrative recounts,

> Mother and father? She could hardly control her tears as scenes from that terrible night flitted across her mind.
> Her voice shook as she asked, 'Who shall I offer the water to? My mother, father and didi?' ... Still in a daze, Sutara wondered if her mother was actually dead. Did she die that night? Her death had not been reported. Tamij Saheb had informed her only of her father's fate – nobody said anything about her mother and sister ... Sutara's hands shook, she felt parched, she offered up her prayers though she did not understand any of the words she was made to utter. All she remembered were her middle-aged father's last words, 'Keep the door closed,' and his hurried exit into the dark night, her mother's face in the flaming glow of the burning cowshed, the way her sister fell, and shadowy figures invading the house. (111–12)[21]

The relationship between language and referent, life and death, sight and knowledge are all thrown into question by this passage. The only things Sutara is certain of are her father's last words, and four images: her father's exit, her mother's face, her sister's fall, and the house invaded by 'shadowy figures.' However, the repetition of her father's words, 'Keep the door closed,' at this stage in the narrative now seems to refer to much more than the literal action of bolting the door. Instead it becomes a metonym for the patriarchal logic that sustains the discourse of contamination governing 'abducted' women's identities at the time and it also anticipates the gendered nature of the collective violence that unfolds and precipitates her treatment by her extended family.

At the time of the attack, Sutara does not understand why her father wants them to hide in the house. 'But,' as Lyotard argues, 'the silence imposed on knowledge does not impose the silence of forgetting, it imposes a feeling' (56). 'What is at stake in a literature, in a philosophy, in a politics perhaps, is to bear witness to differends by finding idioms for them' (13). The 'trauma,' 'loss as loss,' or 'differend' that Sutara's forgetting points to at this moment in the narrative – the 'feeling' that '[o]ne cannot find the words' – seems to be explained by the idiom of this flashback. After Sutara is rejected by her extended family and community, she comes to understand that the obscure events that unfolded outside her father's patriarchal protection are the cause of her misery. By surrendering to the silence in Sutara's story the reader is alerted to what is effaced from modernist accounts of history in order to allow (masculine) Indian subjects to emerge as autonomous citizens – not the details of Sutara's violation, but the ambiguity of their interpretation. The belief that Sutara was sexually assaulted by members of the other community and the shame associated with what is represented as the 'defilement' of her sexual purity is the rationale that informs both her violation and her 'recovery.' By refusing to fill the gap in Sutara's story, Jyotirmoyee Devi's novel denies the reader 'the evidence' he or she needs to assess whether or not Sutara was sexually polluted and instead redirects 'our' attention to the patriarchal rationale that informs the construction of women's sexuality as polluted or pure. Sutara's predicament deflects the categories that have been established to make sense of her experience in that the gap in her story makes it impossible to identify her as a woman of honour or dishonour. It also becomes apparent that for the reader to begin to understand how these categories have been constructed and normalized in the name of the nation, she or he must move outside Jyotirmoyee Devi's text and the terms in which these events have been interpreted in hegemonic historical accounts of partition.

My focus on the novel's commemoration of partition violence, therefore, meditates on the impossibility of anamnesis, 'a practice that seeks the recovery of what has been lost, neglected, or misplaced' and suggests that 'learning from the past' requires a practice of anagnorisis, a critical practice of remembrance that disrupts the hold of patriarchal modernist views over this history. The gendered violence that Sutara experiences and the nation's and community's attempts to forget or contain are indicative of the identity of the modern nation-state as a site of representation which can only be shared by all citizens if it elides the ambivalences of their experiences.[22] The ethics of my reading of *The River Churning*, therefore, locates the 'abducted' or 'polluted' migrant woman as an aporia in Hindu cultural nationalism by refusing to reconcile or 'recover' her identity or experience within the script dictated by the community and state. In the process, my reading discloses the slippage within the representative status implied by the concepts of the nation-state and the citizen-subject in modernist history and gestures at its gendered connotations. Rather than seek to *restore* (or fill in the blanks of) the experiences of women refugees at the time of partition (the impulse characteristic of modern history that ultimately betrays or appropriates those experiences), my reading of Jyotirmoyee Devi's text meditates on the absent-presence of these details at the core of Sutara's story in order to consider other ways of knowing the history of this period. The autonomy of the nation is haunted by this fact that it would rather leave behind but cannot quite resolve. The silence at the core of 'abducted' women's narratives should not, therefore, be resolved, accounted for, translated, or recovered but understood as a refusal to identify with the project of (patriarchal) modernity that has produced it in the first place.

Conclusion: Recovering the Nation?

Each chapter of this book has attempted to disrupt normalized assumptions about women's experiences at the time of India's partition and independence and, instead, to explore, via literature, how they are structured by the discourses of gender and nationalism. Rather than seek to *restore* the experiences of women refugees at the time of partition (the impulse characteristic of modern history), I have argued that the work of Rajinder Singh Bedi, Bapsi Sidhwa, Attia Hosain, and Jyotirmoyee Devi underscores the absent-presence of these women's stories from the history of independence in South Asia and suggests reasons for this ellipsis.

Unsettling Partition has questioned the sense of promise many scholars of partition narratives associate with a future moment in the practice of history writing. I have argued that it is a misguided project to attempt to recover an 'ideal' history – the sort Jyotirmoyee Devi describes as an (im)possible task in the introduction to *The River Churning*. Of course, this does not imply that history did not happen – material reality and social practices are indelibly marked by its events – but that the interpretation of these markings always takes place in and through language with the attendant problems of translation and representation this involves. By understanding representations of history in these terms, it is possible for the scholar to transform the practices of reading and writing about partition narratives from a search for authenticity (which ultimately ends up silencing someone) to an examination of the multiple determinations of experience. With these limitations in mind, I have read representations of women's experiences at the time of partition as 'intent on occupying an historical void and simultaneously gesturing to the absent presence of any details' (Walcott 5). This critical practice recognizes that reading and writing history are necessarily incomplete, indirect, and politically charged.

I have also endeavoured to show how the effort to 'recover' voices in the meta-narrative of the history of Indian nationalism shares some problematic epistemological assumptions with those underpinning the activities of the Central Recovery Operation. The modernist Truth claims of the Recovery Operation constructed a view of the nation as an archaic and stable construct with clearly identifiable members whose interests the state could speak for. The consequences of these assumptions in the case of 'abducted' women was the erasure of difference within and among the experiences of women affected by the changes wrought by partition and the elision of those experiences that did not conform to the script provided by the nation-state. In more practical terms, women, unlike men, were denied the opportunity to decide for themselves where they would prefer to remain after partition, and the competing patriarchal and elite interests in India and Pakistan wrote their desires for them.

Like the Indian and Pakistani states' recovery of 'abducted' women, the recovery of 'lost' or 'forgotten' narratives concerning partition has been represented in modernist history (and unwittingly in some historiography) as a way of completing what is an otherwise unproblematic narrative of national history. Where these narratives are invoked their significance has sometimes been unwittingly ventriloquized and read in terms of the researcher's agenda while at the same time the women are represented as 'speaking for themselves.' In both cases, an unproblematic notion of 'recovery' is operating, rendering language as transparent and experience as unmediated. It has been my intention to avoid rehearsing this pattern throughout my own analysis of the situation. Alternatively, I have read these narratives as evidence of the undecidability of texts in general and attempted to track the way subjects are produced by various interpretations of partition. I have suggested that the most productive interpretations – those that acknowledge the limits of any interpretation of events – provide the greatest potential for recognizing 'abducted' women's (and other Others') indirect agency and present possibilities for the emergence of a national imaginary that is porous, fissured, and fragmented.

Efforts to recover 'lost' history and/or 'lost' women of the nation underscore the doubleness of national discourse. Homi Bhabha identifies this doubleness in nationalist discourse as the '"double and split" time of national representation' (*Nation and Narration* 295). Indian nationalists' production of gendered spheres of knowledge distinguished 'their' culture from the colonizers on the basis of what were claimed to be essential differences represented as originary. At the same time, however, their effort to 'recover' the nation in difference simultaneously undercuts the linear, progressive unfolding of history that is supposed to be emblematic of the nation's time. Like the representations of Hindu Science studied by Gyan Prakash, in the case of 'abducted' women, '[w]e can identify this indeterminancy and unease in ... representation[s] of the national subject in its "recovery" from divisions, defeat, and loss; we find the image of cohesion and synchronicity cracked, the solidity of the ... past hollowed out, when the "nationness" of modern India appears in the restoration of archaic unity from contemporary difference' (539).

The representation of 'abducted' women as members of the community who have been lost and who must be recovered in order to restore the nation entails the same kind of double movement that Bhabha argues is characteristic of all totalizing national discourse. 'Homogeneous, empty time' is ruptured by the need to refer to the nation's or the masculine citizen-subject's failure to protect the female members of his family. The events of partition are represented as a sudden blip on the screen of the nation that would otherwise have evolved into a unified whole with a shared sense of identity. Prior to partition, Hindu revivalists represented Hindus as degraded by Muslim hordes and as the guardians of the Indian nation. The violence of partition represents the degradation of the nation, often blamed on the Muslim Other or 'the dark side of human nature,' that can be overcome by a return to the true Indian citizen – the Hindu. Reference to the prior or 'archaic' time of the nation (to use Gyan Prakash's phrase), however, scrambles the modern premise of the nation's past:

> In such a representation the past appears not as an origin but as an anteriority. Unlike the organicist notion, which draws an unbroken line between the origin and the present, the idea of the modern nation as the return of the archaic introduces a sharp break between the past and the present; the past irrupts, it does not evolve, into the present. As the contemporary national self emerges in the differential sign of the 'return,' as its time is expressed in the repetition of another time, an alienating otherness becomes the necessary mode of enunciating the fullness of the nation. In this sense, the representation of the modern nation as the return of the archaic disrupts the language of origins and organicity and invokes

the past as anteriority, as an otherness in which the identification of the national self occurs. (540)

The purity of community identity maintained through the prohibition of intermarriage and extramarital sex outside the liminal spaces of the brothel, represents the archaic past that is invoked as anterior to the 'abduction,' 'pollution,' and 'defilement' of women during partition. Even as the Recovery Operation returned to a construction of 'pure' Hindu, Sikh, and Muslim communities as the justification for the (sometimes forcible) 'recovery' of women to the dominant national community, so also did it have to confront the ambivalence of these women's 'return.' The behaviour of those who participated in the violence against women from the Other community and the ongoing risk that women who did 'return' to the national fold might express ambivalence to being named 'Indians' posed an ongoing threat that had to be contained.

This ambivalence and the power relations expressed through the activities of the Recovery Operation are epitomized in the testimony of a social worker from the Gandhi Vanita Ashram in Jalandhar;[1] the social worker recounts her involvement in a particular case of twenty-one Muslim women required to return to Pakistan by the Tribunal:

> They ['recovered' Muslim women] were determined to stay back because they were very happy. We had to use real force to compel them to go back ... The girls were desperate ... Those women cursed me all the way to Amritsar, loudly and continuously. When we reached Wagah, it was evening and we found that there were about 15 other jeeps that had also accompanied us – all belonging to their relatives! They were hoping that should any one of the girls manage to escape, they would pick her up and take her back. As far as I could see, they were all Sikhs ... Naturally, as soon as we reached Pakistan, the women realised their complete helplessness – what else can you call it? ... When the jeeps came to a halt, the SP dismounted, went round the back of the jeeps, opened the door and rained abuses on those poor women. He shouted at them and said, 'Now tell me, which one of you wants to go back to India? Tell me and I'll let you off right now to find your way back. Let us see how far you get.' They shouted back at me – after all, I was the one who had brought them – They kept saying, 'Why are you destroying our lives?' Earlier, when I had brought them from Jalandhar jail saying, this is a government agreement, our girls are also being returned, they had shouted at me: 'Who are you to meddle in our lives? We don't know you, what business is it of yours?'

In Lahore, the camp for recovered Muslim women was in the Women's Penitentiary. When we reached there, the women got down and each one of them made a burqa of her *chunni* [scarf] and emerged in *parda* [wearing the veil]. They knew that if they protested now they would regret it. (WS5–6)

While I am aware that Bose and Jalal have raised concerns that feminist research on the state's treatment of 'abducted women' 'dramatiz[es], if not romanticiz[es], examples of murderers and rapists turned into besotted husbands by their former victims' (*Modern* 198), I believe the social worker's account offers a more complex view of the experience of abducted women at the time of partition. I have quoted this testimony at length because I think it references all the elements of instability that threaten to erupt on the surface of nationalist discourse in South Asia. First, the presence of Muslim women living in conjugal relationships in Sikh homes in India challenges the archaic notion that these communities lived separate existences, untainted by each other's bloodline. The women's desire to remain with their 'abductors' throws doubts on the community and state's construction of them as mere 'victims' of the events of partition and raises uncomfortable questions about why they might not want to 'return' to their 'original' communities. The resistance the women offer to the forced migration by the government officials signals the ongoing threat their presence may have for patriarchal expectations for their behaviour in Pakistan (and indeed, the women they are being exchanged for in India). On the other hand, their acquiescence to the situation that confronts them when they reach the border, once they realize there is no turning back, represents their physical (the adoption of *purdah*) and discursive (they no longer argue) conformity to a new (feminine) national identity. This incident, and its narrativization by the social worker, is an example of 'recuperation worked through repetition' that Prakash argues is typical of nationalist discourse (552).

Thus, the formal and thematic unfolding of the partition narratives examined in this study points to women refugees' experiences without attempting 'to put them into the orderly and fabricated seamlessness that the scienticity of [modern] history suggests' (Walcott 10). This reading allows for the emergence of 'a cultural trauma which can never be brought to closure nor grasped as it was in the first instance' (8). Mobilizing this strategy for remembrance would seem to represent the task at hand in the project of understanding the events of partition in

South Asia and their representation in literature, testimony, and history. The intersection between the 'crisis of witnessing' (8) and the 'crisis of representation' in the texts I have explored suggests that most partition narratives are informed by an ethics 'much more concerned with a response to a possible future or tomorrow than with a realist return to the past' (8). *Unsettling Partition* has sought to repeat women's experiences of partition in a different, nonrealist, and fragmentary context in an effort to challenge the dominant perception of these events in history. It is the recognition of this instability and constant maintenance of nationalist discourse that promises the most effective critique of the desire to create a monolithic national imaginary.

Appendix A

Advertisement for Parle's Gluco Biscuits, *Times of India*, 3 November 1947.

Notes

Introduction: Unsettling Partition

1 I am grateful to Debali Mookerjea-Leonard's 'Disenfranchised Bodies' for drawing my attention to this quote.
2 The partition and independence of India are often referred to with upper case 'I's' and 'P's.' Although I have retained the spelling used by various writers cited in this book, I prefer the use of the lower case in my own work. I think this avoids the tendency to monumentalize the events in question – one of the key goals of *Unsettling Partition*.
3 See Gyanendra Pandey's *Remembering Partition* for a discussion of how the numbers of those who migrated or were killed at the time of partition, represented in the form of large, rounded statistics, serve as a kind of '*precise* and yet *extravagant*' 'rumour' (71).
4 See Barbara D. Metcalf and Thomas R. Metcalf's *A Concise History of India*, especially chapter 7, 'The 1940's Triumph and Tragedy,' for a good overview of historical events leading up to India's partition.
5 In *Making India Hindu* David Ludden argues that 'before 1980, the political impact of communalism remained limited ... and Hindu nationalist parties won few votes ... After 1980, however, killing classified as "communal" increased rapidly and so did the Muslim body count' (16).
6 Some other novels in English about the partition published in subsequent decades since independence that have enjoyed a high degree of visibility before this period include Manohar Malgonkar, *A Bend in the Ganges* (1964), Chaman Nahal's *Azadi* (1975), Bhisham Sahni's *Tamas* (first published in Hindi in 1974 and in English in 1981 as *Kites Will Fly*), and Amitav Ghosh's *The Shadow Lines* (1988). Sahni published his own translation of *Tamas* in 2001.

7 The importance of this work in prompting research into local experiences of partition is evidenced in Sukeshi Kamra's introduction to her study on partition, *Bearing Witness*: 'It all began with my yearly return to India in December, 1995. At a friend's place I found a book titled *Short Stories About the Partition* [sic], edited by Alok Bhalla ... [T]he stories came as a shock ... Why was I shocked? Because it did not fit my image of the time, which, in India, is always celebrated as a moment of national triumph' (1).
8 This collection was originally published in 1987 under the title *When the British Left: Stories on the Partitioning of India*. Ravishankar Rao cites the reissue of the collection under its most recent title as an 'index' of how interest in narratives about India's independence shifted toward attention to the events of partition in the early 1990s (13).
9 See Jason Francisco's 'In the Heat of Fratricide' for a widely read comparative review of Bhalla and Hasan's collections. Thomas Palakeel reviews Memon's collection in 'Partition Stories.'
10 These essays include Leslie Flemming's 'Riots and Refugees' (1978), N.K. Jain's 'The Partition Theme in Indo-Anglian Novels' (1984), Muhammad Umar Memon's 'Partition Literature' (1980), S.S. Hans's 'The Partition Novels of Nanak Singh' (1984), and Tariq Rahman's 'Critical Prejudices to Aspects of Partition Literature' (1992). Susie Tharu's article 'Rendering Account of the Nation: Partition Narratives and Other Genres of the Passive Revolution' (1994) departs from the humanist and nationalist reading of partition literature found in these essays and looks at the 1940s/50s and the 1980s/90s as parallel moments of the expression of fascism in Indian politics using the Gramscian concept of hegemony.
11 By the 'everyday' I am referring to events that are considered marginal or supplemental to the high political story of partition but nonetheless impact on the articulation of events at the centre. My understanding of the relation between representation, 'everyday experience,' and materiality draws on feminist historiography such as Joan W. Scott's 'The Evidence of Experience' and Kathleen Canning's 'Feminist History after the Linguistic Turn.' I will return to the notion of the 'everyday' in chapter 2 and unfold its significance to my discussion of partition narratives.
12 Ashis Nandy also frames his work on partition in terms of 'bearing witness,' noting, 'I bear witness to it without reading it the way those who have lived by it may like me to' ('Holocaust' 306). See Sukeshi Kamra's *Bearing Witness* for another approach to this task that examines political cartoons, newspapers, diaries, autobiographies, fiction, and trauma theory.
13 For a general discussion of the importance of Gayatri Spivak's work in unpacking this problematic see the special issue of *Cultural Studies*, 17.1

(2003), *Revisiting the Subaltern in the New Empire*, ed. Jill Didur and Teresa Heffernan.
14 The 'we' of Hargrove's article includes references to researchers including Butalia, Das, Menon, Bhasin, and Pandey.
15 Work on testimony about India's partition can be found compiled in several recent books: Ritu Menon and Kamla Bhasin's *Borders and Boundaries*, Veena Das's *Critical Events*, Urvashi Butalia's *The Other Side of Silence*, and Gyanendra Pandey's *Remembering Partition*.

1 Gender and Nationalist Discourse in South Asia

1 See Harveen Mann's '"The Magic Idyll of Antiquated India"' for an analysis of how Narayan's Bharati adheres to an unabashedly patriarchal conception of Woman as nation, thus reproducing the tropes of patriarchal nationalist discourse overviewed in this chapter.
2 Early packaging for Parle's Gluco Biscuits (as seen in this advertisement) included the image of a woman dressed in a sari standing in a field with cows, reminiscent of scenes from Nargis's *Mother India*.
3 For other commentaries on the gendering of home and world in nationalist discourse see Partha Chatterjee's 'The Nationalist Resolution to the Women's Question'; Uma Chakravarti's 'Whatever Happened to the Vedic Dasi?'; Jasodhra Bagchi, ed., *Indian Women: Myth and Reality*; and Mrinalini Sinha, *Colonial Masculinity: The 'Manly Englishman' and the 'Effeminate Bengali' in the Late Nineteenth Century*.
4 See 'TV/Press Ads' on the Parle company website for examples of recent television and print ads.
5 For examples of feminist critiques of Indian nationalist discourse, see Parama Roy's *Indian Traffic*, Kumkum Sangari and Sudesh Vaid's *Recasting Women*, Radha Kumar's *The History of Doing*, Sangeeta Ray's *En-Gendering India*, Tanika Sarkar's *Hindu Wife Hindu Nation*, Partha Chatterjee's *The Nation and Its Fragments*, Gayatri Spivak's *A Critique of Postcolonial Reason*, Susie Tharu and K. Lalita's *Women Writing in India*, and Rajeswari Sunder-Rajan's *Real and Imagined Women*.
6 As an extention of this construct, Roy continues, 'peasants, tribals, and other subalterns are also figured in this way, in their "failure" to be modern' (137).
7 Gayatri Spivak has famously encapsulated the patriarchal dynamics of imperialist ideological formation that shaped the monolithic construction of Indian women as follows: '[w]hite men are saving brown women from brown men' ('Can' 296).

8 For a discussion of Dalit experiences of the partition see chapter 7, 'Margins,' of Urvashi Butalia's *The Other Side of Silence*. Paola Bacchetta expands on this theme in 'Reinterrogating Partition Violence.'
9 Lata Mani has examined how colonial representatives shored up their influence in India by regulating cultural practices like *sati*. See especially 'Contentious Traditions.'
10 Chakravarti draws attention to these quotes from Max Muller's *Chips from a German Workshop*, I, 4 cited in Johannes H. Voight, *Max Muller: The Man and His Ideas*.
11 See Romila Thapar's 'Some Appropriations of the Theory of Aryan Race' for a discussion of how the myth of the Aryan invasion is deployed in the political rhetoric of Hindu nationalist parties.
12 See Vijay Prashad's article 'The Untouchable Question' for how Untouchables were absorbed into the Hindu fold during the nationalist period. Prashad argues that Untouchables were only considered 'Hindus' within the 'anti-Muslim culturalist solution of nationalism' that shaped nationalist discourse in India since the turn of the century (551).
13 For another perspective on how gender played a role in Gandhi's philosophies and actions, see Madhu Kishwar, 'Gandhi on Women.'
14 The women's movement in Britain also exploited its links with the women's movement in India by comparing the 'sad plight' of their southern sisters in racialized terms to the subordination of women in Britain. The intent of this comparison was not to pressure the British to improve the condition of women in England in concert with those in India, but rather to prompt British men to shore up their race privilege by distinguishing their women from the women of the subjugated race. See Antoinette Burton's *Burdens of History* for more examples of this abuse of 'feminist' sentiments and solidarity.
15 Agricultural land was exempted from the Act (Chhachhi 160).
16 See Dipesh Chakrabarty's essay 'Postcoloniality and the Artifice of History' for an explanation of the relationship between violence and idealism in nationalist accounts of History; see especially pages 21 and 22.
17 See especially chapter 3 in *Imagined Communities*, where he comments on 'a half-fortuitous, but explosive, interaction between a system of production and productive relations (capitalism), a technology of communications (print), and the fatality of human linguistic diversity' (42–3).

2 Narratives of India's Partition

1 I use the term 'History' with a capital 'H' to indicate when I am referring to the practice of writing a historical narrative that is not self-reflexive

about the silences it produces and instead naturalizes the perspective it constructs as objective and universal.

2 In this chapter my primary reference for 'Lajwanti' is to Rajinder Singh Bedi's own English translation found in *Contemporary Indian Short Stories 2* published in 1967. I make secondary references to Alok Bhalla's translation found in *Stories about the Partition of India*, Jai Rattan's in *Orphans of the Storm*, and Khushwant Singh's in *Writings on India's Partition*. Numerous other translations are available including Ashraq Ahmad's in Muhammad Umar Memon's *An Epic Unwritten*, and Mark Pegors's in the *The Annual of Urdu Studies*.

3 I use the term 'abducted' in quotes to emphasize the contested status of the identities of women who were separated from their families in the sectarian violence that unfolded at the time of partition. It is unclear that all women separated from their families were taken and/or held against their will. To use this term without a degree of contingency would be to overlook how it is embedded in nationalist and patriarchal readings of partition history.

4 This statement and several others from this article also frame Talbot's analysis in 'The Partition Experience,' chapter 4 of his book *Freedom's Cry*.

5 My sense of this is reinforced by Talbot's decision to place the word 'representation' in quotes when he writes about the qualities of the literature he will discuss (see pages 40 and 41).

6 'In Defence of the Fragment' and 'The Prose of Otherness' are now ubiquitous citations in almost all work interested in considering how literary narratives offer an alternative memory to dominant accounts of partition. With the exception of Sujala Singh's 'Nationalism's Brandings: Women's Bodies and Narratives of the Partition,' they are generally cited without qualification.

7 For the full poem see Manaazir Aashiq Harganvi's *Ankhon Dekhi Bhagalpur ke Bhayanak Fasad ko dekhne ke baad*.

8 See a similar concern raised by Ayesha Jalal in 'Secularists, Subalterns and the Stigma of "Communalism."'

9 For an English translation of another section of *Azadi ki Chhaon Mein*, see Varsha Das's 'Darkness and Light' in Ritu Menon's *No Woman's Land*.

10 This is Pandey's translation. Urvashi Butalia's discussion of Qidwai's memoir cites similarly ambivalent passages; see especially 'Community' WS20.

11 To be fair, Pandey is alert to the ambivalence Qidwai's text expresses. He states: 'The writer refers to many examples of women who were extremely reluctant to return – for fear of ostracism, because they felt they had been "soiled," because they could not bear the thought of being uprooted yet

again and exposed (possibly) to new levels of poverty and uncertainty, or simply because they were grateful to their new husbands and families for having rescued them from (further?) assault and afforded them protection' ('Prose' 216). Nevertheless, Pandey does not pursue the implications of this ambivalence for his larger argument.

12 Similarly, Sujala Singh calls Pandey's conclusion 'trite' and also notes that 'Urvashi Butalia retells another Manto story "Open Up" ("Khol Do") only to conclude, "Sakina's story was not uncommon at the time of partition." As questions of narrative are asked of history, but not of fiction, fiction becomes the desired "Other" of history' (Singh 126; Butalia, 'Community' 63).

13 Scott cites Karen Swann's unpublished paper 'The Social and Political Construction of Reality.'

14 According to M. Asadudin of Jamia Millia University, 'Lajwanti' was first published in Naorang, Karachi, in 1951 (personal correspondence from Alok Bhalla, 28 June 2004).

15 *Bedi Samagra* (The Complete Bedi) (1995) was published in Hindi translation in 1995. Little critical work has been published on 'Lajwanti' in English. Two commentaries on the story are available in *The Annual of Urdu Studies*: Michael Jauch's 'Witnessing Violence' and Thomas Palakeel's 'Partition Stories.'

16 For more information on this movement and its influence on South Asian literature in general, see Carlo Coppola, 'The All India Progressive Writers' Association: The European Phase' in Carlo Coppola ed., *Marxist Influences and South Asian Literature*.

17 In J. Feldman's view, this has resulted in an interesting problem whereby 'readers who have access to the original Urdu texts do not always understand Bedi's use of symbolism, and those who are able to understand his symbolism often cannot read his work in the original and must rely on Hindi translations when available' (120). It is interesting to note that English versions of the story conflict in their translation of references linking Lajwanti to the widow. Where Bedi's own English version reads '[m]ost of the women of *mohalla* Mulla Shukoor, *except* the widow living in house No. 414, dreaded coming to Babu Sunder Lal's house' (my emphasis on 'except') ('Lajwanti' 212–13), Jai Rattan's translation of this sentence reads, '[t]he widow in number 414 wasn't the only one to keep away from Lajwanti's house' (77).

18 Chakrabarty traces the gendered genealogy of freedom in readings of difference in *bhadralok* constructions of the domestic sphere during the nineteenth and early twentieth centuries in Bengal. He explains that

'Lakshmi, regarded as Vishnu's wife by c. AD 400, has long been upheld in puranic Hinduism as the model Hindu wife, united in complete harmony with her husband in a spirit that combined submission with loyalty, devotion and fidelity' ('Difference' 58). Her antithesis, Alakshmi, becomes synonymous with inauspiciousness and domestic unhappiness. Most significantly, texts contemporary with this period of history in *bhadralok* society associate Alakshmi with 'individual assertiveness on the part of women [like that demonstrated by European memsahibs] and its undesirability' (64). Difference in this reformist-nationalist (re)construction of the domestic, therefore, focuses on the interpretation of the modernist notion of 'freedom' within a patriarchal discourse that privileges the security of the extended family over the individual desires of the wife.

19 In fact, Bedi's narrator also 'seals off' the possibility that Lajwanti's Muslim dress and 'plump' appearance represent a preference for or positive alternative to her relationship with Sunder Lal; he tells his readers that Lajwanti 'had no time to think of the dress she was wearing, nor of the manner in which she wore it' (211) and that 'it was suffering which made her look plump ... This was a kind of plumpness which is but an illusion and which makes a person pant if required to walk but a few steps' (212). Other translations leave this point more ambivalent; see, for example, Bhalla's 'Lajwanti,' especially pages 63–4.

20 The narrative's normalization of domestic abuse is most evident at this point in the text. Earlier the narrator indicates that Sunder Lal's physical abuse of Lajwanti was extreme and triggered by any evidence that she may be his physical or psychological equal: 'Sunder Lal, who had a tendency to obesity, had felt diffident at first; as he discovered that Lajo could bear any burden, submit to any form of pain and suffering and even to occasional bouts of thrashing, he had gradually increased his maltreatment of her. Presently, he became so confident of her capacity for tolerance that he even lost sight of those frontiers at which the tolerance and patience of any human being can crack up' (203). That the narrator could suggest, without a sense of irony, that this was a 'normal' aspect of married life and that 'Lajo was indeed helpful in making Sunder Lal forget those frontiers, in making them dimmer, even non-existent' (203) points to the limits of the narrative's critique of patriarchy.

3 Bapsi Sidhwa's *Cracking India*

1 I am grateful to Sujala Singh's fine essay 'Nationalism's Brandings: Women's Bodies and Narratives of the Partition' for drawing my attention to this statement by Spivak.

2 Lenny's practice of identifying Shanta and other characters in the book according to the role they play in her life (Ayah, Mother, Godmother, Slavesister, Father, Ice-candy-man) is one of the many ways her narrative emphasizes the fact that it is an interested and constructed perspective. I have retained this practice in my discussion of the perception of Shanta's actions we get as a way of signalling my awareness that these things come to the reader through Lenny's eyes. Ambreen Hai's suggestion that Ayah is 'named only once as Shanta' (390) when 'she herself functions as a mediating agent of rescue for another victim' (420n26) is misleading; she is also named by Ice-candy-man when he quizzes her about why she doesn't wear 'Punjabi clothes' (38). Here she demonstrates her savvy awareness of how the manipulation of her appearance can influence assumptions about her ethnicity and education; '"*Arrey Baba*," says Ayah ... "do you know what salary ayahs who wear Punjabi clothes get? Half the salary of the Goan ayahs who wear saris! I'm not so simple!"' (38).

3 A selection of critical essays on the novel over the last ten years include: Nandi Bhatia's 'How Long Does Lahore Burn?'; Ambreen Hai's 'Border Work, Border Trouble'; Sangeeta Ray's 'New Women, New Nations,' in *En-Gendering India*; Deepika Bahri's 'Telling Tales'; Jill Didur's 'Cracking the Nation'; and Harveen Sachdeva Mann's '"Cracking India": Minority Women Writers.'

4 While Ambreen Hai also argues that Lenny's 'liminality ... does not dismantle or re-order the hierarchies that she/it inhabits – but reaffirms class/religious/ethnic hierarchies in the uses it makes of a lesser figure [Ayah]' (396), my analysis here suggests that these hierarchies *are* questioned and reordered when attention is paid to how the adult Lenny's rendering of Ayah's experience is framed by a critical reflection on her own complicity in her nanny's ultimate exclusion from the nation and the constructedness of memory and perspective.

5 In her interview with Andrew Whitehead and Urvashi Butalia, Sidhwa states, '[T]he Parsees were not directly involved in the struggle. I felt I could bring dispassion to the subject' (237).

6 A sense that Sidhwa sees a civilizational hierarchy between Parsis and other communities in South Asia is evident in her interview with Montenegro, where she refers to Pathans as 'untamed people' and comments, 'It's taken Pakistan thirty years to tame [them]' (528).

7 The novel's anachronistic reference to Gandhi's Salt March (1930) is another example of how it foregrounds the narrator's subjective construction of history.

8 The definition of discourse that informs this understanding of agency is

what Canning describes as a 'modified Foucauldian one of a convergence of statements, texts, signs, and practices across different, even dispersed, sites (from courtrooms to street corners, e.g.)' (379).

9 Ambreen Hai rightly suggests, 'Ayah's heavily sexualized servant body will become available not only for multiple masculine desires, but also for certain budding feminine ones. Yet female desire for this other female body will always, in this text, forbid itself knowledge of itself, camouflaging itself in a castigation of what it will see insistently as exclusively male violation' (395).

10 Recall the already cited passage in 'Lajwanti.' Similar sentiments are expressed by characters in *The River Churning* and *Sunlight on a Broken Column*, where the general wish is that these women would have been killed or taken their own lives.

4 Attia Hosain's *Sunlight on a Broken Column*

1 For important studies on domesticity see Rosemary George's *Burning Down the House: Recycling Domesticity*, Antoinette Burton's *Dwelling in the Archive*, and, more recently, Judy Walsh's *Domesticity in Colonial India*.

2 In a short article titled 'Second Thoughts: Light in Divided Worlds' published in *The Independent* on 18 August 1988 when the novel had just been reissued by Penguin, Hosain commented, 'I felt I was not capable of writing, in full measure, about the sufferings of divided Muslim families. Yet to some extent, perhaps, I succeeded ... I hope that a new generation will understand that world of the past, and its human warmth that still remains' (Kaul and Jain 219).

3 Hosain's first publication in Britain was a collection of short stories titled *Phoenix Fled* in 1953. Many of these stories focus on parition-related themes. For an anaylsis of one of the best-known stories from this collection, 'After the Storm,' see Harveen Mann's 'South Asian Partition Literature.'

4 Hosain's statements are taken from Bondi's personal conversations with the author on 6 April 1992.

5 See Carlo Coppola's edited volume, *Marxist Influence and South Asian Literature* as well as Shabana Mahmud's '*Angâre* and the Founding of the Progressive Writers' Association' for more background on this movement. See Hogan, 'The Economics of Cultural Identity,' for a discussion of its specific impact on Hosain's work.

6 Recently published commentaries on the novel include: Nilufer E. Bharucha's 'Inhabiting Enclosures and Creating Spaces,' Patrick Colm Hogan's 'The Economics of Cultural Identity,' Vrinda Nabar's 'Frag-

menting Nations and Lives,' R.K. Kaul and Jasbir Jain's *Attia Hosain: A Dyptych Volume*, Naresh Jain's 'The Muslim Polyphony,' Susheila Nasta's 'Points of Departure' in *Home Truths*, and Antoinette Burton's 'A Girlhood among Ghosts' in *Dwelling in the Archive*.

7 Shoba Dé is a well-known contemporary pulp romance writer in India.

8 Sonia Nishat Amin cites several other similar guides available at the time including: *Taujihul Adas* (1925), *Moslem Pocho Shoti* (1926), *Moslem Nari* (1927), *Muslim Birangana* (1936), and *Moqsudul Momenin O Stree Shikkha* (1932) (88n31).

9 *Bihishti Zewar* is available in partial translation with commentary by Barbara Metcalf. Jalal also notes that 'The book remains a best seller in Pakistan to this day. Special "marriage" editions are available at corner bookstalls' ('Convenience' 109n6).

10 Barbara Metcalf points out that *Perfecting Women* was less a response to 'the model of the European woman or Europeanised Indian woman' and more a concern with 'the unreformed, uneducated woman who did not know Islamic doctrine, was caught up in expensive and corrupting ceremonial practices and handled badly the responsibilities of her everyday life' ('Reading' 6). Also of interest is Metcalf's observation that apart from 'the crucial difference of role that placed women squarely in the home,' men and women were 'regarded as one' in terms of their 'essential nature and potential,' thus questioning the assumption that 'any patriarchal system must posit notions of a distinctive female nature ... is clearly wrong' ('Reading' 7).

11 As Hogan explains, 'Laila is forced to marry someone else, but she preserves her virginity. For years, the two lovers long for one another and write love poetry that becomes legendary throughout the world. Majnun lives alone in the desert, mad, befriended only by wild animals, composing exquisite love lyrics, and at one point joining in a desert war in the hope of gaining his beloved. Laila lives miserably in her husband's compound. Eventually, Majnun dies in the desert and Laila dies in her home' (295).

12 Of course, Hosain's reference to romantic love as it is imagined in this myth also cannot help but be anachronistic. As Judy Walsh points out, 'Romantic love (in its nineteenth century incarnation) may have been as new to people in England and America as it was in India. In America a new domesticity emphasized romantic love as distinct from marriage for money; men and women now expected to fall in love before marriage and find a "soul mate, a companion with whom they could share their innermost secrets"' (111n1). Tapan Raychaudhuri notes that many elite Indians

were aware of stories of romantic love: 'both in fictional representations and real life, we have instances of romantic love in and outside marriage, though the disappointed lover [as in the Laila and Majnun legend] rather than requited love [as in Hosain's novel] is the more typical and convincing image projected in nineteenth century writings. Marriage, and arrangement between families rather than individuals, remained in most cases a matter of fact business' (14).

13 I am grateful to an anonymous reader for the University of Toronto Press for emphasizing this point.

14 'For Laila,' Burton argues, 'the house is a sign of privilege, and in Zahra's case, of the inextricability of that privilege with her conjugal choices and her Muslim identity. It is also a sign of how imprisoning, and blinding, the facile, unthinking embrace of home and family remains for Laila at the end of the novel' (*Dwelling* 133).

15 Patrick Colm Hogan reads this detail in the novel as supporting his thesis about Hosain privileging economic factors as the ultimate determinant in social relations (indicating the influence of the Progressive Writers' Association on her fictional worldview) (296). Clearly, however, gendered notions of who should be the breadwinner in the family are what drive Ameer into the army, as Laila indicates she could afford to pay for their expenses.

16 In the interview with Khan, Hosain talks about her family's ties to Nehru and recounts how she questioned Jinnah (another family friend) about the Muslim League's agenda and explains that ultimately she supported the Congress Party '[f]rom the beginning because it stood for something that I felt at the time the Muslim League was lacking' (5). Like Laila in earlier sections of the novel (130), Hosain recalls how she 'used to go at that time with a sari on that was made of handspun cloth ... when I had to go to anything [school-related]' (5).

5 Reading the Silence in Partition Narratives

1 I should take this opportunity to reiterate that I mean to place the category of 'abducted women' under erasure in order to show how this category came to operate as a kind of 'black box' or normalized category in South Asian history until the intervention of the feminist scholars listed above. I underscore its contingency as a way of drawing attention to the possibility that while many women were likely relieved to have the state-sanctioned Recovery Operation intervene on their behalf, removing them from the custody of individuals and communities that may have held them against

their will during the events that led up to and followed the partition, others may not have been so appreciative. While Jyotirmoyee Devi's story characterizes Sutara as initially grateful for being brought to live with her brother and his family in Calcutta, her treatment by them raises questions about whether some women would have been better off remaining where they were. In addition, while the economic independence Sutara and other women at the college achieve is admirable, Sutara's experience of social alienation seems to constantly undermine any sense of accomplishment she may garner from it. Sugata Bose and Ayesha Jalal's concern that the 'dogged anti-statism' of this group of scholars blinds them to 'a historical nuance or two' (*Modern* 198) seems unfair when the substance of their critique of the state rests primarily on the language of the Recovery Bill, which removed the right of women to decide which country they wished to remain in when found outside the company of the extended family. The paternalism of the state in this instance and the subsequent disenfranchisement of women as decision makers is a serious and telling moment about the nature of citizenship in the postcolonial nation-state. At the same time, as my analysis in this chapter suggests, I am uneasy about Veena Das's claim that 'abducted' women were able to successfully reintegrate themselves into their communities in exchange for their silence on their partition experiences. Similarly Debali Mookerjea-Leonard comments, '[p]erhaps some Hindu/ Sikh women, as Das's research demonstrates, found acceptance in their original communities. Sometimes it came in exchange for their silence or after abandoning their children in the custody of social workers' (34).

2 This title was originally used for a short story about partition that Jyotirmoyee Devi published in 1965 in *Amader Gram* (translated as 'Crossing the River' in *The Impermanence of Lies*). In this story a husband is forced to leave his wife at the border while he attempts to collect money in Calcutta in order to bribe the border officials into allowing them to migrate to India. When he returns later than expected he is told she is dead, though he suspects otherwise and insists on remaining to search for her. The story is interesting in that it suggests the husband, Sudam, unlike Sutara's relatives, is not concerned that her 'honour' may be compromised.

3 I am dependent on Chatterjee's translation for my reading of the story.

4 The novel is also linked to the epic through its chapter titles. As Mookerjea-Leonard notes, '[t]he novel is structured in four parts; the last three [parts –] the "Adi Parva" (The Beginning), the "Anusashana Parva"

(The Disciplining), and the "Stree Parva" (The Women Chapter) [–] derive their names from books of the *Mahabharata*' (37).

5   See Subir Roychaudhury and Abhijit Sen, eds., *Rachana Sankalan* (1991), for an anthology of Jyotirmoyee Devi's writing in Bengali. Other English translations of Jyotirmoyee Devi's writing include Debali Mookerjea's '"That Little Boy"' (2002) and the collection *The Impermanence of Lies: Stories of Jyotirmoyee Devi*.

6   For a consideration of the unique characteristics of the partition experience in East Bengal, see Shelly Feldman's 'Feminist Interruptions: The Silence of East Bengal in the Story of Partition' and, more recently, Jashodhara Bagchi and Subhoranjan Dasgupta, 'The Problem,' in *Porous Borders, Divided Selves: A Symposium on Partitions in the East*. The *Seminar* issue has been republished in an expanded form under the title *The Trauma and the Triumph*, Bagchi and Dasgupta, eds (2003).

7   I follow Mario Di Paolantonio in placing 'we' and 'our' in quotation marks throughout this chapter as a way of recalling 'the boundedness of any particular "we" is never an accomplished and given fact, as contradictions and permeations cut through its illusory homogeneous image. Thus, the interface (the rhetorical encounter) between this illusory identification and metaethical language of the other does not take place *directly* in the empirical; rather it stages an *obligation in thought* – an encounter of the limits – that cannot be considered *purely* in constative or descriptive terms' (181n3).

8   The Rashtriya Swayamsevak Sangh (RSS) is a Hindu nationalist organization that is considered a parent organization to the Bharatiya Janata Party (BJP). Since its inception, the RSS has articulated and promoted a Hindu-centric notion of Indian identity. See Tapan Basu et al., *Khaki Shorts and Saffron Flags* for a history of this movement.

9   See Ashish Nandy's 'The Invisible Holocaust and the Journey as an Exodus' for a discussion of similarities between events related to the Holocaust and India's partition. See also Viney Lal's 'Partitioned Selves, Partitioned Pasts' and 'Genocide, Barbaric Others, and the Violence of Categories.'

10 When asked in her interview with Kanaganyakam 'Does the fact that you are a Parsi give you a very different perspective? In certain ways you belong to a marginalized group,' Sidhwa replies, 'Yes, being a Parsi marginalizes but it also gives a better perspective. My family and my community were not hurt during the Partition; and the Christians weren't. The fight was between people who were to gain by it, who were going to be

empowered by it, the Hindus, Muslims and Sikhs. The battle was theirs and as a Parsi, my emotions were not aligned one way or the other. I could keep an objective point of view to some extent' (45).

11 'The *Manavadharmasatra*,' Mookerjea-Leonard comments, was 'the ur-text on Hindu domesticity during the nineteenth century – was understood to decree the policing of women's sexuality, which was to be harnessed and legitimized through marriage' (17). See Madhu Kishwar's 'Manusmriti to Madhusmriti' and 'Codified Hindu Law' for discussions of how colonialism influenced eighteenth- and nineteenth-century interpretations of this text.

12 In this particular case Das comments: 'This view of life is clearly in contrast with the view that it is by being able to express a trauma through language that one may overcome it. I want to emphasise that I am not asserting that silence is therapeutic. Indeed, it was known that Manjeet's [a pseudonym for the woman she interviewed] husband sometimes got drunk and accused her of being a prostitute, but he was not the only man who hurled accusations of a wild nature in a state of drunkenness. Therefore, the society of women around Manjeet could continue to ignore this; allowing an existence, however fragmented, however poisoned, to continue' ('Composition' 70).

13 In an earlier speech at a prayer meeting on 24 October 1946 it was reported that Gandhi commented on 'disturbances in East Bengal' and advised women 'to learn to be brave.' Pyarelal's 'Weekly Letter' reports that Gandhi felt '[h]is advice to them [women] to commit suicide rather than allow themselves to be dishonoured had been much misunderstood. They could keep a dagger for self-defence if they wished to: But a dagger was no use against overwhelming odds. He had advised them to take poison and end their lives rather than submit to dishonour. Their very preparedness should make them brave. No one could dishonour a woman who was fearless of death. They had two ways of self-defence – to kill and be killed or to die without killing. He could teach them the latter, not the former. Above all he wanted them to be fearless. There was no sin like cowardice' (*Collected Works* 27).

14 See Rajeswari Sunder-Rajan's 'Life after Rape' in *Real and Imagined Women* for a discussion of how '[f]eminist texts of rape counter narrative determinism ... by structuring a post-rape narrative that traces her strategies of survival instead of a rape-centred narrative that privileges chastity and leads inexorably to trials to establish it' (76–7).

15 Susie Tharu points to a growing trend in India to blame Muslims for the partition that mirrors the rise in Hindu chauvinism in contemporary

India: 'The 1950s and 60s position on partition would certainly include a sense of the culpability of colonial rule and of betrayal by the British. But the extent to which the hold of this interpretation has weakened in the late 1980s and 90s is remarkable. The antagonists now are Muslims, with their 'sub'/pre-national religiosity who take on the role of enemy within and symbolize the evils of a 'soft' (Nehruvian/socialist) state' ('Rendering' 74–5). Jyotirmoyee Devi's novel, written in 1967, certainly reflects this shift in perception.

16 The *Ramayana* is an epic poem that depicts the life of Rama, including the story of his search for his wife, Sita, who is abducted by Ravana, the evil king of Lanka. See Paula Richman's *Many Ramayanas: The Diversity of Narrative Traditions in South Asia* for a discussion of how this story has been reinterpreted throughout history.

17 K.S. Srinivasan translates Valmiki and Kamban's versions of this incident in the *Ramayana* as follows: 'Eyes downcast, Sita walked round Rama and went up to the fire. With folded hands she swore, "If my heart can never stray away from Rama, may this fire – eternal witness – grant me full redemption," and in total detachment she entered the flaming fire ... As Bhrama spoke, Agni, the fire-god, emerged with Sita on his lap, unscathed. Handing her over to Rama, Agni said, "this is your Vaidehi, free of fault – not by word or thought nor even a look"' (276).

18 I am grateful to Alok Bhalla for pointing this out to me.

19 Mookerjea-Leonard's translation of this same section also supports this reading: 'At the edges of the garden [surrounding the women's dormitory] a few Eucalyptus trees stood straight and tall, apart and lonely. Like the residents of the [women's] hostel. Solitary trees lacking shrubbery, fruits and flowers, branches and twigs. Cyclones would bend but couldn't break them' ('Disenfranchised' 44). Mookerjea-Leonard comments, 'Recontextualizing Sutara within bourgeois domesticity, Jyotirmoyee Devi immediately undermines the happy-ending by returning to themes of the solitude of socially excluded women (hinting also at their non-reproductivity)' (44).

20 See Das's 'Composition of the Personal Voice' for accounts of these women's lives.

21 Jyotirmoyee Devi also builds this productive uncertainty into her short story 'That Little Boy,' in which Raj, a young woman who was separated from her mother during partition, wonders if a beggar she met in the street could be her: 'she asked herself, "Couldn't Mother escape, she didn't die? She's alive?" Suddenly alert, she checked these thoughts. No, she was mistaken' (Mookerjea 139).

22 It is here that my thoughts intersect with what Chakrabarty has described as the project of 'provincializing Europe' ('Postcoloniality' 22). This project proposes a displacement of a hyper-real Europe, which Chakrabarty argues has occupied the centre of historical imagination, in favour of 'a history that deliberately makes visible, within the very structure of its narrative forms, its own repressive strategies and practices' (23).

Conclusion: Recovering the Nation?

1 'The Gandhi Vanita Ashram in Jalandhar was set up for the rehabilitation of destitute women after Partition' (Menon and Bhasin, 'Recovery' WS11n16).

Bibliography

Ahmad, Aijaz. *In Theory: Classes Nations Literatures*. London: Verso, 1992.
– *Lineages of the Present: Political Essays*. New Delhi: Tulika Print Communication Services, 1996.
Amin, Sonia Nishat. 'Childhood and Role Models in the Andar Mahal: Muslim Women in the Private Sphere in Colonial Bengal.' *Embodied Violence: Communalizing Women's Sexuality in South Asia*. Ed. Kumari Jaywardena and Malathi de Alwis. London: Zed Books, 1996. 71–88.
Anand, Mulk Raj. 'Profile of Attia Hosain.' *Commonwealth Quarterly: Special Issue on Women Writers of Indian English* 3.9 (1978): 1–12.
Anderson, Benedict. *Imagined Communities: Reflections on the Origin and Spread of Nationalism*. London: Verso, 1991.
Bacchetta, Paola '"Reinterrogating Partition Violence": Voices of Women/Children/Dalits in India's Partition.' *Feminist Studies* 26.3 (2000): 567–86.
Bagchi, Jasodhara, ed. *Indian Women: Myth and Reality*. Calcutta: Sangam Books, 1993.
– 'Introduction.' *The River Churning*. Delhi: Kali for Women Press, 1995. xxv–xxxiii.
Bagchi, Jashodhara, and Subhoranjan Dasgupta. 'The Problem.' *Seminar: Porous Borders Divided Selves, A Symposium on Partitions in the East* 510 (2002): 12–14.
– *The Trauma and the Triumph: Gender and Partition in Eastern India*. Kolkata: STREE, 2003.
Bahri, Deepika. 'Telling Tales: Women and the Trauma of Partition in Sidhwa's *Cracking India*.' *Interventions: International Journal of Postcolonial Studies* 1.2 (1999): 217–34.
Basu, Tapan, Pradip Datta, Sumit Sarkar, Tanika Sarkar, Sambuddha Sen. *Khaki Shorts and Saffron Flags: A Critique of the Hindu Right*. Hyderabad: Orient Longman, 1993.

Bedi, Rajinder Singh. 'Lajwanti.' *Contemporary Indian Short Stories 2*. Trans. Rajinder Singh Bedi. Ed. Bhabani Bhattacharya. Delhi: Sahitya Akademi, 1967. 201–14. Trans. of 'Lajwant.' *Naorang*. 1951.
- 'Lajwanti.' *Writings on India's Partition*. Ed. Ramesh Mathur and Mahendra Kulasrestha. Trans. Khushwant Singh. Calcutta: Simant Publications, 1976. 126–35.
- 'Lajwanti.' Trans. Mark Pegors. *The Annual of Urdu Studies* 5 (1985): 67–76.
- 'Lajwanti.' *Stories about the Partition of India*. Ed. Alok Bhalla. Trans. Alok Bhalla. New Delhi: Harper Collins, 1994. 55–66.
- *I Take This Woman*. Trans. Kushwant Singh. Delhi: Penguin Books, 1995. Trans. of *Ek Chadar Maili Si*. Maktaba Jamia, 1962.
- 'Lajwanti.' *Orphans of the Storm: Stories on the Partition of India*. Ed. Saros Cowasjee and K.S. Duggal. Trans. Jai Rattan. New Delhi: USBSD, 1995. 67–78.
- *Bedi Samagra: Volume 1 and 2*. Delhi: Rajkamal Parkashan, 1995.

Bhabha, Homi K., ed. *Nation and Narration*. London: Routledge, 1990.

Bharucha, Nulifer E. 'Inhabiting Enclosures and Creating Spaces: The Worlds of Women in Indian Literature in English.' *ARIEL: A Review of International English Literature* 29.1 (1998): 93–107.
- 'An Interview with Attia Hosain.' *Biblio: A Review of Books* 3.7–8 (1998): 20–1.

Bhatia, Nandi. 'How Long Does Lahore Burn? History Memory and Literature Representations of the Partition.' *Pangs of Partition II*. New Delhi: Indian Council of Historical Research, 2002. 191–208

Bondi, Laura. 'An Image of India by an Indian Woman: Attia Hosain's Life and Fiction.' MA thesis. Facoltà di Lingue e Letterature Straniere, Universita' Degli Studi di Venezia, 1993.

Bose, Sugata, and Ayesha Jalal. *Modern South Asia: History Culture Political Economy*. New York: Routledge, 1998.

Burton, Antoinette. *Burdens of History: British Feminists, Indian Women, and Imperial Culture, 1865–1915*. Chapel Hill: The University of North Carolina Press, 1994.
- *Dwelling in the Archive: Women Writing House, Home and History in Late Colonial India*. Oxford: Oxford University Press, 2003.

Butalia, Urvashi. 'Community, State and Gender: On Women's Agency during Partition.' *Economic and Political Weekly* 24 April 1993: WS12–24.
- 'Muslims and Hindus, Men and Women: Communal Stereotypes and the Partition of India.' *Women and Right-Wing Movements: Indian Experiences*. Ed. Tanika Sarkar and Urvashi Butalia. London: Zed Books, 1995. 58–81.
- *The Other Side of Silence: Voices from the Partition of India*. New Delhi: Penguin, 1998.

Canning, Kathleen. 'Feminist History after the Linguistic Turn: Historicizing Discourse and Experience.' *Signs* 19.2 (1994): 368–404.
Caruth, Cathy. 'Introduction.' *Psycoanalysis, Culture, and Trauma*. Special Issue of *American Imago: Studies in Psychoanalysis and Culture* 48.4 (1991): 1–12.
– 'Trauma and Experience: Introduction.' *Trauma: Explorations in Memory*. Ed. Cathy Caruth. Baltimore: The Johns Hopkins University Press, 1995.
– *Unclaimed Experience: Trauma, Narrative and History*. Baltimore: The Johns Hopkins University Press, 1996.
Chakrabarty, Dipesh. 'Postcoloniality and the Artifice of History: Who Speaks for "Indian" Pasts?' *Representations* 37 (1992): 1–26.
– 'The Difference – Deferral of a Colonial Modernity: Public Debates on Domesticity in British Bengal.' *Subaltern Studies* 8 (1994): 50–88.
Chakravarti, Uma. 'Whatever Happened to the Vedic *Dasi*? Orientalism, Nationalism and a Script for the Past.' *Recasting Women: Essays in Colonial History*. Ed. Kumkum Sangari and Sudesh Vaid. New Delhi: Kali for Women, 1989. 27–87.
Chatterjee, Partha. *Nationalist Thought and the Colonial World: A Derivative Discourse*. London: Zed Press, 1986.
– 'The Nationalist Resolution to the Women's Question.' *Recasting Women*. Ed. Kumkum Sangari and Sudesh Vaid. New Deli: Kali for Women Press, 1989. 233–53.
– *The Nation and Its Fragments: Colonial and Postcolonial Histories*. Princeton: Princeton University Press, 1993.
Chelkowski, Peter J. 'Commentary: Laila and Majnun.' *Mirror of the Invisible World: Tales from the Khamseh of Nizami*. New York: Metropolitan Museum of Art. 1975. 49–68.
Chhachhi, Amrita. 'Forced Identities: The State, Communalism, Fundamentalism and Women in India.' *Woman, Islam, and the State*. Ed. Deniz Kandiyoti. Philadelphia: Temple University Press, 1992. 144–75.
Cleary, Joe. *Literature, Partition and the Nation State: Culture and Conflict in Ireland, Israel and Palestine*. Cambridge: Cambridge University Press, 2002.
Coppola, Carlo. 'The All India Progressive Writers' Association: The European Phase.' *Marxist Influences and South Asian Literature*. Ed. Carlo Coppola. Michigan: Michigan State University, 1974. 1–34.
Cowasjee, Saros, and K.S. Duggal, eds. *Orphans of the Storm: Stories on the Partition of India*. Trans. Jai Rattan. New Delhi: USBSD, 1995. Rept. *When the British Left: Stories on the Paritioning of India*. London: Arnold-Heinemann, 1987.
Das, Veena. 'Composition of the Personal Voice: Violence and Migration.' *Studies in History* 7.1 (1991): 65–77.

- *Critical Events.* New Delhi: Oxford University Press, 1994.
- 'Review of *Stories about the Partition of India.*' *Seminar* 420 August 1994: 56–8.
- 'Language and Body: Transactions in the Construction of Pain.' *Social Suffering.* Ed. A. Kleinman, V. Das, and M.M. Lock. Berkeley: University of California Press, 1997. 47–67.

Das, Veena, and Ashis Nandy. 'Violence, Victimhood and the Language of Silence.' *The Word and the World: Fantasy, Symbol and Record.* Ed. Veena Das. Delhi: Sage Press, 1986. 178–207.

de Certeau, Michel. *Heterologies: Discourse on the Other.* Trans. Brian Massumi. Minneapolis: University of Minnesota Press, 1986.

de Man, Paul. *Allegories of Reading: Figural Language in Rousseau, Nietzsche, Rilke, and Proust.* New Haven: Yale University Press, 1979.
- *The Resistance to Theory.* Minneapolis: University of Minnesota Press, 1986.

Derrida, Jacques. *Of Grammatology.* Trans. Gayatri Chakravorty Spivak. Baltimore: The Johns Hopkins University Press, 1974. Trans. of *De la Grammatologie.* Paris: Les Éditions de Minuit, 1967.

Desai, Anita. 'Introduction.' *Sunlight on a Broken Column.* Delhi: Penguin Books, 1961. v–xv.

Devi, Jyotirmoyee. *The River Churning.* Trans. Enakshi Chatterjee. New Delhi: Kali for Women Press, 1995. Trans. of *Itihashe Stree Parva.* Prabashi 1966.
- 'Beginnings.' *The River Churning.* Trans. Rimli Bhattacharya. Delhi: Kali for Women Press, 1995. vii–xxiv. Trans. of *'Amar lekhar gorar korina.'* Sakhi Sambad. 1969.
- *The Impermanence of Lies: Stories by Jyotirmoyee Devi.* Calcutta: Stree, 1998.

Devi, Mahasweta. 'Preface.' Trans. Rimi Chatterjee. *The Impermanence of Lies: Stories by Jyotirmoyee Devi.* Calcutta: Stree, 1998. Trans. of *'Jyuotirmoyee Devi. Shatbarsher Alotey.'* Jyotirmoyee Debir Rachana – Sankalan. Vol. 2. 1994.

Didur, Jill. 'Fragments of Imagination: Rethinking the Literary in Historiography through Narratives of India's Partition.' *Jouvert: A Journal of Postcolonial Studies* 1.2 (1997): 27 par. http://social.chass.ncsu.edu/jouvert/v1i2/Didur.htm.
- 'Cracking the Nation: Gender, Minorities and Agency in Bapsi Sidhwa's *Cracking India.*' *ARIEL: A Review of International English Literature* 29:3 (1998): 43–64.
- 'At a Loss for Words: Reading the Silence in South Asian Women's Partition Narratives.' *Topia: A Journal for Canadian Cultural Studies* 4 (2000): 53–71.
- 'Lifting the Veil? Reconsidering the Task of Literary Historiography.' *Interventions: International Journal of Postcolonial Studies* 3.3 (2001): 446–51.

Didur, Jill, and Teresa Heffernan. 'Revisiting the Subaltern in the New Empire.' *Cultural Studies* 17.1 (2003): 1–15.

Di Paolantonio, M.D. 'Loss in Present Terms: Reading the Limits of Post-dictatorship Argentina's National Conciliation.' *Between Hope and Despair: Pedagogy and the Remembrance of Historical Trauma*. Ed. R. Simon, S. Rosenberg, and C. Eppert. Lanham, MD: Rowman and Littlefield, 2000. 153–85.

Donzelot, Jaques. *The Policing of Families*. Trans. Robert Hurley. London: Hutchinson, 1980. Trans. of *La Police des familles*. Paris: Les Éditions de Minuit, 1977.

Duggal, K.S. *Twice Born, Twice Dead*. Trans. J. Ara. New Delhi: Orient Paperbacks, 1979.

Feldman, Jamila Linda Ruth. 'Mentioning the Unmentionable: Sexually Frustrated Wives in the Stories of Rajendar Singh Bedi.' *Bridging Worlds: Studies on Women in South Asia*. Delhi: Oxford University Press, 1991. 119–36.

Feldman, Shelley. 'Feminist Interruptions: The Silence of East Bengal in the Story of Partition.' *Interventions: International Journal of Postcolonial Studies* 1.2 (1999): 167–82.

Flemming, Leslie. '*Mahfil* interviews Ismat Chughtai.' *Mahfil* 8.2–3 (1972): 169–88.

– '*Mahfil* interviews Rajinder Singh Bedi.' *Mahfil* 8.1–2 (1972): 139–58.

– 'Riots and Refugees: The Post-Partition Stories of Saadat Hasan Manto.' *Journal of South Asian Literature* 13.4 (1978): 99–109.

– 'Progressive Writer, Progressive Filmmaker: The Films of Rajinder Singh Bedi.' *The Annual of Urdu Studies* 5 (1985): 81–97.

Foucault, Michel. *The History of Sexuality: An Introduction*. Trans. Robert Hurley. Vol. 1. New York: Random House, 1980. Trans. of *Histoire de la sexualité*. Rept. *La Volenté de savoir*. Paris: Gallimard, 1976.

– 'The Subject and Power.' *Critical Inquiry* 8 (1992): 777–95.

Francisco, Jason. 'In the Heat of Fratricide: The Literature of India's Partition Burning Freshly.' *The Annual of Urdu Studies*. 11 (1996): 227–50.

Gandhi, Mohandas K. '37 Speech at Prayer Meeting.' *Collected Works of Mahatma Gandhi*. Vol. 76. Delhi: Publications Division, Ministry of Information and Broadcasting, Govt. of India, 1958–94. 26–7.

– '223 Speech at Prayer Meeting.' *Collected Works of Mahatma Gandhi*. Vol. 89. Delhi: Publications Division, Ministry of Information and Broadcasting, Govt. of India, 1958–94. 200–2.

George, Rosemary Marangoly. *Burning Down the House: Recycling Domesticity*. Boulder: Westview Press, 1998.

Ghosh, Amitav. *The Shadow Lines*. Delhi: Ravi Dayal, 1988.

Gupta, Ashoka, and Anjali Chatterjee. 'Note by the Author's Daughters.' *The Impermanence of Lies: Stories by Jyotirmoyee Devi*. Calcutta: Stree, 1998. v–viii.

Hai, Ambreen. 'Border Work, Border Trouble: Postcolonial Feminism and the Ayah in Bapsi Sidhwa's *Cracking India.*' *Modern Fiction Studies* 46.2 (2000): 379–426.

Hans, S.S. 'The Partition Novels of Nanak Singh.' *Myth and Reality.* Ed. Ravinder Kumar. Delhi: Nehru Memorial Museum and Library, 1984. 365–77.

Haraway, Donna J. 'Promises of Monsters: A Regenerative Politics for Inappropriate/d Others.' *Cultural Studies* Ed. Lawrence Grossberg, Cary Nelson, and Paula A. Treichler. New York: Routledge, 1992. 295–337.

Harganvi, Manazir Aashiq. *Ankhon Dekhi Bhagalpur ke Bhayanak Fasad ko dekhne ke baad.* Bhagalpur: Maktaba Kohsar, 1989.

Hargrove, Anne. 'South Asian Women's Communal Identities.' *Economic and Political Weekly* 30 September 1995: 2427–30.

Hasan, Mushirul, ed. *India's Partition: Process, Strategy, and Mobilization.* New Delhi: Oxford University Press, 1993.

– *India Partitioned: The Other Face of Freedom.* Vols. I and II. Delhi: Roli Books, 1995.

Haynes, Douglas. 'From Tribute to Philanthropy: The Politics of Gift Giving in a Western Indian City.' *The Journal of Asian Studies* 46.2 (1987): 459–92.

Haynes, Douglas, and Gyan Prakash, eds. *Contesting Power: Resistance and Everyday Social Relations in South Asia.* New Delhi: Oxford University Press, 1991.

Heffernan, Teresa. 'The (Post)apocalypse and the Reflexive Text.' Diss. University of Toronto, 1995.

Hogan, Patrick Colm. 'The Economics of Cultural Identity: Attia Hosain's *SunLight on a Broken Column.*' *Colonialism and Cultural Identity: Crises of Tradition in the Anglophone Literatures of India, Africa and the Caribbean.* SUNY Press, 2000. 257–302.

Hosain, Attia. *Phoenix Fled and Other Stories.* London: Chatoo & Windus, 1953.

– *Sunlight on a Broken Column.* New Delhi: Penguin Books India, 1961.

– 'Journey to No End.' *Wasafiri* 26 (1997): 64–5.

– 'Deep Roots.' *Voices of the Crossing: The Impact of Britain on Writers from Asia, the Caribbean and Africa.* Ed. Ferdinand Dennis and Naseem Khan. London: Serpent's Tail, 2000. 19–27.

– 'Second Thoughts: Light in Divided Worlds.' *Attia Hosain: A Diptych Volume.* Ed. R.K. Kaul and Jasbir Jain. Delhi: Rawat Publications, 2001. 218–19.

Hurtado, Aida. 'Relating to Privilege: Seduction and Rejection in the Subordination of White Women and Women of Color.' *Signs* 14.4 (1989): 833–55.

Jain, Naresh. 'The Muslim Polyphony in Attia Hosain's *Sunlight on a Broken Column.*' *Pangs of Partition, Vol. II: The Human Dimension.* Ed. S. Settar and

Indira Baptista Gupta. Delhi: Indian Council of Historical Research, 2002. 283–90.

Jain, N.K. 'The Partition Theme in Indo-Anglian Novels.' *Myth and Reality*. Ed. Ravinder Kumar. Delhi: Nehru Memorial Museum and Library, 1984. 378–93.

Jalal, Ayesha. 'The Convenience of Subservience: Women and the State of Pakistan.' *Women, Islam, and the State*. Ed. Deniz Kandiyoti. Philadelphia: Temple University Press, 1992. 77–113.

– *The Sole Spokesman: Jinnah, the Muslim League and the Demand for Pakistan*. Cambridge: Cambridge University Press, 1994.

– 'Secularists, Subalterns and the Stigma of "Communalism": Partition Historiography Revisited.' *The Indian Economic and Social History Review* 33.1 (1996): 93–104.

Jameson, Frederic. 'World Literature in an Age of Multinational Capitalism.' *The Current in Criticism*. Ed. Clayton Koelb and Virgil Lokke. West Lafayette: Purdue University Press, 1987. 139–58.

Jauch, Michael. 'Witnessing Violence: Perspectives on Sa'adat Hasan Manot's "Khol Do" and Rajinder Singh Bedi's "Lajvanti."' *The Annual of Urdu Studies* 13 (1998): 189–202.

Jayawardena, Kumari. *Feminism and Nationalism in the Third World*. London: Zed Books, 1986.

Jussawalla, Feroza. 'Bapsi Sidhwa.' *Interviews with Writers of the Postcolonial World*. Ed. Feroza Jusawalla and Reed Dasenbrock. Jackson: University Press of Mississippi, 1992. 197–221.

– 'Bapsi Sidhwa.' *South Asian Novelists in English*. Ed. Jaina C. Sanga. Westport, CT: Greenwood Press, 2003.

Kamra, Sukeshi. *Bearing Witness: Partition, Independence, End of the Raj*. Calgary: University of Calgary Press, 2002.

Kanaganayakam, Chelva. 'Interview with Bapsi Sidhwa.' *The Toronto South Asian Review* (1992): 43–52.

Katrak, Ketu. 'Decolonizing Culture: Toward a Theory for Postcolonial Women's Texts.' *Modern Fiction Studies* 55.1 (1989): 157–79.

– 'Indian Nationalism, Gandhian "Satyagraha" and Representations of Female Sexuality.' *Nationalism and Sexuality*. Ed. Andrew Parker. New York: Routledge, 1992. 395–406.

Kaul, R.K., and Jasbir Jain. *Attia Hosain: A Diptych Volume*. Delhi: Rawat Publications, 2001.

Kaul, Suvir. *The Partitions of Memory: The Afterlife of the Division of India*. Bloomington: Indiana University Press, 2001.

Khan, Omar. 'Attia Hosain: Interview, May 19, 1991.' *Harappa*. 23 August 2004. http://www.harappa.com/attia/growingup.html.

Khosla, G.D. *Stern Reckoning: A Survey of Events Leading up to and Following the Partition of India*. Delhi: Oxford University Press, 1948.
Kishwar, Madhu. 'Gandhi on Women.' *Economic and Political Weekly* 5 October 1985: 1691–1702; 12 October 1985: 1753–8.
– 'Codified Hindu Law: Myth and Reality.' *Economic and Political Weekly* 29.33 13 August 1994: 2145–61.
– 'From Manusmriti to Madhusmriti: Flagellating a Mythical Enemy.' *Manushi* 117 (2000): 1–5.
Kumar, Radha. *The History of Doing: An Illustrated Account of Movements for Women's Rights and Feminism in India 1880–1990*. London: Verso, 1993.
Lal, Vinay. 'Genocide, Barbaric Others, and the Violence of Categories: A Response to Omer Bartov.' *American Historical Review* 103.4 (1998): 1187–90.
–'Partitioned Selves, Partitioned Pasts: A Commentary on Ashis Nandy's *Death of an Empire*.' *Manas*. 5 March 2004. http://www.sscnet.ucla.edu/southasia/History/Independent/Partitionselves.html.
'Leaguers Meet Mr. Gandhi.' *Times of India* 8 March 1947: 7.
Liddle, Joanna, and Rama Joshi. *Daughters of Independence: Gender, Caste and Class in India*. New Jersey: Rutgers University Press, 1986.
Loomba, Ania. *Colonialism/Postcolonialism*. New York: Routledge, 1998.
Ludden, David. *Making India Hindu: Religion, Community and the Politics of Democracy in India*. Delhi: Oxford University Press, 1996.
Lüdtke, Alf. 'Organizational Order or *Eigensinn*? Workers' Privacy and Workers' Politics in Imperial Germany.' *Rites of Power, Symbolism, Ritual and Politics since the Middle Ages*. Ed. Sean Wilentz. Philadelphia: Temple University Press, 1985. 303–33.
Luhrmann, Tanya. *The Good Parsi: The Fate of a Postcolonial Elite*. Boston: Harvard University Press, 1996.
Lyotard, J. *The Differend: Phrases in Dispute*. Minneapolis: University of Minnesota Press, 1988.
Mahmud, Shabana '*Angāre* and the Founding of the Progressive Writers' Association.' *Modern Asian Studies* 30.2 (1996): 447–67.
Major, Andrew J. '"The Chief Sufferers": Abduction of Women during the Partition of the Punjab.' *South Asia* 18 (1995): 57–72.
Malgonkar, Manohar. *A Bend in the Ganges*. London: Hamish Hamilton, 1964.
Mani, Lata. 'Contentious Traditions: The Debate on *Sati* in Colonial India.' *Recasting Women: Essays in Colonial History*. Ed. Kumkum Sangari and Sudesh Vaid. New Delhi: Kali for Women Press, 1989. 88–126.
– 'Multiple Mediations: Feminist Scholarship in the Age of Multinational Reception.' *Feminist Review* 55 (1990): 24–41.
– 'Cultural Theory, Colonial Texts: Reading Eyewitness Accounts of Widow

Burning.' *Cultural Studies*. Ed. Lawrence Grossberg, Cary Nelson, and Paula Treichler. New York: Routledge, 1992. 392–408.

Mann, Harveen Sachdeva. '"Cracking India": Minority Women Writers and the Contentious Margins of Indian Nationalist Discourse.' *The Journal of Commonwealth Literature* 24.2 (1994): 71–94.

– '"The Magic Idyll of Antiquated India": Patriarchal Nationalism in R.K. Narayan's Fiction.' *ARIEL: A Review of International English Literature* 31.3 (2000): 1–17.

– 'South Asian Partition Literature and the Gendered Rape and Silence of the National Body.' *South Asian Review* 12 (2001): 3–22.

Manto, Saadat Hasan. 'Toba Tek Singh.' *Manto ke Numaindah Afsaneh*. Ed. Atahar Parvev. New Delhi: Aligarh, 1981.

McClintock, Anne. 'Family Feuds: Gender Nationalism and the Family.' *Feminist Review* 44 (1993): 61–80.

Mehta, Uday S. 'Liberal Strategies of Exclusion.' *Politics and Society* 18.4 (1990): 427–54.

Memon, Muhammad Umar. 'Partition Literature: A Study of Intizar Husain.' *Modern Asian Studies* 14.3 (1980): 377–410.

– *An Epic Unwritten: The Penguin Book of Partition Stories from Urdu*. Delhi: Penguin Books, 1998.

Menon, Ritu. *No Woman's Land: Women from Pakistan, India and Bangladesh Write on the Partition of India*. Delhi: Women Unlimited, 2004.

Menon, Ritu, and Kamla Bhasin. 'Recovery, Rupture, Resistance: India State and Abduction of Women during Partition.' *Economic and Political Weekly* 24 April 1993: WS2–11.

– 'Abducted Women, the State and Questions of Honour.' *Embodied Violence: Communalizing Women's Sexuality in South Asia*. Ed. Kumari Jayawardena and Malathi de Alwis. London: Zed Books, 1996. 1–31.

– *Borders and Boundaries: Women in India's Partition*. New Brunswick, NJ: Rutgers University Press, 1998.

Metcalf, Barbara. *Perfecting Women: Maulana Sharaf Ali Thanawi's Bihishti Zewar: A Partial Translation with Commentary*. Berkeley: University of California Press, 1990.

– 'Reading and Writing about Muslim Women in British India.' *Forging Identities: Gender, Communities and the State in India*. Ed. Zoya Hasan. Boulder: Westview Press, 1994. 1–21.

Metcalf, Barbara D., and Thomas R. Metcalf. *A Concise History of India*. Cambridge: Cambridge University Press, 2002.

Mill, James. *The History of British India*. 10 vols. 5th ed. London: J. Madden, 1858.

Miller, J. Hillis. *The Ethics of Reading: Kant, de Man, Eliot, Trollope, James, and Benjamin*. New York: Columbia University Press, 1987.
Montenegro, David. 'Bapsi Sidhwa: An Interview.' *The Massachusetts Review* 31 (1990): 513–33.
Mookerjea, Debali. '"That Little Boy": An English Translation of Jyotirmoyee Devi's Bengali Short Story "Shei Chheleta."' *Meridians: Feminism, Race, Transnationalism* 2.2 (2002): 128–45. Trans. of 'Shei Chheleta.' *Prabasi* 1962.
Mookerjea-Leonard, Debali. 'Disenfranchised Bodies: Jyotirmoyee Devi's Writings on the Partition.' *Genders* 38 (2003): 46 par., 9 January 2004. http://www.genders.org/g38/g38_leonard.html.
Morris, Meaghan. 'Metamorphosis at Sydney Tower.' *New Formations* 11 (1990): 5–18.
Morrison, Toni. 'In the Realm of Responsibility.' *The Women's Review of Books* March 1988: 5–6.
Mouffe, Chantal. 'Feminism, Citizenship and Radical Democratic Politics.' *Feminists Theorize the Political*. Ed. Joan W. Scott and Judith Butler. New York: Routledge, 1992. 74–89.
Mufti, Aamir R. 'Auerbach in Istanbul: Edward Said, Secular Criticism, and the Question of Minority Culture.' *Edward Said and the Work of the Critic: Speaking Truth to Power*. Durham: Duke University Press, 2000. 229–56.
– 'A Greater Story-Writer than God: Genre, Gender and Minority in Late Colonial India.' *Subaltern Studies 9*. New York: Columbia University Press, 2002. 1–36.
Mukherjee, A. 'Devi, Jyotirmoyee.' *Encyclopaedia of Indian Literature*. Ed. Devraj-Jyoti. Vol. 2. Delhi: Sahitya Akademi, 1987. 942–3.
Mukherjee, Arun Prabha. *Oppositional Aesthetics: Readings from a Hyphenated Space*. Toronto: TSAR Publications, 1995.
Mukherjee, Meenakshi. *Twice Born Fiction: Themes and Techniques of the Indian Novel in English*. Delhi: Heinemann, 1971.
– 'Pawn in the Game.' *The Book Review* 18.12 (1994):14–15.
Muller, F. Max. *History of Sanskrit Literature*. London: Longmans Green, 1859.
– *Chips from a German Workshop*. 4 vols. London, 1867–75.
Nabar, Vrinda. 'Fragmenting Nations and Lives: *Sunlight on a Broken Column*.' *Literature and the Nation: Britain and India 1800–1990*. Ed. Richard Allen and Harish Trivedi. London: Routledge, 2000. 121–37.
Nahal, Chaman. *Azadi*. New Delhi: Orient Paperbacks, 1975.
Nairn, Tom. *The Break-Up of Britain*. 2nd ed. London: Verso, 1977.
Nandy, Ashis. 'The Invisible Holocaust and the Journey as an Exodus: The Poisoned Village and the Stranger City.' *Postcolonial Studies* 2.3 (1999): 305–29.

Narayan, R.K. *Waiting for the Mahatma*. Chennai: Indian Thought Publications, 1999.
Nasta, Susheila. 'Points of Departure: Early Visions of "Home" and "Abroad."' *Home Truths: Fictions of the South Asian Diaspora in Britain*. New York: Palgrave, 2002. 15–55.
Needham, Anuradha Dingwaney. 'Multiple Forms of (National) Belonging: Attia Hosain's Sunlight on a Broken Column.' *Modern Fiction Studies* 39.1 (1993): 93–111.
Oldenburg, Veena Talwar. *The Making of Colonial Lucknow: 1856–1857*. Princeton: Princeton University Press, 1994.
Ortner, Sherry B. 'Resistance and the Problem of Ethnographic Refusal.' *The Historic Turn in the Human Sciences*. Ed. Terrence J. McDonald. Ann Arbor: University of Michigan Press, 1996. 281–304.
Palakeel, Thomas 'Partition Stories: Epic Fragments and Revenge Tragedies.' *The Annual of Urdu Studies* 16 (2001): 329–44.
Pandey, Gyanendra. 'In Defence of the Fragment: Writing about Hindu-Muslim Riots in India Today.' *Economic and Political Weekly* March 1991: 559–72.
– *The Construction of Communalism in Colonial North India*. Delhi: Oxford University Press, 1992.
– 'The Prose of Otherness.' *Subaltern Studies* 8 (1994): 188–221.
– 'Community and Violence: Recalling Partition.' *Economic and Political Weekly* August 1997: 2037–45.
– 'Partition and Independence in Delhi: 1947–48.' *Economic and Political Weekly* 6 September 1997: 2261–72.
– *Remembering Partition: Violence, Nationalism and History in India*. London: Cambridge University Press, 2001.
Parle's Gluco Biscuits. *The Times of India* 3 November 1947: 1.
– 'Parle Story: Introduction.' Parle company website. 25 August 2004. http://www.parleproducts.com/parlestory.html.
– 'TV/Press Ads.' Parle company website. 25 August 2004. http://www.parleproducts.com/adcampaigns.html.
Poovey, Mary. 'Feminism and Deconstruction.' *Feminist Studies* 14.1 (1988): 51–65.
Prakash, Gyan. 'The Modern Nation's Return in the Archaic.' *Critical Inquiry* 23 (1997): 536–56.
Prasad, Madhava. 'On the Question of a Theory of (Third World) Literature.' *Social Text* 31.32 (1992): 57–83.
Prashad, Vijay. 'The Untouchable Question.' *Economic and Political Weekly* 2 March 1996: 551–9.

Qidwai, Anees. *Azadi ki Chhaon Mein*. New Delhi: National Book Trust, 1990.
Rahman, Tariq. 'Critical Prejudices to Aspects of Partition Literature: Universal versus Ethnocentric Values.' *Toronto South Asian Review* 11.1 (1992): 69–78.
Randhawa, Mohindar Singh. *Out of the Ashes: An Account of the Rehabilitation of Refugees from West Pakistan in Rural Area of East Punjab*. Chandigarh: Public Relations Department, 1954.
Rao, Ravishankar. Crossing the Barrier: A Study of Partition Fiction. Diss. Mangalore University, April 2003.
Ray, Sangeeta. 'Gender and the Discourse of Nationalism in Anita Desai's *Clear Light of Day*.' *Genders* 20 (1994): 96–119.
– *En-Gendering India: Woman and Nation in Colonial and Postcolonial Narratives*. Durham: Duke University Press, 2000.
Raychaudhuri, Tapan. *Perceptions, Emotions, Sensibilities: Essays in India's Colonial and Post-Colonial Experiences*. New Delhi: Oxford University Press, 1999.
Richman, Paula. *Many Rāmāyanas: The Diversity of a Narrative Tradition in South Asia*. Berkeley: University of California Press, 1991.
Rose, Sonya O. 'Text and Context: A "Double Vision" as Historical Method.' Paper presented at the annual conference of the Social Science History Association, New Orleans, 1–3 November 1991.
Rouse, Shahnaz. 'Gender, Nationalism(s) and Cultural Identity: Discursive Strategies and Exclusivities.' *Embodied Violence: Communalizing Women's Sexuality in South Asia*. Ed. Kumari Jaywardena and Malathi de Alwis. London: Zed Books, 1996. 43–69.
Roy, Parama. *Indian Traffic: Identities in Question in Colonial and Postcolonial India*. Berkeley: University of California Press, 1998.
Roychaudhury, Subir, and Abhijit Sen. *Rachana Sankalan*. Calcutta: School of Women Studies, Jadavpur University, 1991.
Sahni, Bhisham. *Tamas*. Trans. Jai Ratan. Rev. ed. New Delhi: Penguin Books India, 1988. Rept. of *Kites Will Fly*. Trans. of *Tamas*. 1974.
– *Tamas*. Trans. Bhisham Sahni. New Delhi: Penguin Books India, 2001. Trans. of *Tamas*, 1974.
Saint, Ravikant and Tarun K. Saint, eds. *Translating Partition*. Delhi: Katha Books, 2001.
Sangari, Kumkum. 'Consent, Agency and Rhetorics of Incitement.' *Economic and Political Weekly* May 1 1993: 867–82.
Sangari, Kumkum, and Sudesh Vaid, eds. *Recasting Women: Essays in Colonial History*. Delhi: Kali for Women, 1989.
Sarkar, Sumit. 'The Condition and Nature of Subaltern Militancy: Bengal from

Swadeshi to Non-cooperation, c. 1905–1922.' *Subaltern Studies* 3 (1988): 271–320.
Sarkar, Tanika. *Hindu Wife, Hindu Nation: Community, Religion, and Cultural Nationalism*. London: Hurst & Company, 2001.
Scott, Joan W. 'The Evidence of Experience.' *Critical Inquiry* 17 (1991): 773–97.
Seminar: Memories of Partition 420 (1994).
Seminar: Porous Borders, Divided Selves: A Symposium on Partitions in the East 510 (2002).
Settar, S., and Indira Baptista Gupta, eds. *Pangs of Partition*, vol. 2: *The Human Dimension*. Manohar: Indian Council of Historical Research, 2002.
Sidhwa, Bapsi. *Cracking India*. Minneapolis: Milkweed Editions, 1991. Rpt. of *Ice-Candy Man*. London: William Heinemann, 1988.
Simon, R. 'Testimony as Aesthetics: Teaching and the Interminable Working through of Collective Remembrance.' Conference paper delivered 29 December 1996 at the Modern Language Association Convention, in Washington, DC.
– 'The Paradoxical Practice of Zakhor: Memories of "What Has Never Been My Fault or Deed."' *Between Hope and Despair: Pedagogy and the Remembrance of Historical Trauma*. Ed. R. Simon, S. Rosenberg, and C. Eppert. Maryland: Rowman and Littlefield, 2000. 9–25.
Simon, R., C. Eppert, M. Clamen, and L. Beres. 'Witness-As-Study: The Difficult Inheritance of Testimony.' *The Review of Education/Pedagogy/Cultural Studies* 22.4 (2002): 285–322.
Simon, R., S. Rosenberg, and C. Eppert. 'Introduction: The Pedagogical Encounter of Historical Remembrance.' *Between Hope and Despair: Pedagogy and the Remembrance of Historical Trauma*. Ed. R. Simon, S. Rosenberg, and C. Eppert. Maryland: Rowman and Littlefield, 2000.
Singh, Anita Inder. *The Origins of the Partition of India*. Delhi: Oxford University Press, 1987.
Singh, Khushwant. *Train to Pakistan*. New Delhi: Ravi Dayal Publisher, 1956.
Singh, Kirpal. *Partition of the Punjab*. Patiala: Punjabi University, 1972.
Singh, Mangal. 'Our Honour, Their Honour.' *Seminar* 420 (1994): 17–19.
Singh, Sujala. 'Nationalism's Brandings: Women's Bodies and Narratives of the Partition.' *Comparing Postcolonial Literatures: Dislocations*. New York: Macmillian: St Martin's Press, 2000. 122–33.
Sinha, Mrinalini. *Colonial Masculinity: The 'Manly Englishman' and the 'Effeminate Bengali' in the Late Nineteenth Century*. Manchester: Manchester University Press, 1995.
Skurski, Julie. 'The Ambiguities of Authenticity in Latin America: *Dona Barbara* and the Construction of National Identity.' *Poetics Today* 15.5 (1994): 604–42.

Spivak, Gayatri Chakravorty. 'A Literary Representation of the Subaltern: A Woman's Text from the Third World.' *In Other Worlds: Essays in Cultural Politics*. New York: Routledge, 1988. 241–68.
– 'Can the Subaltern Speak?' *Marxism and the Interpretation of Culture*. Ed. Cary Nelson and Lawrence Grossberg. Illinois: University of Illinois Press, 1989. 271–313.
– 'The Post-modern Condition: The End of Politics.' *The Postcolonial Critic: Interviews, Strategies, Dialogues*. Ed. Sarah Harasym. New York: Routledge, 1990. 17–34.
– *A Critique of Postcolonial Reason*. Cambridge, Massachusetts: Harvard University Press, 1999.
– 'Thinking Cultural Questions in "Pure" Literary Terms.' *Without Guarantees: In Honour of Stuart Hall*. Ed. Paul Gilroy et al. London: Verso, 2000. 335–57.
Srinivasan K.S. *Ramayana as Told by Valmiki and Kamban*. New Delhi: Abhinav Publications, 1994.
Stoler, Ann Laura. *Race and the Education of Desire*. Durham: Duke University Press, 1995.
Sunder-Rajan, Rajeswari. 'Life after Rape: Narrative, Rape and Feminism.' *Real and Imagined Women: Gender, Culture and Postcolonialism*. London: Routledge, 1993. 64–82.
Swann, Karen. 'The Social and Political Construction of Reality.' Paper presented January 1991 at the Little Three Faculty Colloquium at Wesleyan University.
Talbot, Ian. 'Literature and the Human Drama of the 1947 Partition.' *South Asia* 18 (1995): 37–56.
– *Freedom's Cry: The Popular Dimension in the Pakistan Movement and Partition Experience in North-West India*. Karachi: Oxford University Press, 1996.
Thanawi, Maulana Ashraf Ali. *Bihishti Zewar*. Lahore: Taj Company, 1923.
Thapar, Romila. 'Some Appropriations of the Theory of Aryan Race Relating to the Beginnings of Indian History.' *Invoking the Past: The Uses of History in South Asia*. Ed. Daud Ali. Delhi: Oxford University Press, 1999. 15–35.
Tharu, Susie. 'Rendering Account of the Nation: Partition Narratives and Other Genres of the Passive Revolution.' *Oxford Literary Review* 16.1–2 (1994): 69–91.
Tharu, Susie, and K. Lalita, eds. *Women Writing in India 600 B.C. to the Early 20th Century*. 2 vols. New York: The Feminist Press, 1991.
Verma, Balraj. 'Rajinder Singh Bedi.' *The Encyclopaedia of Indian Literature*. Vol. 1. Ed. A. Dev. Delhi: Sahitya Akademi, 1987. 411.
Voight, Johannes H. *Max Muller: The Man and His Ideas*. Calcutta: Firma K.L. Mukhopadhyay, 1967.

Walcott, Rinaldo. '"Middle Passages," Articulating Race and Trauma: Possibilities, Limits, Stakes.' MLA Convention, Royal York Hotel, Toronto, 28 December 1997.

Walkowitz, Judith R., Myra Jehlen, and Bell Chevigny. 'Patrolling the Borders: Feminist Historiography and the New Historicism.' *Radical History Review* 43 (1989): 23–42.

Walsh, Judith E. *Domesticity in Colonial India: What Women Learned When Men Gave Them Advice*. New York: Rowman and Littlefield, 2004.

Weedon, Chris. *Feminist Practice and Poststructuralist Theory*. Oxford and New York: Basil Blackwell, 1987.

White, Hayden. *The Content of the Form: Narrative Discourse and Historical Representation*. Baltimore: Johns Hopkins University Press, 1987.

Whitehead, Andrew. 'Cross-channel: *The River Churning*.' *Biblio: A Review of Books* 2:9 (1996): 19.

– 'History on the Line: Bapsi Sidhwa and Urvashi Butalia Discuss the Partition of India.' *History Workshop Journal* 50 (2000): 230–238.

Winant, Howard. 'Interview: Gayatri Spivak on the Politics of the Subaltern.' *Socialist Review* 90.3 (1990): 81–97.

Woolf, Virgina. *A Room of One's Own*. London: Granada Publishing, 1983.

Wyrick, Deborah. 'Editor's Introduction.' *Jouvert: A Journal of Postcolonial Studies* 1.2 (1997): 16 par. 4 June 2004. http://social.chass.ncsu.edu/jouvert/v1i2/int12.htm.

Yeğenoğlu, Meyda. *Colonial Fantasies: Towards a Feminist Reading of Orientalism*. Cambridge: Cambridge University Press 1998.

Index

abducted women, 9, 11, 12, 15, 17, 18, 19, 24, 36–40, 44, 51–4, 56–8, 60, 61–6, 68–9, 73, 88–92, 126, 129, 131–56
Ahmad, Aijaz, 64
Amin, Sonia Nishat, 104–5
Anand, Mulk Raj, 96, 100, 112
Anderson, Benedict, 14, 25–6, 40

Bacchetta Paola, 168n8
Bagchi, Jashodhara, 126, 136, 147; and Suhoranjan Dasgupta, 128
Bahri, Deepika, 135–8
Bangladesh, 6, 128
Basu, Tapan, and Pradip Datta, Sumit Sarkar, and Sambbudha Sen, 177n8
Bedi, Rajinder Singh, 13, 17, 44, 57–66, 127, 157, 169n2, 170nn15, 17, 171n19; biographical information, 57–8; *Lajwanti*, 13, 17, 44, 57–66, 126, 169n2, 170nn14, 15, 17, 171nn19, 20, 173n10; on the Progressive Writers' Association (PWA), 58–9
Bengal, 2, 19, 23, 74, 102, 108, 127–9, 167n3, 170–1n18, 177nn5, 6, 178n13

Bhabha, Homi K., 39–41, 158–9
Bhalla, Alok, 4, 6, 9, 65–6, 166nn7, 9, 169n2, 170n14, 171n19, 179n18
Bharucha, Nulifer E., 99, 118
Bhatia, Nandi, 68, 172n3
Bondi, Laura, 98, 112, 121
Bose, Sugata, and Ayesha Jalal, 161, 175–6n1
Burton, Antoinette, 5, 94, 96–8, 106, 112, 114, 119, 121, 122
Butalia, Urvashi, 4, 6, 14, 36, 38, 39, 44, 55, 63, 70, 125, 129, 131–3, 144, 148, 167n15

Canning, Kathleen, 36, 44, 56–7, 68, 78, 80
Caruth, Cathy, 137–9, 142
Chakrabarty, Dipesh, 36, 39, 61, 66, 130–2, 168n16, 170–1n18, 180n22
Chakravarti, Uma, 29–32, 167n3, 168n10
Chatterjee, Partha, 16, 23–4, 26–9, 102, 109–10, 126, 167nn3, 5, 176n3
Chelkowski, Peter J., 113
Chhachhi, Amrita, 35–6, 108
Cleary, Joe, 5, 26–7

198   Index

communalism, 4, 8–98, 57, 165n5, 169n8
conduct manuals, 18, 29–32, 103–5, 107
Coppola, Carlo, 170n16, 173n5
Cowasjee, Saros, and K.S. Duggal, 4, 10

Das, Veena, 11–12, 14, 36, 44, 55, 66, 125, 129, 131, 132, 140–1, 144–6, 149, 167nn14, 15, 169n9, 175–6n1, 178n12, 179n20
de Certeau, Michel, 46
de Man, Paul, 43, 50
Derrida, Jacques, 41
Desai, Anita, 96, 97
Didur, Jill, 172n3; and Teresa Heffernan, 79, 166–7n13
Di Paolantonio, M.D., 125, 139
Donzelot, Jacques, 149
Duggal, K.S., 4, 45–6

experience as evidence, 46–50, 55–6, 134–6, 155–6, 158

Feldman, Jamila Linda Ruth, 58–9, 170n17
Feldman, Shelley, 129
Flemming, Leslie, 58–9, 98
Foucault, Michel, 63, 85
Francisco, Jason, 166n9

Gandhi, Mohandas, 3, 7, 21, 32–4, 70, 77–8, 108, 122, 145–6; on nationalism, 3, 7, 21, 32–4, 77–8, 108, 122, 145–6; and partition, 3, 7; on women's sexuality, 3, 7, 32–4, 145–6
gender, 6–7, 11, 13, 15–20, 21–41, 51, 57, 64, 68, 79, 81–2, 84, 87, 94–5, 102–4, 106, 109, 126–7, 131–2, 149, 151, 155, 156, 157, 159, 167nn3, 5, 168n13, 170–1n18, 173n3, 175n15, 177n6
George, Rosemary Marangoly, 173n1
Ghosh, Amitav, 165n6
Gupta, Ashoka, 8; and Anjali Chatterjee, 126–7

Hai, Ambreen, 69, 71, 80, 87–8, 90–1, 126
Hans, S.S., 166n10
Haraway, Donna J., 50–1
Harganvi, Manazir Aashiq, 48–52, 169n7
Hargrove, Anne, 13
Hasan, Mushirul, 4–5, 166n9
Haynes, Douglas, 75; and Gyan Prakash, 81
Heffernan, Teresa, 139
Hinduism, 12, 17–18, 23, 28–32, 35–6, 42, 46, 53, 59, 71, 75, 86, 89, 101–3, 108, 111–12, 118, 127–8, 132, 142, 144–9, 150–6, 159, 160, 165n5, 167n5, 168nn11, 12, 170–1n18, 175–6n1, 177n8, 177–8nn10, 11, 178–9n15
Hindu revivalism, 29–32, 103, 108
historical memory, 129–31, 136–7; amanuensis, 137; anagnorisis, 130, 156; anamnesis, 129, 155
historiography, 7, 12, 16–17, 19, 42–4, 48–57, 64, 130–1, 136–8, 158, 166n11
Hogan, Patrick Colm, 99, 113, 118, 123, 173n5, 173–4n6, 174n11, 175n15
Hosain, Attia, 13, 18, 94–124, 157, 173nn2–5, 174n12, 175nn15, 16; Mulk Raj Anand, 96, 100; 'Deep Roots,' 97; early life; 97–8; and

partition, 96–7, 119–20, 122, 124, 173nn2, 3; *Phoenix Fled*, 112, 173n3; PWA; 98–9; romance 101, 102, 111–13, 117–19, 121, 123–4, 174–5n12; *Sunlight on a Broken Column*, 13, 18, 94–124, 173n10, 173–4n6; use of English, 99, 111–13

Islam, 3, 35, 104–6, 113–14, 123–4, 174n10; Muslim reform, 18, 28, 94–5, 102–13, 115–18, 170–1n18, 174n10

Jain, Naresh, 173–4n6
Jain, N.K., 166n10
Jalal, Ayesha, 52–4, 103–4, 169n8, 174n9
Jauch, Michael, 170n15
Jayawardena, Kumari, 32
Jussawalla, Feroza, 70, 90
Jyotirmoyee Devi, 13, 19, 38, 126–9, 136, 141–4, 147–56, 157, 165n1, 175–6n1, 176nn2, 3, 177n5, 178–9n15, 179nn19, 21; biographical information, 126–7; *The River Churning*, 13, 19, 38, 126–56, 157; women's issues; 126–7

Kamra, Sukeshi, 166nn7, 12
Kanaganayakam, Chelva, 137
Katrak, Ketu, 32–3
Kaul, R.K., 173–4n6
Kaul, Suvir, 6–8, 173n2
Khan, Omar, 96–100, 106, 167n5
Kishwar, Madhu, 168n13, 178n11
Kumar, Radha, 33–4, 167n5

Lal, Vinay, 177n9
Liddle, Joanna, and Rama Joshi, 34–5
literariness, 10, 13, 20, 43, 50

Loomba, Ania, 14
Ludden, David, 165n5
Lüdtke, Alf, 56
Luhrmann, Tanya, 74–6, 78
Lyotard J., 134–5, 139, 141, 155

Mahasweta Devi, 127
Mahmud, Shabana, 99, 165n6
Malgonkar, Manohar, 165n6
Mani, Lata, 67, 72
Mann, Harveen, 167n1, 172n3, 173n3
Manto, Saadat Hasan, 4, 9, 15–16, 54–5, 59, 166n10, 170nn12, 15; and partition 54–5
McClintock, Anne, 27
Memon, Muhammad, 4, 166nn9, 10, 169n2
Menon, Ritu, 36, 131, 169n9; and Kamla Bhasin: 4, 6, 24, 36–8, 44, 51–2, 55, 125, 131–2, 153, 160–1, 167nn14, 15, 180n1
Metcalf, Barbara, 103, 106, 174nn9, 10
Metcalf, Barbara D., and Thomas R. Metcalf, 165n4
Mill, James, 30
Miller, J. Hillis, 6
Montenegro, David, 70, 90, 172n6
Mookerjea, Debali, 34, 177n5, 179n21
Mookerjea-Leonard, Debali, 127, 128, 147, 150, 152, 165n1, 175–6n1, 176–7n4, 178n11, 179n19
Morris, Meaghan, 131
Mufti, Aamir R., 15–16, 42, 59
Mukherjee, A., 127
Mukherjee, Meenakshi, 121, 129
Muller, F. Max, 29–31, 168n10

Nabar, Vrinda, 97–8, 100, 114, 173–4n6

Nahal, Chaman, 165n6
Nandy, Ashis, 166n12, 177n9
Narayan, R.K., 21, 167n1
Nasta, Susheila, 94, 100, 121, 173–4n6
nationalism, 5–6, 15, 16–17, 20, 24–34, 40, 41, 57, 59, 71, 87, 94–5, 100, 102, 124, 128, 140, 156, 157, 158, 167n15, 167nn1, 5, 168n12, 169n6, 171–2n1
nationalist discourse, 7, 9–10, 11, 12–20, 21–41, 51, 68, 72, 78, 81, 94, 103, 123, 158, 161, 162
Needham, Anuradha Dingwaney, 100, 108

Oldenburg, Veena Talwar, 108
Ortner, Sherry B., 80

Pakistan, 3, 4, 6, 12, 17–19, 26, 37, 42, 53, 54–5, 68, 70–3, 76, 85–6, 88, 91, 93, 100, 119, 121, 124, 132, 146–7, 151, 153, 158, 160, 161, 169n4, 172n6, 174n9
Palakeel, Thomas, 166n9, 170n15
Pandey, Gyanendra, 3, 5, 8–9, 13–14, 42, 43, 48–56, 132, 133–4, 165n1, 175–6n1, 176n2, 177n5, 178–9n15, 179nn19, 21; communalism; 8–9; 'Defence of the Fragment,' 4, 9, 42, 48–51, 169n6; 'Prose of Otherness,' 5, 42–3, 52–4, 169n6, 169–70n11
Parle, 21–4, 26, 32, 41
Parsi identity, 17–18, 70–8, 90, 93, 137–8, 172n6, 177–8n10
partition anthologies, 4–5, 7, 8, 10, 24, 166nn8, 9
patriarchy, 34, 38, 54, 57, 106, 110, 127, 171n20
Poovey, Mary, 78
Prakash, Gyan, 39–40, 81, 159, 161

Prashad, Vijay, 168n12
Progressive Writers' Association (PWA), 58, 98, 170n16, 173n5, 175n15; short stories, 98

Qidwai, Anees, 52–5, 169nn10, 11

Rahman, Tariq, 166n10
Rao, Ravishankar, 166n8
Ray, Sangeeta, 25, 28, 69, 71–2, 91, 93, 167n5, 172n3
Raychaudhuri, Tapan, 174–5n12
Recovery Bill, 36–8, 175–6n1
recovery operation, 6, 11, 12, 15, 17–19, 24, 36–40, 44, 51–4, 56–8, 60, 61–6, 68–9, 73, 88–92, 126, 129, 131–56
Richman, Paula, 179n16
Rose, Sonya O., 56
Rouse, Shahnaz, 102–3, 105–6
Roy, Parama, 27, 167nn5, 6
Roychaudhury, Subir, 177n5

Sahni, Bhisham, 165n6
Saint, Ravikant, and Tarun K. Saint, 8–9, 55
Sangari, Kumkum, 24, 71, 81, 83, 85, 121, 167n5
Sarkar, Sumit, 81
Sarkar, Tanika, 22, 28, 167n5
Scott, Joan, 44, 46, 49–50, 54, 55–6, 90–1, 166n11, 170n13
Settar, S., and Indira Baptista Gupta, 8
Sidhwa, Bapsi, 13, 17–18, 47, 67–93, 97, 99, 135, 137–8, 157, 172nn3, 5, 6, 177–8n10; *Cracking India*, 13, 17, 47, 67–93, 135, 138, 172n3; early life, 70–1; personal views on partition, 70, 73–4

silences in women's narratives, 9, 10–11, 14, 18, 48, 63–65, 125–56, 167n15, 168n8, 168–9n1, 173n3, 175–6n1, 177n6, 178n12
Simon, R., 129–30, 138, 141–2; and S. Rosenberg and C. Eppert, 129–30
Singh, Khushwant, 4, 65, 169n2
Singh, Sujala, 55, 69, 169n6, 170n12, 171n1
Sinha, Mrinalini, 167n3
Skurski, Julie, 95, 123
Spivak, Gayatri Chakravorty, 10, 43, 54, 67, 79–80, 84–5, 87, 92, 135, 136, 137, 139, 166–7n13, 167nn5, 7, 171n53; 'Can the Subaltern Speak?' 79–80, 92, 136–7
Stoler, Ann Laura, 18, 76, 85
subaltern speech, 78–80, 92, 136–7, 166–7n13
Sunder-Rajan, Rajeswari, 167n5, 178n14
Swann, Karen, 90, 170n13

Talbot, Ian, 5, 45–51, 169nn4, 5
testimony, 11, 19, 94, 130, 133–9, 160–2, 167n15
Thanawi, Maulana Ashraf Ali, 104, 174n10
Thapar, Romila, 168n11

Tharu, Susie, 166n10, 178–9n15; and K. Lalita, 15, 28, 167n5
'Toba Tek Singh,' 5, 54–5

Urdu, 17, 58, 59, 98, 99, 108, 112, 169n2, 170nn15, 17

Verma, Balraj, 58
Voight, Johannes H., 168n10

Walcott, Rinaldo, 157, 161–2
Walkowitz, Judith R., 57
Walsh, Judith E., 173n1, 174–5n12
Weedon, Chris, 80
White, Hayden, 3
Whitehead, Andrew, 4, 70–1, 129, 172n5
Winant, Howard, 79
women question, the, 14–15, 18, 53–4, 59, 130–52, 156, 160–1, 167nn3, 5, 170n12, 174n10, 175–6n1
women's education, 95, 102–5, 107, 123, 174n10
Woolf, Virginia, 150
Wyrick, Deborah, 44

Yeğenoğlu, Meyda, 136

Zoroastrianism, 71, 74–6

www.ingramcontent.com/pod-product-compliance
Lightning Source LLC
Chambersburg PA
CBHW030320080526
44584CB00012B/636